The Meaning ❧ of the ❧ Constitution

The Meaning of the Constitution

THIRD EDITION

Angela Roddey Holder, LL.M.

Member of the Bars of South Carolina,
Louisiana, and Connecticut
Formerly, Department of Political Science
Winthrop College
Clinical Professor of Pediatrics (Law)
Yale University School of Medicine
and

John Thomas Roddey Holder, M. Phil.

Lecturer in Political Science
Winthrop University

Foreword by Henry Steele Commager

BARRON'S

All inquiries should be addressed to:
Barron's Educational Series, Inc.
250 Wireless Blvd.
Hauppauge, NY 11788
http://www.barronseduc.com

Library of Congress Catalog Card No. 97-74678

ISBN-13: 978-0-7641-0099-4
ISBN-10: 0-7641-0099-8

Printed in the United States of America
19 18 17 16 15 14 13 12 11

To David

and

for our students

Contents

JUSTITIA EST CONSTANS

ET PERPETUA VOLUNTAS JUS

SUUM CUIQUE TRIBUENDI

(Justice is the constant

and perpetual will to

render to each man

his due before the courts)

Foreword

IN THE FIRST OF THE FEDERALIST PAPERS, Alexander Hamilton wrote that

> It has been frequently remarked that it seems to have been reserved to the people of this country, by their conduct and example, to decide the important question whether societies of men are really capable or not of establishing good government from reflection and choice, or whether they are forever destined to depend for their political constitutions on accident and force.

The government they did establish, "by reflection and choice," was the first of written national constitutions, the first to be made by "we the people," the first to inaugurate a federal system that worked, the first to embrace a Bill of Rights that was not merely procedural, the first to separate formally Church and State, the first to expand not by "colonies" but by admitting new settlements as coordinated States. It was the first, too, to create an independent judiciary and to prescribe "judicial review" of legislation binding on State and Nation alike.

Thus, from the beginnings of our national history, the courts undertook the task of expounding not only the Law but also the Constitution itself, until eventually it came to be pretty generally accepted that, as Chief Justice Hughes once said, "the Constitution is what the Judges say it is." American courts, unlike those of other nations, were expected to preside over litigation, work out solutions in conflict of laws, umpire the Federal system, rule on international law, prescribe the bounds of both State and Federal authority and of the popular will, and educate a heterogeneous people to the most complicated government ever devised by the ingenuity of man. Thanks to the wisdom of the Framers, the Judges assigned these heavy responsibilities were immunized from the most dangerous buffetings of popular opinion and politics. Because the courts played so crucial a role, Presidents and Senators have pretty consistently avoided partisanship in appointments, and thus have attracted to the Bench men of the highest talent and integrity. If we have an aristocracy in America, it is, as de Tocqueville observed [over] 150 years ago, "the aristocracy of the robe." At the very beginnings of our judicial history, American courts adopted the habit of elaborate written opinions, of seriatim opinions [several opinions, each written by a different judge hearing the same case] and, a practice all but unknown elsewhere, of dissenting opinions. These were, in effect, appeals from the present to the future, but courts were not invariably dependent on precedent. They could override earlier decisions in order to accommodate the Constitution to the necessities of the time—thus making sure it would be a living instrument. With infinite patience, they accorded to every case and every plaintiff the most scrupulous attention and the ripest wisdom. Over the years—[more than] two centuries—they have built up, case by case, the most imposing body of constitutional law known to history. If we confine ourselves to secular literature, we can say with confidence that nothing compares with this affluent enterprise. When we contemplate this record, we can say, with Justice Holmes, that "our eyes dazzle."

* * * * * * * * * * * *

Students are fortunate to have for their guidance [Angela and John Holder's] book *The Meaning of the Constitution*. It is concise but comprehensive. Notable for its clarity of statement, its accuracy of summation and of clause-by-clause explanation—almost word-by-word—it provides, at almost every level, the essentials for understanding not only the significance of the words and clauses of the Constitution, but also the adjudication of these words and clauses. Its selection of key cases is at once catholic and discriminating. It provides, too, an admirable working bibliography. Finally, it is aware of the changing meaning of such terms as "equal protection of the laws," "regulation of commerce," or "establishment of religion." In all this, it observes a nice impartiality. I know of no other handbook that will prove as useful and sound as *The Meaning of the Constitution*.

HENRY STEELE COMMAGER

Preface

THE CONSTITUTION OF THE UNITED STATES exists to provide a system and to enunciate the basic democratic values and principles within which we, the people of a diverse nation, can solve our problems. It is as relevant in solving contemporary political and legal issues as it was when President Jefferson dealt with the Barbary pirates. For each generation of Americans, our problems seem different from what has happened before, but within our Constitutional system, we have the flexibility to find solutions. Our belief in the inalienable rights of all people has been absolute. Our execution of that belief is often woefully unsatisfactory, but the principle is the goal toward which we strive. Our Constitution has already had its 200th birthday, but it remains the declaration of this nation's commitment to the dignity and worth of every person.

Before any generation can solve its problems, it must understand the system in which it exists and its resources for solving those problems. We hope that this book explains our system in such a way that the reader understands his or her rights, and, much more important, his or her responsibilities.

ANGELA RODDEY HOLDER
Yale University School of Medicine

JOHN THOMAS RODDEY HOLDER
Winthrop University

March 1997

Introduction

THE RATIFICATION OF THE 26TH AMENDMENT in 1971 means that most of the readers of this book are eligible to vote. The right to vote means the right (and the responsibility) to participate in the selection of the people who make policies that affect the lives not only of everyone in this country, including the voter, but of most of the other people in the world.

The Amendment giving eighteen year olds the right to vote was proposed and ratified because, at the time, those who were too young to vote for the people who made American foreign policy were not too young to be drafted and to die in Vietnam. Student unrest in the 1960s and 1970s changed the foreign policy of this country.

The 1980s and 1990s have seen a trend away from political interest and activities among young people (and others), but today the influence of citizens is needed more than ever. Many of the issues being debated today will affect not only our own lives but those of future generations. Those who do not participate in politics, by voting or otherwise, are usually ignored when political decisions are made. We hope that the readers of this book will gain an understanding not only of an important historical document, but also of the importance of participating in politics. Your involvement in politics can have an impact not only on your own life but also on the society whose interests you can express and protect.

The Background of the Constitution

POLITICAL PHILOSOPHY had its beginnings in ancient Greece, where Aristotle, in particular, believed in a concept of "absolute justice." He believed in natural law arising from man's power to reason and, through reason, his ability to determine what justice was and to apply it. Absolute justice could never be attained in practice, but it remained the ideal by which men could measure the ethics of their relationships with others, just as the life of Christ remains the unattainable standard by which Christians of today judge their own conduct. Aristotle believed that men throughout the world would, through reason, arrive at the same views on the nature of universal justice just as the idea of "fire" is the same everywhere, but because local conditions varied, the practice of justice would vary, just as a man in Greece and a man in Persia would think of very different things if they thought of "money."

In the 13th century, St. Thomas Aquinas wrote *Summa Theologica* in which he followed Aristotle's idea of the existence of natural law and absolute justice, but Aquinas believed that they were derived from God. He defined natural law as that portion of the eternal and divine law of God that man could discover by the use of his power to reason. Aquinas believed that natural law governed the relationships among men or between men and the state in somewhat the same way that the physical laws of God regulate the planets. Each man's conscience was a gift of God enabling him to determine the difference between good and evil, and this faculty of the human spirit decided what was or was not in keeping with natural law.

Aquinas believed that God instituted governments to meet the needs of mankind and that the state originated in His will. The state was obliged to comply with the will of God and natural law in the same manner as the individual. If the state made laws that contravened a man's conscience, he was theoretically not bound by them, but Aquinas believed that the unjust ruler would receive his punishment in the hereafter and that it was not the business of the citizen to overthrow a tyrant. Disturbance was to be avoided at all cost, even that of injustice, and obedience was more important than liberty.

By the 17th century, Aquinas' ideas, which had been of profound importance in governmental theory for centuries, had developed into the idea that the king rules by Divine Right. Regardless of how unfair he might be, a rebellion against him was considered to be a rebellion against God, who, it was thought, had established that particular king on that particular throne.

In 1689 John Locke, an English philosopher, wrote his *Second Treatise on Civil Government* to justify the English Revolution of the year before, to reject the idea of the "Divine Right of kings," and to dispute Aquinas' view of the origin of the state. Locke's ideas were the basis of the philosophical justification for the American Revolution, and his concept of the rights of man are basic to the Constitution.

Locke agreed with Aquinas that there was something known as "natural law" although he was much less positive about its source. To Locke, natural law meant that men, because of their humanity, have certain inalienable rights that should not be transgressed by the state or other men, and that among these inalienable rights are the right to life, liberty and property. Our Declaration of Independence expresses these ideas of Locke's when it states: "We hold these truths to be self-evident, that all men are created equal, that they are endowed by their Creator with certain unalienable rights, that among these are Life, Liberty and the pursuit of Happiness."

In this sense, natural law and the natural rights that arise from it are still a part of our law. In 1952, for example, the United States Supreme Court held that a policeman who held a suspect down and forcibly pumped his stomach to obtain evidence had violated the suspect's constitutional rights so flagrantly that he had disregarded the principles of "a sense of justice and the requirements of certain decencies of civilized conduct." [1] In 1965 the Court held that a husband and wife have a basic right to privacy in their marital relations.[2] While the Court denies that it rests its decisions on some abstract theory of natural law, it has frequently pointed out that our basic and inalienable rights as listed in the Bill of Rights must be protected and occasionally finds new "natural rights" it deems worthy of protection.

In modern times most countries have such highly developed codes of laws that reliance on abstract natural law alone as a basis for judicial procedure is most unusual. However, the 1962 trial of Adolf Eichmann was entirely the product of natural law. Eichmann, a leader in the Nazi extermination of the Jews, was tried in Israel for his crimes during World War II. At the time he committed his atrocities, there was no state of Israel and consequently no Israeli law. There is a principle of criminal law in all parts of the civilized world that a man should not be tried for something not specifically prohibited by a statute in force at the time he did it. In the Eichmann case, however, there was a consensus among legal experts that natural law and civilized behavior prohibit the extermination of millions of people, and so Eichmann was tried, convicted, and executed under natural law.

Where Locke and Aquinas most strongly disagreed, and where our political philosophy followed Locke, was in the concept of the origin of the state. Locke believed that the source of political power was derived from the people and not, as Aquinas did, that it was imposed from above. In his *Second Treatise on Civil Government,* Locke wrote an allegory about the origin of the state and its government in which he began with a pre-political society, very similar to life in the Garden of Eden. In this society, there were no laws, no rulers, and no government and everyone was quite satisfied with his lot. This society was governed entirely by reason—as Aristotle and Aquinas had also thought that men were governed by reason—and no one was so unreasonable as to interfere with another person. However, a few citizens transgressed others' rights and it became *convenient* to establish some rules and regulations—in other words, a government. The government was established solely for the sake of convenience to permit everyone to live together with a minimum of strife and not, as Aquinas believed, because God willed it. This was called the "social contract" theory because the citizens made a promise or contract to abide by the rules to protect themselves. The basis of Locke's idea was that government existed only by the consent of the governed. In 1620 the Pilgrims wrote and signed the Mayflower Compact before they landed at Plymouth Rock. This agreement, signed by all of the men (but none of the women) on the ship, set up a government and made rules under which the colony would live. This is Locke's "social contract" theory in action.

Under this theory, the only reason government exists is to preserve the life, liberty and property of the citizens and it has no power except that which is used for the good of the people. The basic rights of the people, therefore, limit the power of the ruler, who has no right, divine or otherwise, to interfere with them. Locke's conclusion was that if the government breaks the trust of the people who established it or if it interferes with the liberty of the citizens, they have a right to rebel and make a new contract under which they may govern themselves more conveniently. This right to rebel was the theory behind our Declaration of Independence, which declared that the colonies found government under the king of England to be highly inconvenient as well as detrimental to their liberties.

Our history as an independent nation began on July 4, 1776, when the Declaration of Independence was signed by representatives of the thirteen colonies. At this point, although we declared ourselves free of English rule, there was, of course, no system of national government, so the Second Continental Congress assembled to form one.

The Congress elected a committee of twelve men to draw up a system of government and this committee wrote the Articles of Confederation. The articles were presented to Congress in 1777 and ratified by all the states except Maryland in 1778 and 1779. Since the colonists' objections to the English king had centered around his use of arbitrary power, they were convinced that a strong central government would soon be guilty of the same abuses. The articles were, therefore, written with the idea of restricting the power of the national government as much as possible and of forming a league of states that would work together as separate entities.

Under the articles, the national government was virtually powerless. There was no executive branch of the government, although there was a president of the Congress, and consequently no one to enforce the laws that Congress passed. The states could and did ignore any national laws that did not suit them. The national government could only request the states to send money, troops, and supplies to fight the revolution.

Internal difficulties, such as the competing currencies issued by seven different states, made it obvious that the articles were in need of revision. A conference was called at Mount Vernon in 1788 and another one in Annapolis, Maryland, without substantial improvement. Finally, in 1787, what was to become the Constitutional Convention met in Philadelphia in secret session to decide what to do. They knew that they had to create a system of government in which the national authority would be sufficient to minister to the needs of the nation. The convention had been called to revise the Articles of Confederation, but once the delegates were assembled, they agreed that the same principle of the "right to rebel" that had been invoked against the king would again apply, and since the government established by the articles was no longer suited to the convenience of the people, they would create another one. They wrote our Constitution and developed the system of government under which we have lived for over 200 years.

The Constitution in Our History

OUR SYSTEM of government is a great deal more than the words written by the Constitutional Convention and ratified by the people. A constitution is a framework that establishes the basic principles of government and leaves the brushstrokes and details to the institutions it creates. At the time the new government began in 1789, it operated under a document that asked more questions than it answered. It provided for "due process of law." What is that? What is "interstate commerce"? As these definitions were supplied, so the government grew. Our Constution has survived for the very simple reason that its flexibility and lack of detail have permitted it to change with new patterns of living and new standards of justice and morality as they are accepted by the people. There are those who feel that the Constitution should be interpreted today as it was in 1789, but had it not been allowed to grow and change while preserving our governmental structure, it would long ago have been unworkable and as doomed to dust as the Articles of Confederation. Our Constitution today is the basic authority for federal and state laws that regulate air transportation, television stations, public education, space exploration, generation of electricity, heart transplants, and other aspects of our ordinary lives that the Founding Fathers would have considered miracles beyond belief. This capacity to grow with social conditions and technology while preserving the institutional structure of the government has been the Constitution's triumph and success and proves that we do have "a living Constitution."

The Constitution has been amended very few times because most changes that are required in the methods of government are brought about by the passage of ordinary laws or by new interpretations. The meaning of the words to which the delegates at the Constitutional Convention signed their names is determined by action of the three branches of government and by the customs of doing things that have evolved in the course of American history.

Many aspects of our system that we take for granted are not established by law. We just do them in a certain way and as long as customary procedures function satisfactorily, no one seeks to change them. The nominating conventions of both parties grew by trial and error and are not controlled by federal law at all. Political parties themselves were unknown in the early years of the country. The first three presidential candidates were nominated in a very disorganized fashion and after that, candidates were nominated by congressional caucus. The convention, although unlike those we have today, was invented by the Anti-masonic party in 1832. The use of congressional committees is also based on custom and tradition and is now considered an indispensable part of the legislative process. The president's cabinet is largely governed by tradition and was not created by the Constitution.

The president has enormous influence in interpreting and expanding the Constitution. At the time President William Henry Harrison died and Tyler became president, it was not clear whether a vice president who succeeded to the presidency was really president or whether he was an "acting president" empowered only to conduct a holding operation until the next election. Tyler made it clear that he was the president and exercized all the powers of the office, thus establishing the precedent that has been accepted ever since. Thomas Jefferson completed the Louisiana Purchase first and asked for congressional approval afterwards, thus continuing Washington's precedent that although the Senate has the authority to "advise and consent" to treaties, they are first negotiated by the executive without legislative interference. Theodore Roosevelt invented the concept of an "executive agreement" which, like a treaty, involves relations with other nations, but that does not require confirmation by the Senate. Every president since his time has used this power. Presidents in this century commenced the practice of proposing legislation to Congress instead of waiting for Congress to initiate it, and for many years almost all important legislation has been initiated by the White House. Since the time of Washington, presidents have made use of his interpretation of the executive's right as commander in chief to include the right to dispatch troops at home or abroad without waiting for a congressional declaration of war. The growth through interpretation of presidential power is one of the more obvious ways in which our governmental framework has grown to meet the needs of a growing nation.

Congress has also expanded the Constitution by interpretation. For example, Article I gives Congress the power to "lay and collect taxes." This is a rather meaningless phrase. What kind of taxes? Income taxes? Excise taxes? Sales taxes? What rates will be levied? Will everyone pay the same rate? How will taxes be collected? The constitutional authority behind our system of federal taxation is in four words, but explaining and expanding their meaning requires many volumes devoted to the tax laws passed by Congress. Congress also has the power to "regulate interstate commerce," and this clause has been the authority for more legislation than any other. Under this grant of power and interpretation of what it means, Congress has regulated virtually all labor management relations, prohibited discrimination by race in business enterprises, and prohibited the sale of noxious foods. All these examples serve to show how the meaning of one small phrase has been kept sufficiently flexible to ensure that our Constitution serves us as well now in a time of surrogate parents and space flights and other new wonders as it did in the small and rural nation of 1789.

The greatest burden of constitutional exposition and interpretation, however, has fallen on the judicial branch of the government and particularly on the United States Supreme Court. The history of the Supreme Court is the history of the development of the Constitution and in its decisions can be demonstrated clearly how concepts such as natural rights, freedom, justice, and morality have evolved in a period of more than 200 years. As Chief Justice Charles Evans Hughes wrote in 1907: "The Constitution is what the Judges say it is."

The Court—1789–1835

The first great chief justice of the Supreme Court was John Marshall of Virginia. He established the Supreme Court as a branch of government equal in power to the other two and, under his leadership, our basic principles of government were enunciated. Until Marshall took office in 1801, the Supreme Court had little power and less prestige. George Washington had several prospective appointees for the Court turn him down, primarily because they believed it too insignificant for their notice. John Jay, the first chief justice, resigned to become governor of New York, a job that he felt to be much more important. Marshall, appointed by John Adams, was the fourth chief justice and remained on the Court until his death in 1835. Since he is now accorded a reverent place in American history, it is interesting to note that his appointment narrowly escaped defeat in the Senate.

From 1801 until about 1820, the primary issue in the new nation was the question of the extent of the powers of the federal government. The Founding Fathers had declared that the Constitution was "the supreme law of the land" but they neglected to specify how this idea was to be sustained. The judges of that time were, therefore, very much inclined to place preservation of the young nation high on their list of priorities and to decide cases with that end in view wherever possible. At the time of Marshall's death, that question had been answered, although the Civil War was fought over its practical enforcement.

Marshall's first major case was *Marbury v. Madison*[1] in 1803. Mr. Marbury had been appointed a justice of the peace by President Adams the day before Jefferson's inauguration but had never received his commission, which the new president's staff refused to give to him. Marbury asked the Supreme Court to issue a writ (a court order) ordering that the commission be delivered, as the Court was allowed to do under the Judiciary Act of 1789. Marshall's opinion denied the writ, thus preventing undue political reaction from President Jefferson, but he declared the Judiciary Act itself, the basis of Marbury's suit, unconstitutional. This decision set the precedent, followed ever since, that when any ordinary law is considered, it must be measured by constitutional standards and if it falls short, it is of no effect. This asserted for the first time that the Constitution, as the foundation of the government, prevails over any ordinary law, state or federal. This further gave the courts the power to be the agents of measurement, thus establishing the principle of "judicial review."

Within four years, Marshall had increased the power of the Court to the point where many congressmen became resentful. An attempt was made to impeach Justice Samuel Chase, primarily because the House did not care for his political views. When the impeachment failed, the principle of judicial independence had been firmly entrenched. Thus was established the now-accepted precept that impeachment will only lie in cases of criminal behavior, not political independence.

The year 1819 saw another major case of Marshall's tenure. The national government owned and controlled a national bank (unlike the "national banks" of today, which are owned by private stockholders and regulated by the government) that was hated by many of the states. The state of Maryland attempted to levy a tax on the bank's assets in Baltimore and the ensuing quarrel went before the Supreme Court as *McCulloch v. Maryland*.[2] This case established two fundamental principles of our legal system. The first objection that the states had to the bank was that the national government had no authority to establish it in the first place. Marshall answered that by declaring the doctrine of "implied powers," which is used today in government subsidy and regulation of all parts of our lives. Marshall declared that the "necessary and proper" clause of Article I, conferring power on the federal government, gave the Congress the power to use *any* convenient means to implement the enumerated powers as long as the means of implementation were not specifically prohibited by the Constitution. This decision meant that although Congress had the power to undertake only those ends for which the Constitution provided, it could use any legal means to achieve them. This decision did more than any other to give the federal government the right to expand its power to meet the challenge of changing times and is probably responsible for the fact that our Constitution has survived our evolution from a small, rural nation to an industrial, urban one. After finding that the bank had been established by implication from the clause giving Congress the power to regulate the credit of the United States, Marshall went on to consider whether Maryland had the power to tax the bank, deciding that it did not. He stated the rule that was to become the cornerstone of our government—that a state government's sovereignty does not extend to actions of the federal government, since the federal government was established by all the people and hence is not subject to attack by a small group of them. This case denied for all time the right of a state to control the action of the federal government. National supremacy, as stated in Article VI, is the most essential part of our system and *McCulloch* made it work. Had the case been decided the other way, our federal union would soon have been fragmented into small units, each of which could have taken unto itself the prerogatives of a nation.

Marshall continued to uphold and strengthen the doctrine of national supremacy with *Cohens v. Virginia*[3] in 1821. The Cohens were arrested in Virginia for selling lottery tickets, legal under an act of Congress within the District of Columbia. The decision meant that the Supreme Court had the power to pass on the constitutionality of state, as well as federal laws, and that the power of the states to legislate was subordinate to the provisions of the Constitution. Most of the Court's business from that day to this has involved cases challenging the validity of state laws and the fact that the court does have this power has meant that we have a diversity of state law but a unity of concept throughout all states, and that while states have freedom to enact laws dealing with local matters, all must conform to national guarantees.

From 1815–1860, this country saw an enormous expansion of trade and business. The use of corporations and trading companies, many of which did business in more than one state, produced numerous legal problems, often involving conflicts between the laws of different states. Respect for the Court increased as a growing feeling of nationalism began to replace sectional views, although concepts of sectionalism were to come to the fore again in the 1820s. With the growth of transportation, in particular, problems of multi-state business arose. Most states attempted to protect home-state industries by restricting the right of out-of-state merchants to do business. New York, in an effort to improve the steamboat business of its residents, passed laws providing that only New York steamboats could use its waterways. Steamboat companies from other states brought suit and the question reached the Supreme Court in 1824 as *Gibbons v. Ogden*.[4] Marshall held that Congress's power to regulate commerce "among the several states" meant that the federal government could regulate commerce within a state if it affected that of other states, hence the New York law permitting a monopoly was unconstitutional. It is directly on the doctrine of this case that the Supreme Court upheld Congress's power to legislate such things as the denial of the right of a restaurant owner to discriminate by race.

In order to have orderly expansion of business during this period, corporate stockholders needed assurance that the rights of corporations would be secure from state government's encroachments. The *Dartmouth College*[5] case in 1819 was Marshall's contribution to the growth of American corporation law. Dartmouth had been chartered by King George III in 1769. In 1816 the New Hampshire legislature, incited by Dartmouth's president, who did not care for the ideas of the board of trustees, attempted to alter its charter by adding more board members who presumably would toe the legislature's line and, incidentally, transform the private college into a state university. Marshall's decision held that the charter could not be changed because it was a contract and Article I, Section 10 of the Constitution forbids states governments to "impair the obligation of a contract." As a result of this case, corporate expansion, so necessary to the growth of a predominantly rural nation, was protected from interference by those states in which legislators might prefer a more bucolic existence. When Marshall died in 1835, he had largely completed the job of ensuring the stability of the federal union. Had someone of less ability been chief justice, the union might have failed.

The Taney Court and the Civil War—1835–1866

Marshall's successor, Roger B. Taney, was appointed by President Jackson. By 1835 when Taney took his seat, Marshall had carved out the constitutional principles and his successor had only to consolidate the gains. Judicial supremacy was an unquestioned fact of American life. The industrial revolution was creating a dynamic economy and the new country was well on its way to stable life. However, after the *Dred Scott* decision in 1857, the Court's power and prestige were seriously impaired and the public acceptance of the Court, which marked the beginning of Taney's tenure in office, was severely eroded when he died in 1864.

Taney's first major decision was the 1837 *Charles River Bridge*[6] case. The Massachusetts legislature in 1785 granted authority to the Charles River Bridge Company for construction of a toll bridge across the Charles River from Boston. Tolls were to be collected indefinitely. In 1828 the legislature authorized construction of another bridge nearby and provided that tolls would be levied only to defray construction costs. Owners of the first bridge sought to enjoin construction of the second on the theory that the *Dartmouth* decision gave their company a complete monopoly, since a competing bridge would "impair the obligation of their contract." Taney ruled that the state had never surrendered its right to intervene in contracts on behalf of the public and that in this case the public interest required construction of another bridge. His opinion is still relevant today as we consider the right of an industry to produce in such a manner as to pollute the environment. He wrote, "While the rights of private property are sacredly guarded, we must not forget that the community also have rights and that the happiness and well-being of every citizen depends on their faithful preservation." Taney was the first justice to recognize the doctrine of the "public utility"—that a corporation providing a service vital to the public may be more strictly regulated than one that deals in a non-essential service. This decision aided competition in industrial areas and marked the beginning of a recognition of the state's police power, the right of the state to act to preserve the safety, health, good order, and morals of its citizens. The change in attitude toward contracts that is shown by the contrast between this case and the *Dartmouth* case reflects the slow process by which the Court comes to change its mind on contracts or other matters in the light of economic or social change. This decision reflected the development of this country from a primarily rural society to one concerned with the problems inherent in the development of urban areas.

Our nation's greatest westward expansion occurred during this period. Westerners tended to be nationalistic and supremacy of the national government seemed assured. Slavery, however, had begun to be an important political problem, not only in the original states but in the new territories. The nadir (lowest point) of the Supreme Court's influence came when it tried to impose a legal solution to a political problem in the *Dred Scott* case. In 1820 the Missouri Compromise had admitted Maine as a free state and Missouri as slave, but all of the territories carved from the Louisiana Purchase north of southern Missouri were declared to be free. The Compromise of 1850 admitted California as a free state, forbade slave trading in the District of Columbia and other territories were to be allowed to determine for themselves if they were slave or free. This compromise quieted the fears of the slave states since it repealed the Missouri Compromise by implication and some of the states that chose to have slavery were north of the Southern boundary of Missouri. The Kansas-Nebraska Act of 1854 gave those two new territories the same choice and specifically repealed the Missouri Compromise.

Against that background the Supreme Court heard the *Dred Scott*[7] case in 1857. It involved a slave whose master had taken him to a free territory and had then returned him to a slave state. Scott sued to be declared free on the ground that he had gained irrevocable freedom as soon as he was on free soil. The case could have been settled by declaring that since Scott was a slave in the state in which he sued, he was not entitled to sue in the courts. The Court actually had precedent for refusing to hear the case at all. However, Chief Justice Taney, supported by a majority of his fellow justices, in a misguided effort to settle the question of slavery forever, succeeded in precipitating a judicial disaster. He delivered the majority opinion, which declared that since Scott was not a citizen in any state, he could not sue, and Taney concluded that the framers of the Constitution never intended blacks to be citizens at all. Secondly, the Court annulled Congress's efforts to legislate restrictions on slavery by declaring that since slaves were the property of their owners, freeing them deprived the owners of their property without due process of law. Reaction to this decision was immediate and severely damaged the Court's prestige. Anti-slavery people refused to recognize it and therefore the rule of law no longer served as a brake on emotionalism on either side of the argument. Congress could, of course, have amended the Constitution in substantially the same form as eventually enacted in the citizenship provisions of the 14th Amendment of 1868, but neither side was in a mood to be reasonable. President Buchanan made no effort to lead the people to calmness.

To Americans in 1861 it must have seemed that the Constitution was dead forever and none would have believed that the Court would ever have the prestige that it had enjoyed in Marshall's day. Between the election of Lincoln and his inauguration, seven states seceded. Buchanan announced that secession was unconstitutional but took no further action. The Civil War began on April 6, 1861.

Taney died in 1864 and was succeeded by Salmon P. Chase. Legal problems inevitably accompany war and never more than in a civil war. President Lincoln suspended the writ of habeas corpus and allowed searches and seizures without warrants and military arrests, all of which were at least constitutionally questionable, since Congress had never declared war, taking the position that since secession was illegal, no war existed against a hostile force. In 1861 in *ex parte Merryman*[8] the Court held that Lincoln's suspension of habeas corpus was unconstitutional, but he ignored the decision and, of course, then as now, the Court is powerless to enforce its orders without executive cooperation. Lincoln also put vast areas of the country under martial law and substituted courts-martial for civilian trials. In 1866 the Court heard the case of *ex parte Milligan*.[9] Milligan, a prominent Southern sympathizer, was tried and sentenced to death by a military court in Indiana, which had been included under military jurisdiction although far removed from the battle area. The Court struck down the president's action, holding that military commissions could not act against civilians except in areas of open warfare where it was impossible for the civil courts to function. Since the Court's support originally had come from strong federalist areas, mainly the Northeast, which had been aghast at the *Scott* decision and were further infuriated by the Court's attempts to check the president, its prestige dropped to an all-time low.

After the Civil War, the Reconstruction Congress rode over the Constitution, the president, and the Court. President Andrew Johnson was a special object of Congress's scorn because of his resistance to a policy of vengeance toward the South. Congress enacted legislation ending his right to supervise Reconstruction and set up a Joint Committee of the Congress. It passed a Civil Rights bill over his veto which was ratified as the 14th Amendment. Finally, in 1866 the radicals attempted to impeach him, and although he won by one vote, the prestige of the office was enormously degraded. The Court, in its turn, capitulated in attempts to reduce its power, thus reaching the low point of judicial independence in our history. However, as the more vehement firebrands aged and the White House changed hands, the Court and the president began to re-emerge as co-equal branches of the government.

Texas v. White,[10] 1869, was the end of the legal problems caused by secession. Texas had some federal bonds that the secessionist government sold to private investors to finance the war effort. When the investors tried to collect, the federal government refused to pay. The issue before the Court was whether or not Texas had the legal right to secede, since, if it had, it could legally have sold the bonds. The Court held that the Union, once formed by vote of the people, was an indissoluble one and that no state had the legal right to withdraw. Therefore, regardless of the facts, the Southern states had never, as a matter of law, left the Union or ceased to be a part of the United States.

The *Legal Tender*[11] cases of 1871 reflect the growing differential between economic classes in the country. The federal government, in need of money to fight the war, had issued paper money instead of requiring gold as the medium of exchange. Inflation resulted, helping debtors and hurting creditors. When the Court held that the right to issue paper money was a constitutional one implied from the power to regulate currency, railroads and the budding corporations that had issued mortgages on their property to begin their businesses were delighted. Banks and other creditors were not.

After 1866, the economic realignment in this country affected the lives of many more citizens. As industry became more important, it created legal problems that had been unknown before the war. There is, for example, a great legal difference in the regulation of a village shoemaker who makes shoes in the back of his house and sells them in his parlor directly to the consumer and regulation of a giant shoe manufacturing corporation with factories in many states and sales outlets in all. The basic questions of whether the government had the right to regulate business and whether it ought to regulate business were to be the major interest of the Supreme Court for the next 70 years.

The Era of Big Business—1866–1900

After the Civil War, America entered a period of economic expansion, resulting from the combination of abundant resources and the accessibility of railroads to move them. The war expenditures had helped Northern businessmen and, when it was over, they turned their energies to industrial expansion. Republicans were in the White House for most of the period and represented the business viewpoint. Railroads were the paramount industry because of their importance to expanding settlement of the plains areas, and small railroads began to consolidate to cover more territory than each could alone. The oil, mail order, and farm machine industries also thrived. The last twenty years of the 19th century were to become the pinnacle of success for big business. The legal climate was most conducive to enterprise. The courts of that time interpreted the 14th Amendment demand for "due process of law" in state action to include corporations as "citizens" and hence made them virtually immune to state regulation. Cases involving business occupied the Supreme Court continuously. The states had never had the power to regulate interstate railroads, although they frequently tried to do so, and the Interstate Commerce Act of 1887[12] attempted to do so. The income tax law of 1894 and the Sherman Antitrust Act of 1890[13] were all Congressional attempts to moderate the abuses of the new industrial giants, but the Court continued to favor business interests and eviscerated all of the acts.

The 1872 *Slaughterhouse*[14] case was the first blow to federal regulation of business. The Louisiana legislature had given a monopoly on slaughtering animals in New Orleans to one company and hundreds of butchers found themselves without facilities. They asked the federal courts to interpret the "privileges and immunities" clause of the 14th Amendment to incorporate a new federally protected right to make a living, which in turn would declare the monopoly unconstitutional. However, the Supreme Court held that the clause did not add any rights, it merely protected pre-existing federal ones, such as the right of interstate travel; therefore the monopoly was a valid use of state power.

In 1876 in *Munn v. Illinois*,[15] the Supreme Court upheld a state's right of regulation. Chicago was the hub of the grain storage industry, since grain was stored there upon receipt from the Midwest's farmers until it could be distributed through the East. Munn and other warehousemen made agreements with railroads to get a monopoly on each line's incoming shipments and then fixed prices. This was most damaging to the grain merchants, who pressured the Illinois legislature into legislating against these practices in 1871. Warehouse owners claimed that these regulations deprived them of their property rights without due process of law. The Supreme Court decision was rendered by Chief Justice Morrison Waite, who had been appointed by President Grant upon Taney's death. He announced that although railroads were interstate commerce, grain storage was not and therefore the state regulations were valid. This was the last case in which the Supreme Court upheld any state regulation of business until 1937.

In addition to business cases, there were other problems as well. After Reconstruction officials left the South, the states began passing laws directed at the removal of the political rights the blacks had gained. For the first decade after the war, there were few "Jim Crow" laws requiring segregation, and integration was at least tolerated. However, persistent denials of the right to vote alarmed Congress and in 1875 the Civil Rights Act was enacted, which protected the franchise and prohibited segregation in places of public accommodation. Several cases involving blacks who had been denied access to theaters and restaurants in New York City and other areas were decided by the Supreme Court in the *Civil Rights*[16] cases of 1883. The Court, delaying as long as possible, did not hear a case of this type during the 1870s. The Court held that the 14th Amendment, providing that "no state shall deny to any citizen the equal protection of the laws" applied only to state action and therefore, although official discrimination was prohibited, attempts to regulate private discrimination, as in restaurants, were unconstitutional. The results of this decision were the immediate segregation laws passed by every Southern state. Since political parties were not state organizations, the "white primary," in which the political party became a private club, was invented. A great deal of progress toward racial harmony had been achieved during the 1870s but the results of this decision and the one to follow in 1896, *Plessy v. Ferguson*, meant that by 1910 segregation laws were rigidly enforced throughout the South. The ironic aspect of this case is that an almost identical provision was enacted as part of the Civil Rights Act of 1964 and upheld by the Supreme Court, demonstrating again how the Court's attitudes change with changes in popular sentiment.

In 1886 the Supreme Court reached a clear turning point in commerce cases with *Wabash, St. Louis and Pacific Railway*.[17] It reversed the direction of the *Munn* case and held that state laws fixing maximum rates for transportation within the state where the rail line was part of an interstate system were unconstitutional because they violated the federal interstate commerce power. The concept of "laissez-faire" ("to leave alone") treatment of business was continued in 1890 in *Chicago, Milwaukee and St. Paul Railway v. Minnesota*[18] when the Court held that a legislature could not fix rates at all and that the question of "reasonableness" of rates was one that could be determined only by the judiciary.

At this time of minimal regulation of business, social problems caused by industrialization were becoming more acute. After the Civil War, increased industrialization induced many rural workers, both black and white, to migrate to urban areas to work in the mills. In addition to native workers, immigration was unrestricted and foreign workers poured in to swell the labor pool. All of these people converged on the low-rent areas of large cities and life in ghetto areas became deplorable. The erstwhile farm worker, once dependent on his initiative and the weather for his income, was totally dependent on his employer. There was no bargaining on wages or terms of employment. If he complained, he was fired. Employers bore no financial responsibility for industrial accidents and the worker, in addition to his pain, was often unemployable after his accident. Factories demanded long hours of work and child labor was the rule, since wages were so low the children had to help feed the family. The result of these conditions was the rise of the American labor movement and social welfare legislation, but partially because of the attitude of the Supreme Court as well as the rest of the federal government, neither made progress until after 1935. In 1886 Samuel Gompers founded the American Federation of Labor, the first great union to survive until the present. In addition to refusing to recognize the right to strike, the Supreme Court during this period also struck down state attempts to enforce wage and hour laws.

A major event in the early labor movement was the arrest and conviction of Eugene V. Debs, an official of the American Railroad Union. The union was on strike in Chicago and a riot broke out when, although the governor had not asked for his help, President Cleveland dispatched troops. Debs was arrested for violation of an injunction against the strike issued by a federal court in Chicago and the injunction which, in effect, killed the right to any strike, was upheld by the Supreme Court.[19] Only under the Clayton Act,[20] passed during President Wilson's term, was labor given the right to strike unimpeded by federal injunction.

As awareness of social problems caused by unregulated industry increased, Congress passed the Interstate Commerce Act of 1887, establishing the Interstate Commerce Commission, which eventually would be empowered to set rates in transportation. This was followed in 1890 by the Sherman Antitrust Act allowing Congress to regulate monopolies. In 1895, however, the Supreme Court destroyed the effect of the antitrust laws by its decision in the *E. C. Knight*[21] case. That sugar refining company was about to merge with others that would have controlled over a third of the sugar production in the country. Alleging that this was a conspiracy in restraint of trade, the government asked for a court order to stop it. The Supreme Court held that although Congress could regulate transportation and shipment of the sugar after refining, manufacturing was not in inter-

state commerce and any attempt to regulate it was unconstitutional. Since companies involved in the big trusts always had plants in more than one state, the net effect was that manufacturing monopolies were not regulated by either state or federal governments.

Also in 1895, the Court struck down the graduated income tax that had been enacted by Congress in 1894. The Court held in *Pollock v. Farmer's Loan and Trust Company*[22] that a graduated income tax (one in which the tax rate goes up as the taxable income rises) was an unconstitutional violation of the provision in Article I that direct taxes had to be uniform throughout the states. This decision was overcome by the 16th Amendment, but it was not ratified until 1913. This case struck at the Marshall doctrine in *McCulloch* that the federal government could intervene in state business whenever the ends were national. At this point, with very little restriction on business and very insignificant taxes, big business was in its heyday. It is at this period that J. P. Morgan, the financier, was supposed to have said "the public be damned," an attitude that was not uncommon in his social circle.

The Court reached the end of the 19th century with the case of *Plessy v. Ferguson*.[23] After the *Civil Rights* case, most Southern states had enacted segregation laws requiring blacks to sit in separate cars on trains traveling intrastate. Since all states in the South had them, it was, in effect, an interstate ban. Plessy, a New Orleans black, was arrested for sitting in a "white" car on a train. When he challenged the law before the Supreme Court, it held that the 14th Amendment only forbade *unequal* protection of the laws and as long as facilities were equivalent, separate-but-equal statutes were constitutional. As a result of this case, those states that had neglected to pass segregation laws after the *Civil Rights* cases hastened to do so, and by 1910, "Jim Crow" reigned throughout the South. Separate-but-equal remained the law of the land until 1954 when the Supreme Court held that "separate" was inherently "unequal."

As the century closed, the Court virtually killed the Interstate Commerce Commission's powers in the 1897 case of *Cincinnati, New Orleans and Texas Railway v. I.C.C.*[24] by denying the commission the power to set rates. The decision of the sixteen cases from 1897 to 1906 involving the commission before the Supreme Court resulted in only one victory for the commission and at the turn of the century it was completely powerless.

1900–1937

Theodore Roosevelt became president in 1901 and spearheaded a revival of the concept of nationalism. Within the next decade a reform movement against business abuses began bringing about a new concept of federal police power in prosecution of monopolies and the revitalization of the Interstate Commerce Commission.

The first case allowing use of the interstate commerce clause to regulate public health, morals, or safety was *Champion v. Ames*[25] of 1903. The Supreme Court upheld federal laws prohibiting interstate transportation of lottery tickets, a statute motivated by Congress's attempts to halt gambling. The following year the Court upheld, in *McCray v. U.S.*,[26] a federal excise tax on colored margarine passed by Congress after lobbying by the dairy industry. This decision opened a vast area for federal social control by taxation, but subsequent cases again narrowed its impact until the 1930s.

Congress enacted a great deal of legislation to control the increasing tendency of business toward monopoly and substandard production. The Interstate Commerce Commission was strengthened by the Elkins Act of 1903[27] and the Hepburn Act of 1906,[28] which gave the commission the power to fix all transportation rates. The Pure Food and Drug Act[29] and the Meat Inspection Act[30] were both passed in 1906, largely as a result of public nausea after reading Upton Sinclair's *The Jungle,* depicting conditions in meat processing plants.

However, in spite of *Champion v. Ames* and the *McCray* case, the Supreme Court, unlike the other two branches of government, held firmly to a policy of non-interference with business and most attempts to regulate it were declared unconstitutional. In 1905 the Court, in *Lochner v. New York*[31] found a state statute limiting the maximum hours a baker could work to 10 a day or 60 a week to be an "unreasonable" use of the state's police power that interfered with the baker's freedom of contract. In 1908, however, the Court accepted the new-fangled notion of state regulation of wages and hours for women in *Muller v. Oregon*.[32] The case involved a state law restricting hours for women workers and the Court upheld it as a reasonable use of the state police power. In addition to the landmark holding, the case was also famous because it was the first one in which a "Brandeis brief" was used. Louis D. Brandeis, to be appointed to the Court by President Wilson in 1916, was the attorney for Oregon. Instead of restricting his argument to law, he demonstrated by medical and sociological evidence what effect long hours of work had on women. Unlike the *Lochner* case, in which the Court concluded that "everybody knew" it did not hurt bakers to work, Brandeis convinced them that there was a social danger if the law were

overturned. This was the first case in many years to break the barrier of the Court's economic theory of laissez-faire, and although there would be a return to conservatism, the Brandeis view would eventually prevail.

From the 1895 E. C. *Knight* case until 1904, the government had been so sure that the Court would knock down attempts to enforce the antitrust laws that it did not bring any suits. However, in 1904 the Court upheld the government's contention that the *Northern Securities Railroad*[33] trust was a conspiracy in restraint of trade. In 1905 the government again won against the *Swift & Co.*[34] meatpacking combine. The Court broadened its view of "interstate commerce," holding that although all the packing houses were in Chicago, they "affected the stream of interstate commerce" and therefore could be regulated. The Court distinguished it from the *Knight* case by declaring that Swift was engaged in sales, not production. The Court's inclination to permit regulation of business continued as it recognized the authority of the Interstate Commerce Commission in *ICC v. Illinois Central Railroad*[35] in 1910 and in 1914 *U.S. v. Atchison, Topeka & Santa Fe.*[36] Finally realizing that the social and economic problems occasioned by big business required a new look at the Constitution, the Court paved the way for President Wilson to ask Congress for legislation establishing other regulatory commissions, including the Federal Trade Commission, the Tariff Commission, and the Federal Reserve Board.

In 1911, however, the Court returned to its views of laissez-faire economics. In *Standard Oil v. U.S.*,[37] the Court held that the Sherman Antitrust Act did not automatically prohibit all monopoly, it just permitted restraint of "unreasonable" monopolies and the Court did not find that Standard Oil was "unreasonable." This again made it almost impossible to break a monopoly, since all of them could argue that they were "reasonable." However, the Court at the same time was willing to accept government regulation for which it could apply the concept of "reasonableness." In the *Hipolite Egg Co.*[38] case of 1911, the Court agreed that the Pure Food and Drug Administration had the authority to seize contaminated food.

President Wilson's term began in 1913 with a desire for more control over big business. During his tenure in office, the Clayton Antitrust Act[39] was passed in 1915 forbidding price discrimination and other conspiracies. It also was the first federal law that granted any power to labor and denied the federal courts the right of injunction to stop a nonviolent strike, thus reversing the Supreme Court's 1895 *Debs* decision. The Adamson Act[40] of 1916 provided an eight-hour day for railway workers, again under the interstate commerce clause, and the Court upheld it in 1917 in *Wilson v. New.*[41] However, in 1918 the Court minimized the effect of the *Muller* case by outlawing, in *Hammer v. Dagenhart,*[42] a child labor law that Congress had passed in 1916. Since the *Knight* ruling prohibited regulation of manufacturing, Congress attempted to restrict shipment of goods that had been made by children. The theory behind the act was that goods that were not shipped could not be sold, hence child labor would become unprofitable. However, the Court invalidated the act, although they admitted the right of the government to seize goods in the *Hipolite Egg* case. The difference, according to the Court, was that the contaminated eggs were harmful in themselves but that the goods made by the children were not, thus the indirect attempt to regulate manufacturing impinged upon the reserve powers of the states under the 10th Amendment. This case was not reversed until 1941 in *U.S. v. Darby.*

For the first time since the Civil War, major civil liberties cases came to the Court during and after World War I. Oliver Wendell Holmes, Jr. had been appointed to the Court in 1902 by President Roosevelt and he won his name as "The Great Dissenter" in cases involving freedom of expression in wartime. Holmes, whose opinions are widely considered the most literary in the Court's history, frequently disagreed with his fellow justices, but time and changing attitudes have seen his opinions become the law of the land within several decades. During World War I, there was considerable hysteria in the country about anything suspected of being "unpatriotic." Violent reactions against anything German meant that study of the German language was made illegal in numerous states and German operas were never sung. Any difference of opinion was labeled "sedition" and Wilson, as Lincoln had done, attempted to impose conformity by legislation. The Espionage Act of 1917 banned anything the postmaster general, using any standard he chose, thought was "seditious" from the mail, and at one point both the *New York Times* and the *Saturday Evening Post* were included. With Holmes writing the opinion, the Espionage Act was found unconstitutional as a violation of the right of free speech in *Schenck v. U.S.*[43] in 1919. It was this opinion that established the "clear and present danger" rule— that basic freedoms in this country cannot be restricted unless the government can prove an obvious and immediate danger. However, since the war was over before the Court's decision was rendered, it was of little practical effect.

The theory of nationalism was still predominant in federal-state relations. In 1920 the Court upheld a treaty made with Canada dealing with migratory birds. A previous law prohibiting hunting of certain species of birds had been declared unconstitutional on the grounds that there was no implied power on this subject (birds, since they did not belong to anyone, were not in interstate commerce). However, when the same provisions were included in a treaty, the Court held that the inherent powers of government to conduct foreign relations mean that a treaty is valid as long as it does not include something that is specifically prohibited by the Constitution. This decision, *Missouri v. Holland,*[44] strengthened the power of the president to make treaties as he saw fit.

During the 1920s the Court again retreated to its laissez-faire view of business. The result of the Court's decisions since the 1880s meant that widespread fraud in stock manipulations could not be regulated, although Congress made no effort to do so in any case, and there was almost no control over credit. Instead of a solid economy, the American business scene was much more like a balloon, as the Crash of 1929 demonstrated, but the Court remained aloof from the realities of the situation and refused to allow any more regulation of business until the *Nebbia* case of 1934.

In 1923 in *Adkins v. Children's Hospital*[45] the Court ignored its decision in the *Muller* case and invalidated a law that restricted hours of work for female employees in the District of Columbia. Again, as in the *Lochner* case, the Court held that this was a denial of the right of women to work and interference with their "liberty of contract." The language of this decision is the classic exposition of the traditional doctrine of laissez-faire economics. This case was eventually overruled in 1937 in *West Coast Hotel Co. v. Parrish*, but laws prohibiting overtime for female employees are now challenged by women themselves, who no longer want extra protection.

The Court's respect for individualism went beyond contracts and into the field of civil liberties. In 1883 the Court had held in *Hurtado v. California*[46] that the 14th Amendment did not require states to abide by the procedural restraints in the 4th, 5th, 6th, and 8th Amendments that applied to federal criminal prosecutions, and the period of the 1920s was the first sign that this view would be altered. As a reaction to anti-German feeling during World War I, states had passed laws forbidding the teaching of foreign languages to children in public schools. *Myer v. Nebraska*[47] in 1923 declared these to be unconstitutional restrictions on the right of a parent to bring up his children according to his individual conscience. In 1925 this was followed by *Pierce v. Society of Sisters,*[48] which invalidated laws forbidding parents to send their children to private schools. The main themes of these cases, that a parent has a right to educate his child, were picked up in the "School Prayer" cases several decades later. These two cases were decided under the 14th Amendment alone. However, the first case in which a specific right in the Bill of Rights was declared applicable to the states was *Gitlow v. New York*[49] in 1925. This case, involving freedom of speech, was a landmark decision of the court and paved the way for most of the civil liberties cases of the past thirty years. The Court overruled the *Hurtado* decision and declared that when a state denied free speech it denied to its people "due process of law" as required by the 14th Amendment. This concept of "incorporation" of the Bill of Rights by the 14th Amendment is now almost complete. *Gitlow* was expanded in 1938 by *Near v. Minnesota*[50] and *Powell v. Alahanuz*,[51] which incorporated the basic rights of criminal procedure, declaring that defendants who are denied counsel are denied a federally protected right. The concept of incorporation of provisions of the Bill of Rights as restrictions on state police power was almost uniformly accepted by 1932, although not until the 1960s were all major rights incorporated.

The president's powers also grew in the 1920s. The *Missouri* case had strengthened his hand in treaty-making and *Myers v. U.S.*[52] in 1926 increased his power in dealing with the government. Myers, a postmaster, had been appointed by the president and confirmed by the Senate but before his term was up, the president fired him. He sued for his lost salary and the Supreme Court upheld the president's right to dismiss an employee of the executive branch. A 1935 case was to restrict this right as to employees of independent commissions, but the president had vast new control over the bureaucracy.

In 1929 the glorious dream of economic abundance burst and the Great Depression was at hand. President Hoover, although lamenting the problems, took an extremely limited view of his constitutional authority to act and so intervened in only limited ways as banks, business, and necessary production collapsed. Things did not improve, and President Franklin Roosevelt's victory was a vote for immediate federal intervention in the crisis. Roosevelt sent numerous proposals to Congress designed to stop the collapse of the economy and used his executive authority to close the banks and to stop mortgage foreclosures. The "New Deal" concepts as his proposals were termed, were enacted at an extremely rapid rate by Congress, which was beyond the point of reflection on the possible unconstitutionality of the measures as long as they would work.

In 1934 the Supreme Court upheld, in *Nebbia v. New York*,[53] a state statute creating a board to fix milk prices. This marked the reversal of the decisions of the 1920s in which the Court had struck down most statutes of this type. The *Nebbia* case allowed a state, within its police power, to make any regulations it deemed necessary for the public welfare, again demonstrating that the Court's view of new situations requires it to adopt new interpretations.

The regulatory agencies gained tremendous independence as a result of *Humphrey's Executor v. U.S.*[54] Humphrey had been appointed to the Federal Trade Commission by President Hoover, but before his term expired, President Roosevelt fired him. The Court, denying this power to the executive, distinguished this from the *Myers* case by holding that Myers was an employee of the executive department but that regulatory commissioners were not, since they were answerable only to the judicial and legislative branches of government and that, in fact, the commissions had been established to be as remote from presidential political influence as possible. The *Humphrey* case did for the commissions as much as the attempt to impeach Justice Chase in 1805 had done to sustain the principle of judicial independence.

The Court construed many New Deal laws as an unconstitutional delegation of legislative power to the executive. In January 1935, the Court issued ten decisions on New Deal legislation and struck down eight laws. In particular, the *Panama Refining Company*[55] case throttled the president's plan to regulate the oil industry. The Court held that when Congress passed a law giving the executive the right to regulate an industry without fixing standards, it had unconstitutionally delegated its lawmaking powers. The Court also struck down the National Industrial Recovery Act of 1933 in the *Schechter Poultry Co.*[56] case. The NIRA had used codes of wages, prices and marketing procedures that the president had allowed the affected industries to compose and again the Court said that these regulations were an unconstitutional delegation of Congress's power. The Agricultural Adjustment Act and the Bituminous Coal Act, both of which also regulated marketing procedures, were declared unconstitutional for the same reason. In *Carter v. Carter Coal Co.*,[57] the Court also said that regulation of coal production was per se invalid under the doctrine of the *Knight* case.

The basic issue in the country as the result of these decisions was the Court's refusal, at a crucial time in American life, to accept the concept of constitutional growth. Roosevelt and many of those of his political persuasion were furious with the Court, and the president's method of retaliation was known as the "Court-packing plan." Roosevelt interpreted his re-election in 1936 as a mandate from the people to continue his policies. In hopes of strengthening his position with the Court, he proposed to Congress that a new federal judge be named for each remaining on the Court after reaching age 70, which would have increased the membership of the Supreme Court to fifteen.

Tampering with the structure of the judicial branch was too much for Congress, even though a majority of its members disagreed with the Court, so the plan went down to defeat. However, the Court realized in the face of this threat that unless they bowed to the wishes of the people, the effectiveness of the judicial branch would be lost forever. Thus occurred "the switch in time which saved nine." In March, 1937, the Court reversed the *Adkins* case of 1923 and upheld minimum wages and maximum hours for women in *West Coast Hotel Co. v. Parrish.*[58] In *National Labor Relations Board v. Jones & Laughlin Steel Co.*[59] they upheld the right of the National Labor Relations Board to regulate all aspects of commerce, including production of goods that would be shipped in interstate commerce, thus finally overruling the doctrine of the *Knight* case. The Court also upheld the Social Security Act,[60] reversing its old idea that taxation could not be used to promote social welfare. These cases marked a definite break with the restrictive interpretation of "interstate commerce" that the Court had espoused for many years.

The year 1937 marked the end of a period of American history in which one group, business, dominated the economic scene, and by the end of that year, a more balanced social structure, with regard for the farmer and the worker, had replaced one-group rule. This was the end of the concept of the application of "due process" in economic matters and from that time until the present, "due process" has been used exclusively in cases involving individual liberties under the Bill of Rights. A new era of federal regulatory power was at hand. The New Deal changed the public's concept of the role the federal government should play in the economic sphere and "dual federalism," which left large areas of regulation to the states, was almost entirely dead. These constitutional changes were wide in their ramifications and today the federal government exercises wide control over our lives, but all these changes have taken place within the established structures of our government, and again, a flexible Constitution had met and overcome national problems.

1938–1953

Continuing its new economic policy, in 1938 the Court upheld federal enforcement of the rights of labor in a series of cases involving the National Labor Relations Board. The Court held that if interstate commerce were even remotely affected, the national

government could regulate production. In the 1938 case of *U.S. v. Carolene Products Co.,*[61] the Court said "regulatory legislation affecting ordinary commercial transactions is not to be pronounced unconstitutional unless it is of such a character as to preclude the assumption that it rests upon some rational basis within the knowledge of the legislature." Since it is almost impossible to show that a legislature is irrational, few, if any, attempts have been successful. In 1941 the Court upheld the child labor provisions of the Fair Labor Standard Act[62] in *U.S. v. Darby,*[63] thus overruling *Hammer v. Dagenhart. Mulford v. Smith,*[64] 1939, established the constitutionality of federal agriculture regulation and the Court also permitted federal regulation of public utilities. In 1940, in *Madden v. Kentucky*[65] the Court finally said that the concept that a corporation was a "citizen" for purposes of 14th Amendment protection was overruled and the era of the Court's efforts to block industrial regulation was over.

With the end of its preoccupation with economics cases, the Court entered a period of attention to individual liberties under the Bill of Rights. Since the beginning of this period, the Court has tried to establish a system of justice that will eventually realize the promises of liberty for which our revolution had been fought.

The Civil Liberties Era began with *Palko v. Connecticut*[66] in 1937. This case, involving the constitutionality of state laws affecting freedom of speech, incorporated for all time those provisions in the Bill of Rights "essential to the concept of ordered liberty" into the 14th Amendment. *DeJonge v. Oregon*[67] held that the right to participate in orderly political meetings was a federally protected right under the 1st Amendment and unless there was open advocacy of violence, the state could not restrict it. *Herndon v. Lowry,*[68] the third free-speech case that year, re-established Justice Holmes's "clear and present danger" rule, which had been ignored for many years. The 1937 case of *Senn v. Tile Layers Union*[69] added to the list of "incorporated rights" the right of peaceful picketing and *Hague v. C.I.O.*[70] added the right of peaceable assembly. *Cantwell v. Connecticut*[71] added freedom of religion to the list of rights with which the state could not interfere, and *Thornhill v. Alabama*[72] and *Lovell v. Griffin,*[73] both of 1938, added the right to distribute pamphlets and to organize politically. These concepts were carried over in the 1943 "Flag Salute"[74] cases in which the Court held that children who have religious objections to saluting the flag at school cannot, by any stretch of the imagination, be held to present a "clear and present danger" to the community. *Bridges v. California*[75] extended 1st Amendment protection to newspapers, declaring unconstitutional California laws that provided criminal penalties for newspapers that criticized the government. In 1946 the Court declared[76] that an attempt by Congress to cut the salaries of three government employees whom the House Un-American Activities Committee had declared "subversive" was an attempt to use the constitutionally forbidden device of a bill of attainder. All these cases throughout the 1940s and early 50s rested on a very broad interpretation of 1st Amendment freedoms.

In addition to the 1st Amendment cases, the late 30s and early 40s saw the genesis of a trend of civil rights cases that culminated in 1954 in *Brown v. Board of Education*,[77] which held that racial discrimination was unconstitutional. In 1938, although the Court did not specifically overrule "separate but equal," it held in *Missouri ex rel. Gaines v. Canada*[78] that facilities had to be equal in fact. Missouri had no law school for blacks and refused to admit them to the white law school, so the Court held that it must either build a new one for blacks immediately or admit them to the one it had. This decision marked the beginning of a new judicial mood toward blacks and was followed by *Sweatt v. Painter*[79] in 1950, which held that the black law school in Texas was inherently unequal because unless all law students have the same opportunities to meet those with whom they would later practice, they did not have an equal chance for education. *McLaurin v. Oklahoma*[80] in the same year held that students, once admitted, must be treated equally and may not be segregated in classes, the library, or the cafeteria.

Under the concept of "state action" in the 1875 *Civil Rights* cases, the Southern political parties had declared themselves to be private clubs and restricted the right to vote in the primaries to whites. *Smith v. Allwright*[81] in 1944 held that since the primary was an integral part of the electoral process, it had to be open to all. In addition to political rights, the Court also made new restrictions on "separate-but-equal." In 1941, *Mitchell v. U.S.*[82] held that denial of Pullman berths on trains to Negroes when they were provided for whites was a denial of equal protection of the laws, and in 1950 *Henderson v. U.S.*[83] forbade discrimination in railroad dining cars, since railroads were within the power of the federal government to regulate.

In the field of property rights, the 1948 case of *Shelley v. Kraemer*[84] forbade the judicial enforcement by civil suits of restrictive covenants in deeds. The Court could not outlaw provisions in deeds requiring purchasers to agree to resell only to whites, but it did declare that when lawsuits were brought to enforce them, state action was involved and hence the 14th Amendment was violated. The stage was thus set for the far-reaching decision of the Warren Court in the mid 50s and beyond that effectively rendered all segregation unconstitutional.

World War II again saw the country in crisis. President Roosevelt adopted the theory that war gave the executive sweeping emergency powers and the Supreme Court usually backed him up. As far back as 1936 in *U.S. v. Curtiss-Wright*,[85] the Court had held that the president's inherent powers in the field of foreign relations gave him the power to provide criminal penalties for shipping arms to foreign nations. This concept of "inherent executive power" was adhered to by the Court throughout the war. Roosevelt, as commander in chief, dispatched destroyers to our European Allies before we actually entered the war. After Pearl Harbor, by executive order derived from broad grants of authority from Congress, he created innumerable boards to regulate rationing, price control, production, labor disputes, and hundreds of other areas of life. In 1944 the Court sustained them in *Yakus v. U.S.*[86]

The civil liberties of 112,000 Japanese-Americans were completely ignored by an executive order that permitted the Army to remove them from their homes on the West Coast and intern them in detention camps for periods of up to four years, solely on the grounds that they were of Japanese descent. There was no attempt to distinguish between the loyal and the disloyal and they were just herded away. The 1944 case of *Korematsu v. U.S.*[87] upheld the detention on the theory that in a time of national emergency, the Army and the president have powers that they do not ordinarily possess, and that the suspension of the right to habeas corpus was therefore valid. Such orders would not be declared constitutional today, but during the fever that affected the Court as well as the country in wartime, constitutional "niceties" were sometimes overlooked. *Ex parte Quirin*[88] of 1942 held that a German spy in this country could be court-martialed instead of being tried in federal court and *In re Yamashita*[89] held that a Japanese general on trial for war crimes had no constitutional rights at all. The 1945 cases of *Cramer v. U.S.*[90] had held that before any American citizen could be tried for treason, it had to be shown that he actively helped the enemy's agents instead of just hiding them, but in 1947 *Haupt v. U.S.*[91] held that merely housing a spy was enough.

Although in retrospect what was done to the Japanese-Americans who were not guilty of anything except not being white sounds as if the country was not interested in any constitutional rights, with that most unbelievable exception (since the war was being fought to oppose race hatred), the Constitution did survive the war and its flexibility was demonstrated.

After the war this country embarked on a period of unparalleled involvement with the rest of the world. The period saw our involvement in the birth of the United Nations, a far cry from the isolationism abroad in the land when the Senate refused to ratify the treaty that would have let the United States join the League of Nations. The beginnings of the "Cold War" brought numerous defense treaties, such as our NATO involvement, in which we pledged our aid to our allies if attacked.

The Korean War was not a declared war, but President Truman dispatched troops to fight under his authority as commander in chief, asking afterwards for a congressional resolution of support, which he got after heated debate. The president's power in time of a "police action" was, however, not to equal the emergency powers held by a president in a declared war. During World War II President Roosevelt had seized several companies during time of labor difficulties in an effort to keep war materials production going. President Truman attempted to do the same thing to the steel mills when the Steelworkers' Union went out on strike during the Korean Conflict. However in 1952 in *Youngstown Sheet & Tube Co. v. Sawyer*[92] the Court found no statutory authority for his action and thus the seizure was unconstitutional. This was the first substantial check on presidential power since the New Deal days.

During the early 50s, the country embarked on a rather hysterical subversive witch-hunt spearheaded by Senator Joseph McCarthy, who was eventually censured by the Senate for his actions. The Congress passed numerous laws dealing with subversive activity and put new teeth into the Smith Act[93] of 1940, which had regulated speech that might be construed as an attempt to overthrow the government. Between 1948 and 1954, the Supreme Court upheld most of the laws as constitutional, although subsequently the Warren Court watered them down. In *American Communications Ass'n v. Douds*[94] in 1950 the Court upheld the constitutionality of a requirement in the Taft-Hartley Act that required unions to sign non-communist affidavits, on the theory that this was a valid use of the interstate commerce power. In *Dennis v. U.S.*,[95] 1951, the Court upheld the Smith Act provision requiring registration of those belonging to organizations that the attorney general thought subversive. This case was extremely significant, since the previous law, to which the Warren Court was to return, had been that before one could be prosecuted for belonging to an organization, it had to be proven that not only did one

belong, he had joined knowing that the organization sought to overthrow the government and had actively participated personally in illegal activities. The Smith Act declared that mere membership was enough to prove subversion, but *Wieman v. Updegraff*[96] in 1952 partially returned to the "knowledge" rule.

Other than in the field of sedition, the post-war Court rapidly increased the number of provisions in the Bill of Rights that it protected from state intervention by incorporation into the 14th Amendment. The 1949 decision in *Terminiello v. Chicago*[97] declared that a speaker whose remarks result in a riot is not liable for prosecution if the riot is caused by those who disagree with him as long as he himself is peaceable. In *Roth v. U.S.*[98] the Court sharply curtailed the right of censorship of allegedly "obscene" material and in *Burstyn v. Wilson*,[99] 1952, the Court held that movies may not be censured on the grounds that they are "sacreligious." In the field of freedom of religion, the Court enunciated many new cases upholding the doctrine of separation of church and state, and upheld the idea that the individual has the right to his own religious belief even if it is abhorrent to the rest of the community. *Everson v. Board of Education*,[100] 1947, in dealing with a state law providing free school bus transportation to children attending parochial schools, upheld the practice as an aid to the children, not to religion. However in 1948 in *McCollum v. Board of Education*,[101] the Court declared that a state could not impose religious ideas on children by using public school facilities for teaching religion, although in 1952 it upheld "released time" whereby children could be excused from school to go to a church for religious instruction.

Thus at the mid-point of the 1950s, while the Court was not willing to adopt the position that a possible political subversive had 1st Amendment rights that could overcome the danger he presented to the community, the 1st Amendment in other contexts was brought more firmly under the "preferred position" doctrine, in which, before a state or the federal government could infringe on 1st Amendment rights, it had to demonstrate a more overwhelming necessity than it was required to use in other areas.

1953–1969

The "Warren Court" began in 1953 when President Eisenhower appointed Earl Warren as chief justice, a position that he held until his retirement in 1969. In general terms, the Warren Court gave an emphasis new in American history to the personal rights of citizens. In the areas of civil rights, 1st Amendment freedoms, restrictions on the states' use of criminal procedures to deny fair trials and political rights, the Warren Court focused on the individual in society.

1969–1986

Chief Justice Warren E. Burger took office on June 24, 1969, and the "Warren Court" era was over. He resigned in 1986 to chair the nation's celebration of the Bicentennial of the Constitution.

1986–1997

In 1981, Justice Sandra Day O'Connor, who had not been able to get a job with a law firm at the time she graduated with honors from Stanford Law School, (because almost no law firms hired women in the 1950s), became the first woman member of the Supreme Court of the United States. President Clinton nominated Justice Ruth Bader Ginsburg, and she became the second woman justice in 1993. In the early 1970s the number of women in law schools and entering the practice of law and teaching increased remarkably. Today, almost all law schools have classes that are at least 40 percent women and in some law schools, women students are a majority. As these women, who studied law in the 1960s and 1970s (including Hillary Rodham Clinton and Elizabeth Hansford Dole), reach positions of responsibility within the legal profession and as elected officials, it will be very interesting to see what changes, if any, occur in the American legal and political systems.

President Ronald Reagan named Justice William H. Rehnquist as chief justice in 1986 to succeed Chief Justice Burger. Justice Rehnquist had been appointed to the Supreme Court by President Nixon in 1981 and began service on the Court in January 1982.

Presidents Reagan and Bush served for a total of 12 years, and made six appointments to the Supreme Court. Combined with the remaining appointees of Presidents Nixon and Ford, this meant that eight of the nine justices who sat on the Court when President Clinton came into office had been appointed by Republicans and, at least in theory, would be expected to hold more "conservative" views. However, this has not always been the case.

The Supreme Court under the leadership of Chief Justice Rehnquist was expected to be less protective of individual liberties than the Court had been during the Warren era. In some cases, this has proved to be true. The Rehnquist Court has been more willing than its predecessors to uphold criminal convictions in cases where the convicted person claimed violations of his or her 4th Amendment rights by the police. However, there are other areas in which the Rehnquist Court ruled in favor of individual rights and against the constitutionality of state criminal laws or other restrictions on personal behavior. For example, in a series of cases beginning in 1989, the Court upheld specific restrictions established by state legislatures on abortion rights. Other restrictions, however, were overturned as "burdensome," and the Court explicitly refused to overturn the basic right to abortion that was established in *Roe v. Wade*. In 1989, as well, the Court struck down laws in 48 states that prohibited the burning or desecration of the American flag. The Court held that this activity fell under the category of political speech and was protected by the 1st Amendment.

As we come to the 21st century, we will live in a world where the Internet changes the ability to communicate, not only within communities but within the world. When medical science can do miraculous things to keep people alive, whereas others are denied even minimal medical care and die needless deaths while they are young; when within the lifetime of the students reading this book, it will be possible to clone humans; how will the legal system respond? Who owns a frozen embryo? What are the limits parents can place on what public schools teach their children and, therefore, the children of others? We cannot foresee the answers, but we know that the Constitution will ensure that the questions will be dealt with in a manner that will value the individual and respect the process by which the solutions are found.

The Preamble

WE THE PEOPLE of the United States, in Order to form a more perfect Union, establish Justice, insure domestic Tranquility, provide for the common defence, promote the general Welfare, and secure the Blessings of Liberty to ourselves and our Posterity, do ordain and establish this CONSTITUTION for the United States of America.

THE AUTHORITY of our Constitution was given by the consent of the people of all the states and was not the act of the independent state governments. Although delegates to the Constitutional Convention had been elected by the state legislatures, the Constitution was submitted to the people for ratification, not to the legislatures. Our government, therefore, proceeds directly from the people and was established by them. In 1819 the Supreme Court upheld this view of the source of the Constitution's authority in *McCulloch v. Maryland*,[1] probably the most famous judicial decision in our history.

Whether the Constitution was established by the people or by an agreement among the states is not an unimportant question. Throughout our history some people have felt that the United States government and its Constitution came into being by action of the state governments. This is known as the "states' rights" or "compact" view of constitutional interpretation. Implied in the theory that all the national government's powers come from grants by the states is an idea known as "interposition." Those who believe in interposition believe that the United States is nothing more than a group of 50 states and that any state may impose its power within its borders against any decision of the Supreme Court or any act of Congress. In effect, this doctrine holds that a state does not have to respect those decisions of the United States Supreme Court with which it does not agree. This is, as you can see, a theory very similar to that which existed at the time of the Articles of Confederation. The keystone of this thesis was disavowed in the Preamble of our Constitution and by Article VI.[2]

Although the Preamble indicates by whom the Constitution was established and the general purposes for which the people ordained it, it has never been regarded as the source of any specific powers conferred on any branch of the government.[3] Such powers arise only from specific grants in the body of the Constitution or those that may be implied from those specific grants.

The purpose of the Preamble is to expound the nature, extent, and application of the powers actually conferred by the Constitution and not to create them.

The Preamble is a clear indication that the founders were not just a group of men creating a government that would serve their own narrow, selfish interests, but that they were statesmen dedicated to establishing a government that would serve the common good for many generations. Two hundred years of success prove the wisdom of their political theories.

Article One

ARTICLE I of the Constitution deals with the Congress, the legislative branch of the federal government. The Congress, rather than the president, is vested by the Constitution with the lawmaking function and the president is restricted to recommending laws thought wise, vetoing of laws considered bad, and seeing to the faithful execution of laws properly enacted by Congress.[1] This article describes the composition of the two Houses of Congress (the Senate and the House of Representatives), the requirements for election to either House and the powers and duties of this branch of the government. It also specifically forbids Congress and the states to do certain specified things.

The framers of the Constitution envisioned the Congress as the most important and most powerful branch of the government. Our constitutional practice grows by custom and usage as well as by amendment, and the growth of the legislative power of the president is one way in which it has been quite startling. Today much of the important legislation is initiated by the president and members of his executive departments. When you read in the newspaper that "The president sent a bill to Congress today," you should remember that George Washington never sent bills to Congress. Historically speaking, this is a recent use of presidential power.

One of the major political questions at the present time is the proper division of power between the president and the Congress, particularly in matters relating to the conduct of military affairs. Representatives and senators on committees such as Foreign Affairs and Armed Services are often in conflict with the president's representatives, such as the secretaries of defense and state, about whose business it is to send troops and carry on military operations.

The Gramm-Rudman Hollings Act, designed to reduce the federal financial deficit that by 1986 had begun to cause the nation serious economic problems, required reductions in federal spending. If Congress and the president did not agree on spending cuts, they would be made automatically by the comptroller-general of the United States based on percentages specified in the legislation. The Supreme Court held the act unconstitutionally in violation of the doctrine of separation of powers, since it vested executive authority, which belongs to the president, in the hands of the comptroller-general, who is subservient to Congress.[2]

SECTION 1

All legislative Powers herein granted shall be vested in a Congress of the United States, which shall consist of a Senate and House of Representatives.

There are two Houses of Congress. The Senate has two members from each state and the House of Representatives consists of members apportioned on the basis of population. Every ten years the federal government takes a census to determine how many people live in each state, and a state may gain or lose representatives on the basis of this survey.

The bicameral system was fixed at the Constitutional Convention as a result of the "Connecticut Compromise." The big states, quite naturally, wanted a Congress whose membership would be determined by population. The smaller states wanted a legislature in which each state would have the same number of representatives. When the convention was about to collapse on this very fundamental issue, the Connecticut Compromise saved the day, the convention, and our system of government.

SECTION 2

1 The House of Representatives shall be composed of Members chosen every second Year by the People of the several States, and the Electors in each State shall have the Qualifications requisite for Electors of the most numerous Branch of the State Legislature.

2 No Person shall be a Representative who shall not have attained to the Age of twenty-five Years, and been seven Years a Citizen of the United States, and who shall not, when elected, be an Inhabitant of that State in which he shall be chosen.

3 [Representatives and direct Taxes shall be apportioned among the several States which may be included within this Union, according to their respective Numbers, which shall be determined by adding to the whole Number of free Persons, including those bound to Service for a Term of Years, and excluding Indians not taxed, three fifths of all other Persons.]* The actual Enumeration shall be made within three Years after the first Meeting of the Congress of the United States, and within every subsequent Term of ten Years, in such Manner as they shall by Law direct. The Number of Representatives shall not exceed one for every thirty Thousand, but each State shall have at Least one Representative; and until such enumeration shall be made, the State of New Hampshire shall be entitled to chuse three, Massachusetts eight, Rhode-Island and Providence Plantations one, Connecticut five, New-York six, New Jersey four, Pennsylvania eight, Delaware one, Maryland six, Virginia ten, North Carolina five, South Carolina five, and Georgia three.

4 When vacancies happen in the Representation from any State, the Executive Authority thereof shall issue Writs of Election to fill such Vacancies.

5 The House of Representatives shall chuse their Speaker and other Officers; and shall have the sole Power of Impeachment

---

*Bracketed text means that this portion of text has been altered by an amendment or is no longer applicable.

CLAUSE 1 Elections are held every two years for all 435 members of the House of Representatives. The men who wrote the Constitution felt that a short term of office would force the representatives to remain in close touch with the people whom they represent and would ensure that at least this branch of the Congress would remain in close contact with the will of the people.

This section also points out that to be an elector (voter) in a congressional election, one must abide by the qualifications set by the *state* for voting for state legislators. All qualified voters have a constitutionally protected right to cast their ballots and have them counted in a congressional election,[3] but both state and federal laws are involved. Each may make regulations on the same subject. The paramount character of those made by Congress, however, has the effect of superseding those made by the state if there is any inconsistency between them.[4] Various amendments to the Constitution and supplementary acts of Congress passed immediately after the Civil War and in recent years ensure that voters must be registered by the states without discrimination because of race, creed, color or sex, but even with such federal requirements, registration of voters and regulation of elections are still primarily state powers.

CLAUSE 2 There is a legal difference between being an "inhabitant" and a "legal resident" of a state, and it is interesting to note that the only requirement in the Constitution is that a candidate for Congress must be an inhabitant.

Students whose colleges are outside their home

states remain legal residents of the states from which they came. They probably have drivers' licenses from their home states, are usually registered to vote at home and, when someone asks them where they are from, they give their home states. This and other criteria, such as an intention to remain there, make one a legal resident of a state. On the other hand, one is an inhabitant of a state in which one is physically present. The same student, while at school, is an inhabitant of the state where the college is located. The same rule applies to members of the Armed Forces stationed in the United States. They are legal residents of the state from which they came, but they are inhabitants of the state where they are stationed.

CLAUSE 3 "Direct taxes" are those imposed directly on property according to its value. "Other persons" meant slaves, and this clause has been obsolete since slavery was abolished. The entire bracketed portion of this clause was changed by Section 2 of the 14th Amendment.

The rest of this clause set up the original House of Representatives before the first census could be taken. If we had one representative for every 30,000 people today, the House would be so enormous that no work could be done. Some years ago the House itself set its quota of members at 435, and that number of representatives is distributed among the states on the basis of population, although all states have at least one representative.

CLAUSE 4 This clause gives the governor of a state the authority to call a special election in case of the death or resignation of one of the state's representatives.

CLAUSE 5 The Speaker of the House, the presiding officer of that body, is, as a matter of practice, chosen by the majority party.

When the House exercises its power of impeachment, it brings charges against a federal officer. In other words, the House acts in the same way that a grand jury acts in respect to an ordinary person accused of a crime. It issues a statement of charges against the official and presents the evidence of guilt to the Senate. House members do not determine the guilt or innocence of a person under impeachment. They only decide if the facts indicate a trial and present them to the Senate.

SECTION 3

1 The Senate of the United States shall be composed of two Senators from each State, [chosen by the Legislature thereof,] for six Years; and each Senator shall have one Vote.

2 Immediately after they shall be assembled in Consequence of the first Election, they shall be divided as equally as may be into three Classes. The Seats of the Senators of the first Class shall be vacated at the Expiration of the second Year, of the second Class at the Expiration of the fourth Year, and of the third Class at the Expiration of the sixth Year, so that one-third may be chosen every second Year; [and if Vacancies happen by Resignation, or otherwise, during the Recess of the Legislature of any State, the Executive thereof may make temporary Appointments until the next Meeting of the Legislature, which shall then fill such Vacancies.]

3 No Person shall be a Senator who shall not have attained to the Age of thirty Years, and been nine Years a Citizen of the United States, and who shall not, when elected, be an Inhabitant of that State for which he shall be chosen.

4 The Vice President of the United States shall be President of the Senate, but shall have no Vote, unless they be equally divided.

5 The Senate shall chuse their other Officers, and also a President pro tempore, in the Absence of the Vice President, or when he shall exercise the Office of President of the United States.

6 The Senate shall have the sole Power to try all Impeachments. When sitting for that Purpose, they shall be on Oath or Affirmation. When the President of the United States is tried, the Chief Justice shall preside: And no Person shall be convicted without the Concurrence of two thirds of the Members present.

7 Judgment in Cases of Impeachment shall not extend further than to removal from Office, and disqualification to hold and enjoy any Office of honor, Trust or Profit under the United States: but the Party convicted shall nevertheless be liable and subject to Indictment, Trial, Judgment and Punishment, according to Law.

CLAUSE 1 The Senate is composed of two members from each state. At one time, the state legislatures elected senators, but the 17th Amendment provided that the citizens of each state would elect senators directly, just as they do members of the House of Representatives.

Unlike the House of Representatives, senators serve for six years and only one-third of that body is elected in each general election. It is, therefore, a continuous body. This ensures, or so the framers of the Constitution believed, a continuity of policy that we would not have if it were possible to elect entirely new members of both Houses of Congress in any one election.

CLAUSE 2 The bracketed portion of this clause was changed by the 17th Amendment. In case of a vacancy in the Senate, the governor of the state in which the vacancy occurs *appoints* someone to fill the unexpired term of the previous senator. You will note that this differs from the procedure to be followed in case of a vacancy in the House of Representatives. However, the appointment only lasts until the next general election.

Example

Senator Y, from the State of New York, dies after a year of his senatorial term has passed. The governor appoints X to his seat. X serves for another year, until the next general election. If he wishes to remain in the Senate, he must run for the remaining four years of the term.

An election to fill the remainder of a term is the only time it is possible for both Senate seats from the same state to be contested at the same time. The Senate is so composed that the terms for senators from one state expire at different times, but in the case of an election to fill a vacancy, if the other senator's term is regularly expiring at the same time, both seats will be contested in the same election.

CLAUSE 3 The same rules as to inhabitancy apply to the Senate as to the House.

CLAUSE 5 The president pro tempore (called the president pro tem) of the Senate is generally the senator with the longest service.

CLAUSE 6 When a bill of impeachment, which is similar to an indictment, has been drawn by the House of Representatives, it is presented to the Senate, which exercises the same function as a jury in a criminal case. It hears the evidence against the impeached official, any evidence he wishes to present, considers the facts, and finds the official guilty or not guilty. The Senate has the right to compel the attendance of witnesses and to require witnesses to answer in the same way that courts do. They must take an oath, as a juror does, to do their duty fairly and honestly.

CLAUSE 7 In all the history of our country, only seven officials (all federal judges) have been impeached by the Senate. Fourteen bills of impeachment have been brought by the House. In 1974, for the second time in the history of our country, impeachment of a president became a possibility. The House Judiciary Committee voted three articles of impeachment against President Richard Nixon. When President Nixon resigned before the articles could be voted on by the full House, the proceedings where automatically terminated. The sole penalty that flows directly from an impeachment case is removal from office, and the Senate cannot send an impeached official to jail. However, the proper procedure would be to present the evidence on which the impeachment was based to the proper authorities in state or federal courts, who would then see that the official was tried under the ordinary criminal statutes by the ordinary processes of the law.

Examples

1. A federal judge, Walter Nixon, was convicted of two counts of making false statements to a federal grand jury. The grand jury's investigation stemmed from reports that Nixon had accepted a bribe from a man in exchange for asking a local district attorney to stop the prosecution of the

man's son. Nixon was sentenced to prison and was thereafter impeached by the Senate. After he went to prison and before he was impeached, he continued to receive his federal judge's salary.[5]

2. Another federal judge, Alcee L. Hastings, was indicted on charges of conspiracy to accept a bribe. In 1983, he was acquitted by a jury on all charges. Six years later, in 1989, the Senate voted to impeach Judge Hastings on eight articles of impeachment that paralleled the facts that the jury had concluded were not criminal. The district court in Washington, to which Hastings appealed, held that the courts had no jurisdiction to intervene, even if, as the opinion stated, "This Court believes that the events surrounding plaintiff's impeachment are an unfortunate chapter in the history of this country."[6] Mr. Hastings was thereafter elected to the House of Representatives, where he is currently sitting.

SECTION 4

1 The Times, Places and Manner of holding Elections for Senators and Representatives, shall be prescribed in each State by the Legislature thereof; but the Congress may at any time by Law make or alter such Regulations, except as to the Place of Chusing Senators.

2 The Congress shall assemble at least once in every Year, and such Meeting shall [be on the first Monday in December,] unless they shall by Law appoint a different Day.

CLAUSE 1 In 1872 Congress established the first Tuesday after the first Monday in November as election day. As we have already seen, Congress and the states have joint control of election practices and requirements, and this section, Amendments 14, 15, 17, and additional federal legislation have set the standards that Congress requires in federal elections.

CLAUSE 2 This clause has been superseded by Amendment Twenty.

SECTION 5

1 Each House shall be the Judge of the Elections, Returns and Qualifications of its own Members, and a Majority of each shall constitute a Quorum to do Business; but a smaller Number may adjourn from day to day, and may be authorized to compel the Attendance of absent Members, in such Manner, and under such Penalties as each House may provide.

2 Each House may determine the Rules of its Proceedings, punish its Members for disorderly Behavior, and with the Concurrence of two thirds, expel a Member.

3 Each House shall keep a Journal of its Proceedings, and from time to time publish the same, excepting such Parts as may in their Judgment require Secrecy; and the Yeas and Nays of the Members of either House on any question shall, at the Desire of one fifth of those Present, be entered on the Journal.

4 Neither House, during the Session of Congress, shall, without the Consent of the other, adjourn for more than three days, nor to any other Place than that in which the two Houses shall be sitting.

CLAUSE 1 Until 1969 the House and the Senate had the power to refuse to seat a duly elected representative who had come to sit in either House, and the courts had no power to intervene on behalf of a representative who had been refused his or her seat. However, on June 16, 1969 in an historic decision, the Supreme Court of the United States substantially restricted the power of either House of Congress to refuse to seat a duly elected member. Representative Adam Clayton Powell of New York had been denied his seat in the 90th Congress in 1967–68 as a result of his conviction of contempt of a New York court as well as alleged misappropriation of federal funds during the 89th Congress. In *Powell v. McCormack*[7] the Supreme Court interpreted Congress's power to judge "the qualifications of its members" to be restricted to a determination of those qualifications specifically set forth in Article I of the Constitution. In other words, it now appears that Congress can refuse to seat an elected member *only* if it finds that he or she does not meet the requirements of age, citizenship, and inhabitancy that are stated in Article I, Section 2, Clause 2 for the House and Section 3, Clause 3 for the Senate. The Court stated, however, that once a member has been seated, the House of which he or she is a member may expel or discipline that member as it sees fit.

Either House may still exercise some control over the elections of its members. An incumbent senator's re-election margin was so close that his opponent was entitled to a recount under state law. The senator sought to enjoin the recount on the theory that this clause made the Senate the only body that could determine the outcome of the election. The Supreme Court held that the state had the authority to conduct a recount under its own law, since the Senate's authority to undertake an independent one if it wished to do so was not affected by any action the state might choose to take.[8]

Examples

1. Henry Horrid, a notorious gangster, is elected to the House of Representatives. The other members of the House are quite upset about this. Under the ruling in the *Powell* case, as long as Henry is 25, has been a citizen for 7 years, and is an inhabitant of the state from which he was elected, he must be given the oath and allowed to take his seat. However, once this has been done, he may be expelled by a two-thirds vote of the House.

2. Yvette Youngster is only 23 when she is elected to the House. Since she does not meet the specific requirements for membership set forth in the Constitution, the House may, by a simple majority vote, deny her her seat.

Furthermore, the state has no power to refuse to send a duly elected representative to Washington.

Example

The Supreme Court of Maryland held that disqualification after election of a subversive person seeking to overthrow the federal government by force and violence must be determined by Congress itself and not by the state.[9]

CLAUSE 2 In addition to determining the rules of procedure for day-to-day activity on the floor of the House or Senate, members of the Congress also determine rules and procedures for committee hearings. A congressional committee may investigate in order to determine the necessity or advisability of future legislation, but it must set up rules before it begins and abide by them once the hearings have begun.[10] It may compel disclosures of facts relevant to its inquiry, but it has no constitutional power to expose witnesses or their associations simply for the sake of exposure.[11] A congressional committee is not required to give a witness all the rights that he would have in a federal criminal court.

A member of Congress is not subject to impeachment and the only method of expulsion, once seated, is by a two-thirds vote of a quorum (a majority) of the appropriate house.

Example

Senator Bob Packwood was brought before the Senate Ethics Committee on multiple charges of sexual harassment. During the committee's investigation, it discovered that the senator kept extensive diaries covering all of the time he had been in the Senate. While examining these diaries, the committee's representatives discovered that Senator Packwood may have tried to use his senatorial connections illegally to get his former wife a job (presumably to lower the amount of alimony he would be required to pay). Senator Packwood then said that he would no longer allow inspections of his diaries and the Ethics Committee subpoenaed them. The court held that the Ethics Committee had the power to investigate allegations of misconduct and that a court could not restrict the scope of that investigation. The Court upheld the issuance of the subpoena.[12]

Senator Packwood resigned before he could be expelled.

SECTION 6

1 The Senators and Representatives shall receive a Compensation for their Services, to be ascertained by Law, and paid out of the Treasury of the United States. They shall in all Cases, except Treason, Felony and Breach of the Peace, be privileged from Arrest during their Attendance at the Session of their respective Houses, and in going to and returning from the same; and for any Speech or Debate in either House, they shall not be questioned in any other Place.

2 No Senator or Representative shall, during the Time for which he was elected, be appointed to any civil Office under the Authority of the United States, which shall have been created, or the Emoluments whereof shall have been encreased during such time; and no Person holding any Office under the United States, shall be a Member of either House during his Continuance in Office.

CLAUSE 1 Members of Congress are exempt from arrest in order to protect their independence in the legislature. At one time, a king could deal with dissident members of his legislature by arresting the rebels and holding them in jail until his measures had been passed by a more pliable parliament. It was in order to prevent any such interference that the framers of the Constitution inserted this clause. A member of Congress, however, is not exempt from civil suits or from a serious criminal charge, known as a "felony."

Examples

1. A representative has a wreck on the way to work one morning and in due course, the other driver files a civil suit for damages against him. He is not privileged to ignore the suit.

2. A representative commits murder. Murder is a felony. He may not plead privilege when he is arrested.

Several members of the Congress have been involved in decisions involving congressional immunity from criminal prosecution or investigation. The decision on whether or not immunity existed depended on the nature of the activities in which the senators or representatives were engaged.

A congressman made a speech on the House floor in return for payment of money. His conviction was overturned when the Supreme Court held that any judicial inquiry into a congressman's motivation for making a speech would be unconstitutional.[13]

A former senator was charged with accepting bribes while in office. The bribes were paid him in exchange for his agreement to perform certain acts relating to nonlegislative Senate business. He claimed that since he had been a member of the Senate at the time the acts were supposed to have taken place, he was immune from criminal prosecution. The Supreme Court held that illegal political, as opposed to legislative, actions were not covered by the immunity provisions of this section. The former senator could, therefore, be prosecuted.[14]

Examples

1. Congressman Mel Reynolds was tried and convicted of having a sexual relationship with a minor. He was sentenced to prison, where he is currently confined. His status as a congressman was irrelevant.[15]

2. Senator David Durenberger was indicted for making false claims for reimbursement of expenses while on senatorial business. He was not protected from court action because he was a senator.[16]

3. A congressman was charged with a violation of the Ethics in Government Act because he allegedly willfully failed to file truthful financial statements. He did not report certain loans. He received a Letter of Reproof from the House. The Department of Justice brought a criminal action against him. He challenged the Department of Justice. The courts held that he was not protected by the speech and debate clause because the actions were unrelated to legislative matters and the House rules permitted the attorney general to bring actions to enforce this act.[17]

4. Congressman Dan Rostenkowski was charged with misappropriation of congressional funds. The court held that the criminal prosecution did not violate the speech or debate clause because the misappropriations, many of which involved staff

"kickbacks," did not involve the legislative process. He was not prosecuted for violating House rules, he was prosecuted for violating the criminal law.[18]

The fact that a member of Congress may not be sued for slander (oral defamation of character) for anything he or she says on the floor of Congress is a very important privilege. The basis of the rule of absolute immunity of congressional officials from damage done by their acts or speeches, even though it is knowingly false or wrong when it is done, is that the importance of the individual's hurt is overbalanced by the public necessity for untrammeled legislative activity.[19] A witness may not recover damages for any injury to his or her reputation that occurs in a congressional investigation.[20]

Examples

1. John Doe is a witness before a congressional committee and his appearance is televised. While he is testifying, a member of the committee makes the flat statement that Doe is a murderer. This is not true and the committee member knows it. Doe loses his job and all his friends. The member of the committee is not subject to suit.

2. The same congressman, while addressing a club meeting, makes the same statement about Doe. Doe may file suit against him for slander and defamation of character.

There have been times in the history of our country, some quite recently, when wild accusations have been made in committees and innocent people badly hurt. However, were this power curbed, it is possible that members of Congress would be intimidated by fear of suit from carrying out proper investigations.

Examples

1. The House of Representatives enacted a rule that considerations of raising the income tax required a vote of at least 3/5 of the members voting, instead of a simple majority. This was challenged as unconstitutional by some House members and voters. The Court held that since the Constitution provides that each House may make its own rules, the courts had no authority to review congressional practices.[21]

2. During preparations for a lawsuit against several tobacco companies, a legal assistant in a law firm representing one of the companies made unauthorized copies of important documents damaging to the tobacco companies. He gave copies of the documents to members of Congress who were holding hearings on tobacco-related issues. The company issued subpoenas to two congressmen. The courts held that the speech or debate clause barred enforcement of these subpoenas.[22]

CLAUSE 2 No member of Congress may be a federal judge, act as a member of any part of the executive branch of the government (including the cabinet) or hold an active commission in the Armed Forces while he or she is sitting in Congress.

SECTION 7

1 All Bills for raising Revenue shall originate in the House of Representatives; but the Senate may propose or concur with Amendments as on other Bills.

2 Every Bill which shall have passed the House of Representatives and the Senate, shall, before it become a Law, be presented to the President of the United States; If he approve he shall sign it, but if not he shall return it, with his Objections to that House in which it shall have originated, who shall enter the Objections at large on their Journal, and proceed to reconsider it. If after such Reconsideration two thirds of that House shall agree to pass the Bill, it shall be sent, together with the Objections, to the other House, by which it shall likewise be reconsidered, and if approved by two thirds of that House, it shall become a Law. But in all such Cases the Votes of both Houses shall be determined by Yeas and Nays, and the Names of the Persons voting for and against the Bill shall be entered on the Journal of each House respectively. If any Bill shall not be returned by the President within ten Days (Sundays

excepted) after it shall have been presented to him, the Same shall be a Law, in like Manner as if he had signed it, unless the Congress by their Adjournment prevent its Return, in which Case it shall not be a Law.

3 Every Order, Resolution, or Vote to which the Concurrence of the Senate and House of Representatives may be necessary (except on a question of Adjournment) shall be presented to the President of the United States; and before the Same shall take Effect, shall be approved by him, or being disapproved by him, shall be repassed by two thirds of the Senate and House of Representatives, according to the Rules and Limitations prescribed in the Case of a Bill.

CLAUSE 1 Revenue (tax) bills always originate in the House of Representatives because the authors of the Constitution thought that the members of that body were "closer to the people." At the time the Constitution was written, the members of the Senate were not directly elected by the voters. Even today, with terms of two years, House members can be voted out much faster than the senators with six-year terms, if the voters become angry with them.

CLAUSE 2 This clause describes the procedure by which a bill becomes a law. A member in either house proposes a bill that goes to the appropriate committee (Judiciary, Armed Services, Foreign Relations, and the like) of the House of which he or she is a member. On many occasions identical bills are introduced into the Senate and House at the same time. When the committee under whose jurisdiction the bill falls has approved it by majority vote, it is submitted to the entire body for a vote. It then goes to the other House, where it is also considered by a committee and then considered by the entire body. The procedure in each House varies slightly. The House of Representatives has a Rules Committee to establish the conditions for debate of each bill before it is sent to the floor for debate by the full House. The Senate debates all bills under the same rules, so has no need for a Rules Committee.

If there is a difference in the versions passed by the House and Senate, the bill goes to a "conference committee" composed of members of both Houses. Once the bill leaves that committee, it is repassed in identical form by both Houses. It is then signed by the Speaker of the House and the president of the Senate and sent to the president.

The president may do one of three things to a bill. If he signs it, it becomes law. If he approves of the bill, but for political reasons does not wish to be responsible for it, he may exercise a "pocket veto." In this case, he keeps the bill but does not sign it. If Congress is still in session ten days after he receives the bill and he has not returned it, it becomes law without his sig-

nature. If, however, Congress has adjourned before the expiration of the ten days, the bill is dead. If the president vetoes the bill, he refuses to sign it and sends it back to Congress with his reasons. It may be sent back to the House in which it originated and if it is repassed by both Houses with a two-thirds majority of a quorum, it becomes law without the president's signature and over his objections. In 1997 Congress enacted the Line-Item Veto statute. For the first time in American history, a president may remove specific provisions of a bill and still sign it. President Clinton invoked the new law when he struck three items from the Budget Bill on August 11, 1997 and signed the rest.

In order to allow Congress to legislate as well as to carry out its other responsibilities, it must have the authority to investigate. The power to investigate has become one of Congress's most used and sometimes abused powers. The power to investigate led to the development of the congressional committee system. In recent years, almost any significant issue in American life and politics has been investigated by a congressional committee, from whether or not one should be allowed to sell one's kidney for transplant to the activities of the National Security Council. Congress has used these broad powers to look into every major action of the president. This has led on many occasions to tension between the legislative and executive branches, and each is very protective of its powers.

In particular, Congress has tried to use its power to control the executive branch through the "legislative veto." Congress delegates general powers to the executive branch but may disapprove the plans for implementation. In *Immigration and Naturalization Service v. Chadha*,[23] a 1983 decision, the Supreme Court questioned the constitutionality of legislative vetoes. The full effects of this ruling are not yet clear, but Justice White wrote in dissent that the Court's decision "strikes down in one fell swoop provisions in more laws enacted by Congress than the Court has cumulatively invalidated in its history."

Example

The Clean Water Bill was passed almost without dissenting vote by both Houses of Congress in 1986 but was vetoed by President Ronald Reagan. As soon as the new Congress assembled in January, 1987, both Houses again passed the bill. When President Reagan again vetoed it, both Houses then overrode his veto and the Clean Water Bill became law.

CLAUSE 3 This clause permits Congress to express its opinion on something that is not a proper subject for legislation. A concurrent resolution reflects the sentiment of both Houses in matters such as the Gulf of Tonkin Resolution approving President Johnson's conduct of the Vietnam Conflict.

SECTION 8

Section 8 of Article I deals with specific powers of Congress. Except in the field of foreign relations, Congress has no powers except those specifically granted by some part of the Constitution or that may be implied from those specific grants. As you will see, the courts have taken a very broad view of what "may be implied" means, but in any case a federal law is unconstitutional unless it may be related to some power that Congress has.

By the nature of the federal system, the United States and not the individual states must carry out diplomatic business. Other countries do not send ambassadors to one of our states, they send them to the president, who represents the federal government. If the states carried on foreign relations, we would have no federal system and it is in the nature of our governmental system for Congress to legislate on the subject of foreign relations. The power to conduct foreign relations is therefore known as an "inherent power."

This section of Article I deals with enumerated powers of Congress. Congress also has powers that flow by implication from these enumerated powers, and that are necessary in order to carry out an enumerated power.

Example

Congress has an enumerated power to raise an army. From this may be implied the power to draft men for military service and to decide that women will not be drafted.[24]

1 The Congress shall have Power To lay and collect Taxes, Duties, Imposts and Excises, to pay the Debts and provide for the common Defence and general Welfare of the United States; but all Duties, Imposts and Excises shall be uniform throughout the United States;

2 To borrow Money on the credit of the United States;

3 To regulate Commerce with foreign Nations, and among the several States, and with the Indian Tribes;

4 To establish an uniform Rule of Naturalization, and uniform Laws on the subject of Bankruptcies throughout the United States;

5 To coin Money, regulate the Value thereof, and of foreign Coin, and fix the Standard of Weights and Measures;

6 To provide for the Punishment of counterfeiting the Securities and current Coin of the United States;

7 To establish Post Offices and post Roads;

8 To promote the Progress of Science and useful Arts, by securing for limited Times to Authors and Inventors the exclusive Right to their respective Writings and Discoveries;

9 To constitute Tribunals inferior to the supreme Court;

10 To define and punish Piracies and Felonies committed on the high Seas, and Offences against the Law of Nations;

11 To declare War, grant Letters of Marque and Reprisal, and make Rules concerning Captures on Land and Water;

12 To raise and support Armies, but no Appropriation of Money to that Use shall be for a longer Term than two Years;

13 To provide and maintain a Navy;

14 To make Rules for the Government and Regulation of the land and naval Forces;

15 To provide for calling forth the Militia to execute the Laws of the Union, suppress Insurrections and repel Invasions;

16 To provide for organizing, arming, and disciplining the Militia, and for governing such Part of them as may be employed in the Service of the United States, reserving to the States respectively, the Appointment of the Officers, and the Authority of training the Militia according to the discipline prescribed by Congress;

17 To exercise exclusive Legislation in all Cases whatsoever, over such District (not exceeding ten Miles square) as may, by Cession of particular States, and the Acceptance of Congress, become the Seat of the Government of the United States, and to exercise like Authority over all Places purchased by the Consent of the Legislature of the State in which the Same shall be, for the Erection of Forts, Magazines, Arsenals, dock-Yards, and other needful Buildings;—And

18 To make all Laws which shall be necessary and proper for carrying into Execution the foregoing Powers, and all other Powers vested by this Constitution in the Government of the United States, or in any Department or Officer thereof.

CLAUSE 1 Under our constitutional system, both national and state governments have the power to tax (dual power is known as "concurrent power"). The federal government may tax a state's activities if those activities are not part of the essential government of a state and are a profit-making enterprise.

Example

The state of New York bottled and sold mineral water. The courts held that such an activity was not an essential part of state government and as such was subject to federal taxation.[25]

Instrumentalities of the national government may not, however, be taxed by the states. This ruling was first enunciated by Chief Justice Marshall in the very famous case of *McCulloch v. Maryland*[26] in 1819. The Supreme Court still refuses to allow state taxation of any federal property, such as mail trucks, which do not bear state license tags, which are primarily revenue-raising devices, or federally owned real estate. The Supreme Court has held that a national bank was immune from state sales taxes on purchases made by the bank.[27]

This clause gives Congress the power to collect and levy taxes necessary for any purpose proper under any constitutional power.

The second portion of this clause prohibits duties that are not uniform at all ports.

Example

If you order a sweater from Scotland, the import duty would be the same if it arrived in the port of New York or the port of Charleston.

CLAUSE 2 This clause permits the government to issue savings bonds and paper money.

CLAUSE 3 This is the "interstate commerce" clause and is one of the most important congressional powers. The power of Congress to regulate commerce between the states is the power to enact all appropriate legislation for its protection and advancement.[28] Almost anything you eat or buy is in some way involved with interstate commerce. If you go to the movies, the film was probably sent from another state. If you eat in a restaurant, it is most unlikely that all the food and all the seasoning and all the silverware came from within your state. If you buy something in a store, it probably came from the factory across a state line. All transportation industries are part of interstate commerce.

As you can see, in modern-day America it is virtually impossible to exist without encountering interstate commerce. Where it goes, Congress has the power to regulate it.

Examples

1. Under this clause, Congress was empowered by the 1964 Civil Rights Act to prohibit racial discrimination in public eating establishments.

2. The National Collegiate Athletic Association (NCAA) is a national organization that regulates intercollegiate sports. Each year the member institutions enact rules dealing with recruiting, eligibility, financial aid, and other such issues. After allegations of violations led to an investigation of the University of Nevada at Las Vegas, the Nevada legislature enacted a statute requiring the NCAA to provide special procedural protections in any case involving a Nevada school, student, or employee. The NCAA challenged the state legislature's authority to make such a law, and the federal court held that the law violated the interstate commerce clause.[29]

There is another aspect of this problem that should be noted, which is the power of the states to make laws regarding these subjects. In general, where there has been only partial exercise by the federal government of its power to regulate interstate commerce, the state may legislate on the phases that have been left unregulated, but when the United States exercises its legislative power so as to conflict with state regulation, the state law usually becomes inoperative and the federal legislation is exclusive in its application.[30] This power of the federal government is called "pre-emption."

If a local or state statute or regulation is more stringent than a federal one, however, preemption may not occur. For example,[31] federal regulations governing blood plasma centers do not preempt more stringent county regulations. Thus a state may set a higher standard than the federal government does, but not a lower one. Most areas of labor-management relations, for example, fall into areas that have been pre-empted by federal legislation.

As you can see, Congress has the constitutional power to interject federal legislation into virtually every aspect of all commerce. Whether it should or should not exercise this power is another question, the answer to which depends on your view of the role of the federal government, but it does, quite clearly, have this power if it chooses to use it.

CLAUSE 4 The naturalization clause permits Congress to do two things. It may legislate on the subject of the admission of immigrants to this country and it may legislate on the requirements for naturalization. A "naturalized citizen" is one who was born a citizen of another country and becomes a citizen of the United States by following certain procedures set forth by federal law. Also, this clause gives Congress, by implication, the power to revoke citizenship for a naturalized citizen who has committed certain specific criminal offenses against the United States government. In effect, there are only two differences between the rights of the native-born American citizen and a naturalized citizen. A naturalized citizen is ineligible to become president of the United States and a naturalized citizen may have his citizenship revoked. A native-born American may renounce his citizenship but it may not be revoked against his will.[32]

Bankruptcy laws belong, because of this clause, exclusively in the domain of federal law. A bankrupt person is one who owes more money than he has assets. He may wish to go into voluntary bankruptcy in order to discharge finally these debts or his creditors may throw him into involuntary bankruptcy. The debtor must declare all his assets and the creditors appear and list the debts and the final result is that the creditors are paid a certain percentage of what is owed them and the bankrupt person is discharged from further liability. He is, however, still liable for such debts as alimony payments.

CLAUSE 8 Congress has the power to issue patents to protect an inventor's right in his invention, although to qualify for a patent, the invention must be new and useful. After a patent has been issued, no one may use the device without the permission and payment of royalties to the patentee. Similarly, a writer may get a copyright on a book, a play, a movie, or music, which prohibits others from using what he has created without acknowledging his authorship and payment of a royalty.

Patent and copyright cases now involve topics of which the men who wrote the Constitution would never have dreamed.[33] Is computer software subject to patent or copyright regulation? Is a computer program an invention or creative writing? For example, the Supreme Court held in 1984 that the sale of home videocassette recorders did not infringe the copyrights of television programs.[34]

CLAUSE 9 All federal courts, the subject of Article III, except the Supreme Court, are established and may be abolished by Congress.

CLAUSE 10 Effective use of this clause is difficult because there is no definite code of international law. However, it permits Congress to enact federal laws that make murder or other crimes on the high seas a crime against the government of the United States *as long as* they are committed on United States ships.

CLAUSE 11 Letters of Marque and Reprisal, banned by international agreement in 1856, were issued by a government to private individuals and gave them power to raid enemy shipping without being guilty of piracy.

This clause makes it quite clear that Congress is the proper branch of the government for declaring war and establishing programs necessary for pursuing it. This involves the rule that in wartime, the rights of the individual must yield to the face of necessity and to the extent necessary for the preservation of the state.[35] The war power is the power to wage war successfully and one that permits harnessing of the entire efforts of the people. Congress may, therefore, in time of war, require rationing and price controls. However, the direct interference with liberty and property and abridgement of constitutional guarantees of freedom can be justified only when the danger to the government is real and impending.[36]

The last time Congress declared war was at the beginning of World War II. All military actions by the Armed Forces of the United States since the close of that war have not been "wars" in the legal sense. The president, as commander in chief of the troops, has dispatched them to Korea, Vietnam, and other trouble spots without a declaration of war. He is empowered to do this under Article II. This power of the president was the subject of a great deal of congressional dissatisfaction in the course of the Vietnam Conflict. On the other hand, with present-day weapons on the world scene, an attack upon the United States would require instant dispatch of men and weapons and the president would have no time to request Congress to assemble and issue a declaration of war before retaliation could take place.

CLAUSE 12 This clause gives Congress the power of the purse over the military. The president may send troops as he pleases, but if Congress disapproves, it does not have to issue the money to pay them until he brings them home. This clause also permits Congress, by implication, to establish the draft.

The two-year restriction on appropriations was designed to ensure the civilian supremacy over the military, a cornerstone of the Anglo-Saxon and American legal systems.

CLAUSE 13 The Navy is likewise established and financed by Congress.

CLAUSE 15 The "Militia" in the Constitution refers to what we know as the National Guard. Until it is "federalized" the Guard is a state-supervised organization, but the president and the Congress may call it up into federal service in case of emergency, at which time it becomes a part of the Army. As a result of legislation by Congress delegating its power to him, the president may call up the Guard without consulting Congress, should the need arise.

CLAUSE 16 Although the Guard is a state organization, Congress appropriates money for it and may control it through appropriation.

CLAUSE 17 Congress has exclusive jurisdiction over all federal property. An Armed Forces base in the United States is federal territory, and any crimes committed by civilians thereon are tried in federal court, although the state may exercise concurrent jurisdiction in some respects.

Until 1973, the District of Columbia was governed by a congressional committee and those local officials appointed by that committee. A citizen of the District had no voice in local affairs. The "Home Rule" statute allowed election of a mayor and other officials who handle all local matters in the same way the mayor and other officials operate any other city. Congress still maintains the streets and provides for fire and police protection for the area of the District encompassing federal monuments and buildings.

When the District of Columbia almost became bankrupt in 1995 and city services were drastically curtailed, President Clinton appointed a board of financial overseers to investigate the situation and manage the city's finances. When the situation became even worse, Congress appropriated funds, but provided them on the condition of increased oversight and, thus, a reduction in the authority of the city government.

CLAUSE 18 This clause gives Congress the power to make all laws that are necessary to execute its powers granted by the Constitution or to facilitate the exercise of powers given to the president or the judiciary. However, the term "necessary" includes all appropriate means that are conducive to the end to be accomplished. "Proper" means "convenient.37 It does not mean that Congress has the power to exercise any function that it chooses, although there is no constitutional basis for such.

Example

The Department of Health and Human Services has no authority to regulate biomedical research projects for which it does not provide funding.

SECTION 9

There are certain specified acts that the Constitution expressly prohibits to Congress. These are enumerated in Section 9.

1 The Migration or Importation of such Persons as any of the States now existing shall think proper to admit, shall not be prohibited by the Congress prior to the Year one thousand eight hundred and eight, but a Tax or duty may be imposed on such Importation, not exceeding ten dollars for each Person.

2 The Privilege of the Writ of Habeas Corpus shall not be suspended, unless when in Cases of Rebellion or Invasion the public Safety may require it.

3 No Bill of Attainder or ex post facto Law shall be passed.

4 No Capitation, or other direct, Tax shall be laid, unless in Proportion to the Census or Enumeration herein before directed to be taken.

5 No Tax or Duty shall be laid on Articles exported from any State.

6 No Preference shall be given by any Regulation of Commerce or Revenue to the Ports of one State over those of another: nor shall Vessels bound to, or from, one State, be obliged to enter, clear, or pay Duties in another.

7 No Money shall be drawn from the Treasury, but in Consequence of Appropriations made by Law; and a regular Statement and Account of the Receipts and Expenditures of all public Money shall be published from time to time.

8 No Title of Nobility shall be granted by the United States: And no Person holding any Office of Profit or Trust under them, shall, without the Consent of the Congress, accept of any present, Emolument, Office, or Title, of any kind whatever, from any King, Prince, or foreign State.

CLAUSE 1 This clause referred to the slave trade and is therefore now obsolete.

CLAUSE 2 This clause guarantees one of the most important rights a citizen of the United States can have. "Habeas corpus" means, in Latin, "you have the body" and writs are issued to bring a party in custody before a judge. It is concerned with the legality of the detention and not with the guilt or innocence of the accused if he is charged with a proper crime. Every person, regardless of where he is held, whose liberty has been unlawfully restrained, has an absolute right to test the legality of his detention by use of this writ.[38] Habeas corpus is also the appropri-

ate remedy for a prisoner who is denied the effective assistance of counsel.[39]

If you are in jail and wish to get out, your lawyer would ask a judge to issue a writ of habeas corpus. You and the sheriff or the person who has you in custody would be brought before the judge. The judge would then determine (1) if you were held on a legitimate criminal charge and (2) whether bail should be granted. If the jailor can show that you are properly in custody, the judge will not grant the writ. The judge does not determine whether or not you are guilty of the crime as charged. He merely determines if you are charged with a legitimate crime.

Examples

1. A man is brought before a judge on a writ of habeas corpus and the jailor testifies that the man is being held on a charge of car theft, that bail had been set, and that the man could not pay it. The judge determines that the man is being held on a valid charge and denies the writ.

2. A man is brought before the judge on a writ and the jailor testifies that he is being held because he has red hair. The judge would decide that there is no criminal offense charged and order the man released.

There are times when the national interest in time of war requires suspension of the writ of habeas corpus. It may be suspended for enemy aliens, who are usually interned until the cessation of hostilities.[40] During World War II, many native-born Americans of Japanese ancestry were interned in camps set up by the federal government. Although denial of their right of habeas corpus was upheld at that time by the courts,[41] it is inconceivable that such internments would be permitted in these times.

CLAUSE 3 A bill of attainder is a legislative act passed against a named person or identifiable group pronouncing him, her, or them guilty of a crime without a trial.

Examples

1. Two teenage girls got into a fistfight. One lost jewelry and sustained injuries that required medical care. She filed a criminal complaint against the other girl and asked for an award of damages. In New York, the state where the altercation occurred, there was a statute making parents liable for malicious acts committed by children between the ages of 10 and 18. The victim's mother sued the aggressor's mother for damages. Because the parent could have no conceivable defense to any claim, the Court held that the statute was a bill of attainder. [42]

2. In 1984, the Supreme Court held that a federal statute requiring compliance with draft registration in order for a college student to be eligible for federal financial aid was not a bill of attainder.[43] The statute did not single out an identifiable group and there was no punishment.

Because it is the business of the judicial branch of the government to determine guilt or innocence of criminal acts and the business of the legislative branch to specify behavior, not individuals, as criminal, bills of attainder are forbidden.

An ex post facto law is one that imposes punishment for an act that was not punishable at the time it was committed or that imposes additional punishment. A retroactive law that applies to civil actions and that does not impose a criminal penalty is not an ex post facto law and does not violate this provision of the Constitution.

Examples

1. A student had a federally insured college loan from his college. When he defaulted, the college assigned the note to the federal government, which was authorized by a statute to collect students loans. The government brought suit against him to recover the money. The Court held that the statute was not a criminal one and therefore was not an ex post facto law, even though it was enacted after the loan was made.[44]

2. The president of a pharmaceutical manufacturing company was debarred by the Food and Drug Administration (FDA) from any further involvement in drug development. The man had been convicted of bribing an FDA employee. The debarment provision in the statute under which the FDA acted had been added after the crime had been committed, but the court held that it was not a criminal "punishment," thus, not subject to ex post facto provisions.[45]

3. A man was convicted of a series of misdemeanors, including possession of a weapon and possession of stolen property. He was sentenced to one year's imprisonment for each count. At the time he committed the crime, the maximum punishment for each count was six months. The court held that the longer sentence violated ex post facto guarantees.[46]

4. A sixteen-year-old boy was committed to a juvenile detention facility after he was convicted of murder in February 1990. In December of that year, the state legislature amended the juvenile justice statute and the boy was resentenced under the new statute for a much longer term. When he challenged the resentencing, the Court held that his rights against ex post facto punishment had been violated.[47]

CLAUSE 4 This clause has been modified by the 16th Amendment, which permits the levying of income taxes and is no longer of use. A direct tax is one on real or personal property by reason of its being owned by the taxpayer.

CLAUSE 5 You may not be required to pay a duty on an article that you send to another country.

CLAUSE 6 Import duties must be the same at all ports.

CLAUSE 7 This clause gives Congress the power of the purse strings over all aspects of the federal government's activities. It is a restriction on the power of the executive department to spend, and means simply that no money can be paid out of the Treasury unless it has been appropriated by an act of Congress.

CLAUSE 8 The United States is prohibited from creating a class of peers as was found in England and from granting titles such as duke and earl.

SECTION 10

This section prohibits states from carrying on certain specified activities. In addition to these prohibitions, of course, as we saw in the section on interstate commerce, because of the principle of the supremacy of federal law found in Article VI, the federal government may restrict the operation of state laws by implication by the passage of conflicting federal laws.

1 No State shall enter into any Treaty, Alliance, or Confederation; grant Letters of Marque and Reprisal; coin Money; emit Bills of Credit; make any Thing but gold and silver Coin a Tender in Payment of Debts; pass any Bill of Attainder, ex post facto Law, or Law impairing the Obligation of Contracts, or grant any Title of Nobility.

2 No State shall, without the Consent of the Congress, lay any Imposts or Duties on Imports or Exports, except what may be absolutely necessary for executing its inspection Laws: and the net Produce of all Duties and Imposts, laid by any State on Imports or Exports, shall be for the Use of the Treasury of the United States; and all such Laws shall be subject to the Revision and Controul of the Congress.

3 No State shall, without the Consent of Congress, lay any duty of Tonnage, keep Troops, or Ships of War in time of Peace, enter into any Agreement or Compact with another State, or with a foreign Power, or engage in War, unless actually invaded, or in such imminent Danger as will not admit of delay.

CLAUSE 1 A state would obviously destroy the fundamental system of our government if it made a treaty with a foreign nation. To do so would render the existence of the national government unimportant.

A "bill of credit" is paper that will be redeemed at a later date) issued to be used as money.

A state law that impairs the obligation of a contract is one that alters the legal duty of the parties to abide by an agreement which, at the time it was made, the law recognized as enforceable.

Examples

1. The legal rate of interest in Mr. Doodle Bugg's state is 10 percent. Mr. Bugg borrows money at that rate on Monday. On Tuesday, the state legislature makes a law that the legal rate is 6 percent. If Mr. Bugg were permitted to go to court and ask to have the interest on his note reduced, the state would have impaired the obligation of his contract.

2. A state public service authority operated its finances on a fiscal year that began on July 1. It asked and received from the state legislature permission to change to a fiscal year that conformed to the calendar year. This changed the immediate marketability of its bonds (because they would become due at different dates), and some banks who held its bonds sued to stop the change. The Court held that this legislative action did not impair the obligations of the authority's contracts, because the bond obligations would be met.[48]

A state does have the authority to require the alteration of contracts for reasons of important public policies.

Example

The legislature in Maine enacted a law requiring companies that issued health insurance policies to insure or continue to insure persons with preexisting medical conditions after a wait not to exceed two years. The companies sued, and the Court held that this was not an impairment of contracts forbidden by the Constitution. The new statute provided an answer to a pressing public health problem, which was the number of people who lost their insurance because they became ill, or who could not purchase it in the first place because of health problems.[49]

CLAUSE 2 No state may charge an export duty for goods going out of state or an import duty on goods shipped from out of the country or from another state. However, inspections of incoming goods may be required to protect the health of the citizens. As long as the amount of inspection fee charged is merely to defray expenses, the fee is not unconstitutional.[50]

Examples

1. Some states require inspection of fruit brought from another state in order to control Japanese beetles. A small fee in order to pay expenses of such inspection is valid.

2. A statute providing for the inspection of oil products that required the payment of a fee per barrel to defray expenses did not violate this clause.

3. A fee charged on books shipped into the state would be unconstitutional.

4. Alabama enacted a statute imposing taxes on aircraft fuel oil sold in the state. An oil company loaded fuel to be sent to Canada onto a tanker docked in Mobile, Alabama. The oil company refused to pay the state tax and contested it. The Court held that the tax violated the prohibition against import-export taxes.[51]

CLAUSE 3 A "duty of tonnage" is a fee charged to a vessel before it may enter the ports of a state.

This clause also prohibits states from having their own armies that are not subject to federal regulation.

States are not required to obtain congressional approval to join in a "reciprocity statute."[52] A reciprocity statute is one made by two or more states in which each one gives citizens of the other certain privileges on condition that its citizens enjoy the same privileges while in the other states.

Example

The Uniform Support of Dependents Act has been adopted by most states. If a man deserts his family in New York and moves to California, normal court procedures would require that he be brought back to New York for trial on the question of alimony and child support. This usually takes a great deal of time and in the meantime, the family could suffer severe hardship. The Uniform Act provides that the facts would be sent to a California judge by a New York court, the judge in California would determine the amount of support to be paid, and the California court would collect the money and send it to the New York court for distribution to the family. The New York courts would do the same for a California man who had abandoned his family in California.

On the other hand, an agreement between two states regarding joint land use would require congressional approval.

Example

Agreements on the use of hydroelectric power by states located on a river that ran among them would be a "compact" and would require congressional approval.[53]

Article Two

ARTICLE II deals with the executive branch of the government—the President of the United States—and specifies his powers, duties, responsibilities, and qualifications for office. He has no powers not derived from the Constitution.[1] It is his responsibility, first and foremost, to carry out the laws that have been made by the legislative branch.

The men who wrote the Constitution probably had no idea that the president of the United States would ever exert as much power as present-day presidents do. The executive branch now initiates legislation and is responsible for activities of the governmental departments to which he has delegated some of his powers. The American president is now not only the most powerful individual in our own country, but is one of the most powerful people in the entire world. This growth of the president's power is an excellent example of the ways in which our constitutional government has grown and changed by custom and usage.

SECTION 1

1 The executive Power shall be vested in a President of the United States of America. He shall hold his Office during the Term of four Years, and, together with the Vice-President, chosen for the same Term, be elected, as follows

2 Each State shall appoint, in such Manner as the Legislature thereof may direct, a Number of Electors, equal to the whole Number of Senators and Representatives to which the State may be entitled in the Congress: but no Senator or Representative, or Person holding an Office of Trust or Profit under the United States, shall be appointed an Elector. [The Electors shall meet in their respective States, and vote by Ballot for two persons, of whom one at least shall not be an Inhabitant of the same State with themselves. And they shall make a List of all the Persons voted for, and of the Number of Votes for each; which List they shall sign and certify, and transmit sealed to the Seat of the Government of the United States, directed to the President of the Senate. The President of the Senate shall, in the Presence of the Senate and House of Representatives, open all the Certificates, and the Votes shall then be counted. The Person having the greatest Number of Votes shall be the President, if such Number be a Majority of the whole Number of Electors appointed; and if there be more than one who have such Majority, and have an equal Number of Votes, then the House of Representatives shall immediately chuse by Ballot one of them for President; and if no Person have a Majority, then from the five highest on the List the said House shall in like Manner chuse the President. But in chusing the President, the Votes shall be taken by States, the Representation from each State having one Vote; A quorum for this Purpose shall consist of a Member or Members from two-thirds of the States, and a Majority of all the States shall be necessary to a Choice. In every Case, after the Choice of the President, the Person having the greatest Number of Votes of the Electors shall be the Vice President. But if there should remain two or more who have equal Votes, the Senate Shall chuse from them by Ballot the Vice President.]

3 The Congress may determine the Time of chusing the Electors, and the Day on which they shall give their Votes; which Day shall be the same throughout the United States.

4 No Person except a natural born Citizen, or a Citizen of the United States, at the time of the Adoption of this Constitution, shall be eligible to the Office of President; neither shall any Person be eligible to that Office who shall not have attained to the Age of thirty-five Years, and been fourteen Years a Resident within the United States.

5 In Case of the Removal of the President from Office, or of his Death, Resignation, or Inability to discharge the Powers and Duties of the said Office, the same shall devolve on the Vice President, and the Congress may by Law provide for the Case of Removal, Death, Resignation or Inability, both of the President and Vice President, declaring what Officer shall then act as President, and such Officer shall act accordingly, until the Disability be removed, or a President shall be elected.

6 The President shall, at stated Times, receive for his Services, a Compensation, which shall neither be increased nor diminished during the Period for which he shall have been elected, and he shall not receive within that Period any other Emolument from the United States, or any of them.

7 Before he enter on the Execution of his Office, he shall take the following Oath or Affirmation:— "I do solemnly swear (or affirm) that I will faithfully execute the Office of President of the United States, and will to the best of my Ability, preserve, protect and defend the Constitution of the United States."

CLAUSE 1 Although not specifically mentioned in the Constitution, the doctrine of executive privilege, the power of the president to withhold information from Congress, had been accepted until the time of the Watergate scandals. When Alexander Butterfield, a presidential aide, told the Select Committee investigating Nixon's role in the matter that President Nixon tape recorded all conversations in his office, the committee demanded the tapes. Nixon refused to release them and the matter ended in the Supreme Court. In *United States v. Nixon*,[2] the Court recognized the proper role of executive privilege but declared that when challenged, the burden was on the White House to prove a need to protect diplomatic or military secrets and specifically excluded from it any evidence of criminal wrongdoing in the White House.

Example

During the litigation following the Iran-Contra investigation, one of the defendants, John Poindexter, who had been President Reagan's National Security Advisor, wished to subpoena former President Reagan as a defense witness. He also wished to subpoena the former president's diaries. The Court ordered that Mr. Reagan testify by videotaped deposition, but it did not order him to appear in court. The Court refused to order then-President Bush to testify. The Court found that a current or former president might be required to testify in court, but that the exercise of that power must be done in a way that is least disruptive. Moreover, the relevance of the president's or a cabinet member's testimony must be demonstrated in advance.[3]

The president is absolutely immune from any damage awards in suits brought against him for any activity involving his presidency, even if a court eventually decides that the presidential action that was the subject of the suit violated the plaintiff's rights.[4]

Example

A woman brought a sexual harassment suit against President Clinton. The alleged act occurred while he was governor of Arkansas and she was a state employee. Mr. Clinton did not claim that presidential immunity would apply to this case, but he did argue that the case should be dismissed, subject to reinstatement after his term of office expires. The trial court rejected that claim, but ordered that the action be stayed (delayed) until his term was completed. The appellate court held that pre-trial depositions and other matters could proceed, although the judge supervising scheduling should be respectful of the president's schedule. The issue in this case, which the Supreme Court decided in 1997, is whether the president should be free to go about his official duties or whether a trial judge can exercise some degree of control over his schedule. The Court held that this does not violate the principle of separation of powers.[5]

CLAUSE 2 The method of election of the president will be discussed under Amendment Twelve. It is sufficient to say here that the president and vice president are only indirectly elected by the voters. The second portion of this clause has been entirely superseded by Amendment Twelve.

CLAUSE 3 As we have seen, Congress has chosen the Tuesday after the first Monday in November as election day.

CLAUSE 4 The office of president of the United States is the only one that a naturalized citizen may not hold. A candidate born of American parents in a foreign country would be considered to be a native-born American and is eligible for election as long as he has complied with the fourteen-year residency requirement.

Example

Senator Barry Goldwater, Republican candidate for president in 1964, was born in Arizona when it was still a territory and, of course, was an American citizen by birth.

CLAUSE 5 The problem of an incapacitated president has been one of the more serious constitutional problems in our history and the 25th Amendment was adopted in order to deal with it. When a president dies in office, the vice president succeeds him and assumes the title and the responsibilities of president. The question of whether a vice president actually became president or was merely an acting president was settled in 1841 when Tyler became president and set a precedent for future vice presidents to follow. The difficulties arise, however, when a president is too ill to carry out his duties but the office has not been vacated. President Wilson's illness in 1919 and 1920 is the best example of prolonged incapacitation. Until quite recently, this question was never settled and there have been times when the office of the president was virtually unoccupied. Beginning with President Eisenhower and continuing through Presidents Kennedy and Johnson, each man made an agreement with his vice president as to the circumstances under which the vice president would assume control of presidential duties. However, these agreements were merely stop-gap arrangements, had no legal force, and obviously were not sufficient.

The problem would arise most critically in the event that a president ever became mentally ill or senile. A president who has had a heart attack normally realizes he is too sick to act and is aware of the necessity of relinquishing his duties. However, in some forms of mental disease or senility, the nature of the difficulty would be such that the president would not voluntarily give up his responsibilities and powers. The 25th Amendment provides for involuntary removal of the president from his power (but not from his office) if this tragedy should ever occur.

CLAUSE 6 If Congress were able to reduce the presidential salary, they could starve him out of office if they did not approve of his administration.

CLAUSE 7 Any judicial officer, including a justice of the peace, may administer the presidential oath. When President Lyndon Johnson was sworn in following the assassination of President Kennedy, the oath was administered by a woman, Judge Sarah T. Hughes of the Federal District Court.

The president becomes president when his term begins or, if he succeeds from the vice presidency, when the previous president dies. His office is not assumed from the time he takes the oath.

Example

President Johnson became president at the instant President Kennedy died. The office was not vacant between the president's death and administration of the oath to President Johnson.

SECTION 2

1 The President shall be Commander in Chief of the Army and Navy of the United States, and of the Militia of the several States, when called into the actual Service of the United States; he may require the Opinion in writing, of the principal Officer in each of the executive Departments, upon any subject relating to the Duties of their respective Offices, and he shall have Power to Grant Reprieves and Pardons for Offenses against the United States, except in Cases of Impeachment.

2 He shall have Power, by and with the Advice and Consent of the Senate, to make Treaties, provided two-thirds of the Senators present concur; and he shall nominate, and by and with the Advice and Consent of the Senate, shall appoint Ambassadors, other public Ministers and Consuls, Judges of the supreme Court, and all other Officers of the United States, whose Appointments are not herein otherwise provided for, and which shall be established by Law: but the Congress may by Law vest the Appointment of such inferior Officers, as they think proper, in the President alone, in the Courts of Law, or in the Heads of Departments.

3 The President shall have Power to fill up all Vacancies that may happen during the Recess of the Senate, by granting Commissions which shall expire at the End of their next Session.

CLAUSE 1 This clause invests the president with the right to wage a war that the Congress has declared and to carry into effect all laws passed by Congress for the conduct of war and for the government and regulation of the Armed Forces.[6] The president also has the authority to dispatch troops throughout the world without waiting for a congressional declaration of war. In fact, Congress has only declared war five times in our history, while American troops have fought outside the United States more than 150 times. Our Founding Fathers feared the military establishment so they quite clearly made a civilian the supreme commander.

In August 1990 when Iraq invaded Kuwait, President George Bush sent United States troops to the Persian Gulf. By November of that year, there were about 230,000 American troops in the area and President Bush announced that he intended to increase that number substantially. Fifty-three House members and one senator filed a suit to enjoin further deployment of troops without a declaration of war. The Court held that although the plaintiffs had raised legitimate arguments about the extent of the president's power to commit Armed Forces, the case could not be heard before Congress took legislative action or until a majority of the members of Congress joined the suit.[7] Other recent cases also involved efforts to restrain the president's authority to deploy troops. The governor of Minnesota brought a suit to prevent deployment of the Minnesota National Guard to Central America,[8] a taxpayer sued to prevent troops from being sent to the Persian Gulf,[9] and a National Guard sergeant who had been called to active duty in the Persian Gulf tried to enjoin his deployment.[10] In each case, the courts pointed out that the president had the authority to deploy the Armed Forces and the courts did not have the authority to intervene.

Although the cabinet is not mentioned anywhere in the Constitution, the drafters of the Constitution realized the obvious need for executive departments and assumed that they would exist. The Departments of State, War, and the Treasury were established in 1789.

The president may reprieve or pardon any criminal who has committed a *federal* crime. A pardon, in effect, wipes away the criminal record. It restores all civil rights and releases the offender from all disabilities, such as a sentence of imprisonment, imposed by the offense. It does not, however, impose upon the government any obligation to compensate the offender for anything he may have suffered by reason of his imprisonment.[11] A reprieve merely postponed the execution of the sentence. A president is powerless to pardon a criminal convicted of a *state* crime.[12]

Examples

1. Mr. Bad Mann throws a rock through the post office window. This is a federal crime. He is tried, convicted and sentenced to a term of imprisonment in the federal penitentiary. The president may pardon or reprieve him.

2. Luke Looped is tried, convicted and sentenced for drunk driving in a state court and is serving his term in the state penitentiary. The president may not pardon or reprieve him, but the governor of the state has the power to do so.

After President Nixon resigned, President Ford, citing as his reason a desire to let the nation heal from the wounds of Watergate and to get on to other unsolved national problems, unconditionally pardoned Nixon, even though he had not been indicted for any crime.[13] The pardon created such a national uproar that it was an important factor in President Ford's loss of the next election to Jimmy Carter.

Several persons in the National Security Administration, the Central Intelligence Agency, and other government officials were indicted and convicted in the Iran-Contra affair. President Bush pardoned many of them.[14]

CLAUSE 2 A treaty is a compact made between two or more nations. Because a treaty becomes part of the federal law, a state law that conflicts with it must yield to the treaty.[15] As a matter of practice, instead of asking for senatorial advice, the president and his representatives negotiate treaties and then ask the Senate for ratification. Ratification must be by a two-thirds vote of a quorum of 51 Senators.

In recent years, most of the treaties that the presidents have signed have been ratified, but some of them have not been assured of overwhelming support. Although President Wilson was largely responsible for the drafting of the Charter of the League of Nations, the Senate refused to ratify it.

Examples

1. When General Manuel Noriega was captured during the American invasion of Panama, he claimed to be a prisoner of war at his trial in the federal court in the United States. After he was convicted, this status became relevant when he was to be sentenced. He claimed that he was entitled to the benefits of the Geneva Convention relative to the treatment of prisoners of war in determining the conditions of his confinement. The court in which he was tried held that the Geneva Convention did apply to his case and, upon ratification of that treaty on July 6, 1995, the terms of the Convention had become part of the "supreme law of the land."[16]

2. Sea turtles are often trapped in nets used by commercial shrimpers. Congress enacted a law directing the secretary of state to initiate negotiations with other nations to establish treaties protecting sea turtles. The Earth Island Institute brought suit against Secretary of State Warren Christopher for failing to conduct such negotiations. The Court dismissed the suit and held that the statute violated the separation of powers doctrine. The Congress does not have the authority to direct the president or the executive branch to initiate discussions with foreign nations.[17]

The Constitution is silent about terminating treaties. In 1979 President Carter announced the termination of the treaty between this country and Taiwan. He did this without obtaining congressional approval. Senator Barry Goldwater challenged President Carter's action in court, but the Supreme Court upheld the president.[18]

The president has sidestepped the consent right of the Senate by using executive agreements. Executive agreements are negotiated by the State Department and validated by the president.

Only a majority vote is required to confirm a presidential appointment. The "vacancies" referred to in Clause 3 refer to the list given in Clause 2.

CLAUSE 3 During a recess of the Senate, the president has the power to fill, by temporary commission, a vacancy that occurred during the previous session. A temporary commission continues until the end of the next session of Congress.

Example

The president appoints his son-in-law as ambassador to Great Britain during a recess of the Congress. When Congress comes back into its new session, the Senate unanimously refuses to confirm the appointment. The ambassador remains on his post until the end of the session.

SECTION 3

He shall from time to time give to the Congress Information of the State of the Union, and recommend to their Consideration such Measures as he shall judge necessary and expedient; he may, on extraordinary Occasions, convene both Houses, or either of them, and in Case of Disagreement between them, with Respect to the Time of Adjournment, he may adjourn them to such Time as he shall think proper; he shall receive Ambassadors and other public Ministers; he shall take Care that the Laws be faithfully executed, and shall Commission all the Officers of the United States.

Each year the president must present, in person or otherwise, a "State of the Union" message to Congress in which he reviews national progress during the preceding year and presents, in general terms, his plans for the next year.

The duty of the president to see that the laws are faithfully executed is not limited to the enforcement of acts of Congress, but includes the rights, duties, and obligations growing out of the Constitution, our international relations, and all the protections to citizens implied by the nature of the government under the Constitution.[11]

The president commissions, among others, all officers in the Armed Forces.

SECTION 4

The President, Vice President and all civil Officers of the United States, shall be removed from Office on Impeachment for, and Conviction of, Treason, Bribery, or other high Crimes and Misdemeanors.

All civil officers of the federal government may be impeached. This excludes military officers and members of Congress. As we have seen, impeachment extends only to removal from office, but ordinary proceedings in federal or state criminal courts may follow.

The grounds for impeachment are only that of commission of a crime and not because a majority of the Congress thinks the president or judge involved is of obnoxious political beliefs or has in good faith mismanaged his office. Senility, inability to function for any reason, or other difficulties that do not constitute a criminal offense are not grounds for impeachment. An offense charged in an impeachment must be a criminal act that implies moral turpitude (conduct contrary to justice, honesty, or good morals), which is dangerous to the safety of the state, and which makes an incumbent unfit to remain in his office.[20]

The House Judiciary Committee voted three articles of impeachment against President Richard M. Nixon. Article I charged him with criminal obstruction of justice during the investigations of the Watergate scandal. Article II charged him with criminal violations of the rights of American citizens, alleging his complicity in the Watergate break-ins and wiretaps. Article III charged him with refusing to provide the congressional investigators with tape recordings and records they had subpoenaed. Mr. Nixon resigned before the full House of Representatives voted to send the Bill of Impeachment to the Senate.

Examples

1. If Joseph Blow, president of the United States, accepts a bribe to veto a bill, he has committed a federal crime. He may be impeached.

2. If Joseph Blow, president of the United States, dresses himself in a toga and goes to Congress and tells them he is Emperor Julius Caesar reincarnated, he may not be impeached. Since the adoption of Amendment Twenty-five, Blow's powers would probably be given to the vice president until he recovered.

Article Three

ARTICLE III deals with the third branch of the government—the judicial branch. The Supreme Court is established by this article and, as we have seen, by Article I, but all lower federal courts and the jurisdiction of all federal courts including the Supreme Court, have been established by Congress and may be altered or abolished by it.

Courts have what is known as "judicial power." This means they may decide cases that are actually before them and pronounce judgment between the parties to the case. They may not decide hypothetical questions and they have no investigative power.

Example

Following a 1992 Supreme Court decision that prayers at public school graduations violated the 1st Amendment, the American Civil Liberties Union (ACLU) in Tennessee indicated that if school systems planned such prayers at graduations, the ACLU would represent students and their families who objected and asked the ACLU for help. A high school principal filed suit in the Tennessee state courts against the ACLU and asked that the Court decide if the Tennessee statute on the subject was constitutional. The federal court took jurisdiction of the case and held that the case was only a hypothetical one in the absence of any action by the ACLU.[1]

Alone among the court systems of the world, state and federal courts in the United States exercise a most important power known as "judicial review." There is no mention of judicial review in the Constitution because it grew as a matter of practice and not constitutional or statutory directive. Judicial review is the power of a court to declare a law or act of the executive unconstitutional—that is, to determine the validity of the law or act in relation to the higher constitutional law that binds all branches of the government.

Since they have the power of judicial review, the courts are, in effect, the most powerful of the three branches of government. The federal courts may declare acts of Congress, actions of the president or any part of the executive branch, state statutes, and state court decisions to be in conflict with the Constitution and therefore void. As a matter of fact, most determinations of constitutionality in the Supreme Court involve decisions made by state courts on state laws.

Since it is a grave matter to superimpose the decision of nine justices upon the actions of the elected legislative branch of the government, the Supreme Court has made rules to guide itself and the lower federal courts in determining constitutional cases. In the first place, a real case with damage to a real party must be presented. The Court will neither answer hypothetical questions nor offer advice to anyone, including Congress and the president. The person asking the Court to declare unconstitutional a statute or lower court decision must show that he has actually been damaged by the unconstitutionality.[2] Most important of all, if there is any possibility of construing a statute so as to render it constitutional, the courts must do it.

The organization of the federal court system has been established by Congress. The Supreme Court, which sits in Washington and consists of nine justices, is, of course, the highest court. There are 12 circuit courts of appeal scattered throughout the country and there are 94 federal district courts. Congress frequently increases the number of district courts in order to keep up with the volume of cases and reduce the length of time parties must wait to have their cases heard.

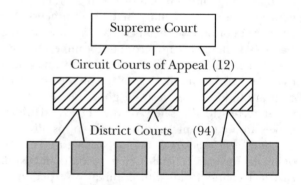

In addition to the system of federal courts, of course all states have court systems. There are state trial courts and state appellate courts usually known as supreme courts, and, in some cases, intermediate courts of appeal.

The federal district court is the first or lowest federal court. It is here that juries hear and determine the guilt of defendants charged with a federal crime. It is here that damages are awarded or denied by juries in civil actions.

Examples

1. You are involved in a collision with a driver from another state and sue him in federal court. The jury in federal district court will hear the evidence and either award damages to you or determine that the other driver was not guilty of negligence.

2. You throw a brick through a post office window. Since this is federal property, you have violated a federal criminal law. You are tried in federal district court by a jury and found guilty or not guilty.

Appeals from the district court go to the circuit court of appeals, but only on matters of law. The jury is the final determiner of the facts (whether or not you threw the brick through the window) and the appeals court hears appeals only on questions involving the law (whether or not there is a criminal statute prohibiting throwing bricks through post office windows). Further appeals would go to the United States Supreme Court. It is very important to note that one may, if a federal question is presented, appeal from the decision of a state supreme court but not from any lower state courts.

Since Congress has the right to fix the jurisdiction of all federal courts, it has established certain requirements before the Supreme Court may hear a case. In some instances, there is a right to have a case heard by the Supreme Court. This is called an "appeal," which is used in a very technical sense in this case.

Appeals to the United States Supreme Court can be made from three types of lower court:

FEDERAL DISTRICT COURTS

a When a federal statute has been held unconstitutional,[2] provided the United States or one of its employees is a party to the suit.

Examples

1. Congress passes a law making it a crime to have red hair. You are arrested and brought before the district court for trial. The judge holds the statute unconstitutional. The government may appeal to the Supreme Court. The Court must hear the case.

2. A federal district court in Alabama decided that certain portions of the 1965 Voting Rights Bill were unconstitutional. An appeal lay to the Supreme Court, which reversed the Alabama judge.

b When judgment has been given in a civil suit involving the anti-trust laws, the Federal Communications Act or the Interstate Commerce Act, the statutes themselves provide for a direct appeal to the Supreme Court, as long as the United States or one of its agents is a party to the action.

The anti-trust laws, in particular, encompass many more areas of our lives than most people might realize.[4]

Example

The Sherman Antitrust Act applied to restraints imposed by the NCAA on televising college football games. When a university's board of trustees brought an action, the Supreme Court held that by imposing limits on televised games, the NCAA restricted the place of intercollegiate athletes in the national life.[4]

Example

You and your best friend buy up all the factories that make compact disc players. The Justice Department files a suit against you under the Sherman Antitrust Act and says you have established a monopoly. If you lose, you may appeal to the Supreme Court.

c When a three-judge court (which is required by some congressional acts) gives an injunction (an order to do something or to stop doing something) in a suit to restrain enforcement of state or federal statutes or orders of some federal agencies.[5]

Example

A three-judge panel is required to hear questions arising from some aspects of the 1964 Civil Rights Act and to issue injunctions. If a panel orders a state to cease enforcement of a state statute requiring segregation, an appeal by the state would lie to the Supreme Court.

FEDERAL CIRCUIT COURTS OF APPEALS

a When a federal law or treaty is held unconstitutional[7] as long as the United States or one of its employees is a party to the suit.

Example

If a circuit court of appeals held the Medicare Amendment to the Social Security Act unconstitutional, an automatic appeal would lie to the Supreme Court.

b When a state statute is declared unconstitutional.[8]

Example

In a labor-management case, if a circuit court declared a state statute unconstitutional as in conflict with federal laws governing union elections, an appeal would lie to the Supreme Court.

STATE SUPREME COURTS[9]

a When it has held unconstitutional a federal law or treaty.

Example

If the supreme court of a state declared a federal civil rights law unconstitutional, an appeal would lie directly to the Supreme Court.

b When a state court has upheld a state law that is in necessary conflict with a federal law and therefore the federal law has been invalidated by implication.

Example

A state law requires children to go to school until they are 18. A boy, 17, is drafted into the Army. The state supreme court upholds his conviction as a juvenile delinquent, based on his truancy from school. An appeal would lie to the Supreme Court.

Those are the instances in which the Supreme Court *must* hear an appeal. They are somewhat rare.

The majority of the Court's cases arise on what is know as "writs of certiorari." This means "to be informed." A person asks the Court to hear his case and the Court issues a writ of certiorari to the lower court to "inform itself" about the case. The Court does not have to hear these cases and in fact only does so if it thinks a substantial question of law that is of national importance is presented.

Examples

1. The state of Virginia, by law, maintained the Virginia Military Institute, a state-supported college, exclusively for male students. The Supreme Court found that this state law presented a substantial federal question and held that it discriminated against women, contrary to the equal protection guarantees of the 14th Amendment.[10]

2. John Doe is in the state penitentiary awaiting execution for murder. If no substantially important legal question is presented in the record of his case, the Supreme Court will not consider it regardless of the obvious importance of the matter to Doe.

These aspects of the jurisdiction of the federal courts are not in the Constitution. They are matters of practice, self-imposed regulations of the Supreme Court or established by acts of Congress. However, all these regulations are established within the framework of constitutional provisions on the subject.

SECTION 1

The judicial Power of the United States, shall be vested in one supreme Court, and in such inferior Courts as the Congress may from time to time ordain and establish. The Judges, both of the supreme and inferior Courts, shall hold their Offices during good Behaviour, and shall, at stated Times, receive for their Services a Compensation, which shall not be diminished during their Continuance in Office.

We have already seen that judicial power is the power to decide an actual case. The courts will not hear a "political question," which is one properly decided by the executive or legislative branches.

Examples

1. The country of Yugoslavia owned an apartment in New York where its ambassadors to the United Nations had lived for years. When the country was dissolved by war, the federal republic of Yugoslavia asked the federal district court in New York to order that it was the rightful owner of the property.

The republics of Slovenia, Bosnia and Herzegovina, Croatia, and Macedonia (all parts of what had been Yugoslavia) opposed the request and asked the Court to rule that they owned the property jointly. The Court held that this was a political question and refused to act.[11]

2. Forty-one members of Congress sued President Clinton after he refused to spend appropriated funds to deploy ballistic missiles. The president thought the expenditure unnecessary and unwise. The congressmen wanted the Court to order him

to restructure the missile system. The Court refused to act, and held that this was a political question.[12]

3. During 1992, several NATO countries, including the United States and Turkey, were involved in combined forces naval exercises. The crew of the USS *Saratoga*, an aircraft carrier, fired two live Sparrow missiles at a Turkish ship, the *Muavenet*. Of course, the "attacks" were supposed to have been simulated. The *Muavenet* was sunk. Survivors of the event and the heirs of those who died sued the United States. The Court held that almost all cases involving foreign affairs raise political questions and that this case certainly did. Therefore, the Court could not act.[13]

A person must have a genuine interest in a matter before the Court before he may bring an action.

Example

A nonprofit environmental organization had standing under the Federal Emergency Planning and Community Right-to-Know Act to bring an enforcement action against a company it claimed was using toxic chemicals without submitting required information to state and federal authorities.[14]

Since Congress could starve a judge into resigning if they had the power to cut his salary if they disagreed with his decisions, this clause of the Constitution is designed to facilitate judicial independence.

SECTION 2

1 a The judicial Power shall extend to all Cases, in Law and Equity, arising under this Constitution, the Laws of the United States, and Treaties made, or which shall be made, under their Authority;

   b to all Cases affecting Ambassadors, other public Ministers and Consuls;

   c to all Cases of admiralty and maritime Jurisdiction;

   d to Controversies to which the United States shall be a Party;

   e to Controversies between two or more States;

   f between a State and Citizens of another State;

   g between Citizens of different States;

   h between Citizens of the same State claiming Lands under Grants of different States, and

   i between a State, or the Citizens thereof, and foreign States, Citizens or Subjects.

2 In all Cases affecting Ambassadors, other public Ministers and Consuls, and those in which a State shall be Party, the supreme Court shall have original Jurisdiction. In all the other Cases before mentioned, the supreme Court shall have appellate Jurisdiction, both as to Law and Fact, with such Exceptions, and under such Regulations as the Congress shall make.

3 The trial of all Crimes, except in Cases of Impeachment, shall be by Jury; and such Trial shall be held in the State where the said Crimes shall have been committed; but when not committed within any State, the Trial shall be at such Place or Places as the Congress may by Law have directed.

CLAUSE 1 a A case arising under the Constitution and laws of the United States is one for which a correct decision depends upon the construction of either. It may be an appeal from a state supreme court.

Example

After the Supreme Court decided in *Roe v. Wade* that state statutes forbidding abortions were unconstitutional, many states enacted statutes that restricted the right even if it could not be prohibited. Women brought suits challenging these state laws and these claims arose "under the Constitution of the United States."[15]

b Ambassadors *from* foreign countries to the United States are tried or sued in federal courts. Our ambassadors to foreign countries are tried, when at home, in ordinary state courts unless another federal question is presented.

Example

The ambassador from the Country of X to this country runs over and kills a child. He is prosecuted for manslaughter in federal court.

However, since ambassadors and other representatives of foreign countries may plead "diplomatic immunity" and legally remove themselves from the reach of our courts, few are successfully tried or sued. If the foreign country waives immunity, however, the legal action may proceed.

c Admiralty and maritime jurisdiction confers the right to try all cases involving shipping in the federal courts.

Example

You are on a United States owned cruise ship. You fall over a rope that was left on the deck and break your leg. You sue the shipping company in federal court.

d The United States may not be sued at all unless it consents, but in most cases it does.

Example

You are run down by a mail truck. You would sue for damages in federal court.

e If one state sues another state, it is heard in federal court in order not to prejudice the cause of the state in whose courts the case would not be heard, nor to benefit the state in whose courts the case would be tried.

Example

Pennsylvania and Ohio sued under the original jurisdiction of the Supreme Court to prevent West Virginia from forbidding producers of natural gas found there to pipe it out of the state.[16]

The Supreme Court usually decides to hear as part of its original jurisdiction suits brought by one state against another involving boundary disputes.[17]

In spite of the fact that most people think that the state boundaries in this country have been fixed since the 18th and 19th centuries, almost every year, the Supreme Court hears at least one boundary case.

Example

The Supreme Court ruled in 1991 in a dispute between Illinois and Kentucky about their boundary. The Supreme Court decided that the boundary between the two states was the low-water mark of the northern shore of the Ohio River as it stood in 1792. The river, of course, had shifted considerably in 199 years.[18]

f The 11th Amendment has modified the clause about suits between a state and citizens of another state.

g A suit between citizens of different states may be tried (but not necessarily) in federal court if the amount in controversy is at least $50,000. Congress imposed this limit in order to reduce the workload of the courts.

Examples

1. You are involved in a collision with a driver from out of state. You sue him for $50,000. The suit may be tried in federal court but it may also be tried in state court.

2. A woman sued her former husband, who lived in a different state, for damages on behalf of her two minor children. She alleged that her former husband had abused the children while they were visiting him. The Supreme Court held that this action could be brought in the federal court system, although most domestic relations and family law disputes are purely matters of state law.[19]

The framers of the Constitution believed that this provision was necessary to secure the rights of the out-of-state citizen against local prejudice in state courts.

h The clause about land grants is now obsolete.

i The last clause has also been modified by the 11th Amendment.

CLAUSE 2 We have already seen what the power to hear an appeal (review) a case entails. The original jurisdiction of the Supreme Court means that in some cases it may hear a case from the beginning, and in this case it, of course, considers the facts as well as the law. Although the Court has the power to hear these cases in its original jurisdiction, it does not have to, and it may refuse a case of original jurisdiction if the state or ambassador can obtain an adequate hearing in a lower federal court.

Example

South Carolina brought a suit in 1965 to have the Voting Rights Act of 1965 declared unconstitu-

tional. The Supreme Court heard the case in original jurisdiction and upheld the constitutionality of the law.[20]

Theoretically, Congress has the power under this clause to remove various sorts of cases from the jurisdiction of the Supreme Court. Whenever the Supreme Court hands down unpopular decisions, such as some of the ones striking down segregated school systems or the abortion cases, there are always harangues from outraged people to abolish that part of the Court's jurisdiction. Fortunately, however, Congress has never done this.

CLAUSE 3 This right is also guaranteed by the 6th Amendment.

SECTION 3

1 Treason against the United States, shall consist only in levying War against them, or in adhering to their Enemies, giving them Aid and Comfort. No Person shall be convicted of Treason unless on the Testimony of two Witnesses to the same overt Act, or on Confession in open Court.

2 The Congress shall have power to declare the Punishment of Treason, but no Attainder of Treason shall work Corruption of Blood, or Forfeiture except during the Life of the Person attainted.

CLAUSE 1 Since treason is the most serious crime known to the law, the framers of the Constitution wished to make absolutely certain that the innocent could not be convicted. A person who is in sympathy with the enemy but does not perform any act to aid them is not a traitor.

A person can only be tried for treason during a declared war. Persons accused of selling secrets or other acts of espionage during times of peace are tried for violating the espionage statutes, the national security laws, or other federal statutes.

Example

Richard Miller, an officer in the FBI, was convicted of espionage. He worked in the Foreign Counter-

Intelligence Squad. He began an affair with a Russian woman who was an intelligence contact. He made plans to fly to Eastern Europe with classified documents and join her there. He was arrested before he left the United States.[21]

CLAUSE 2 This clause was inserted into the Constitution to prevent the effects on the traitor's family that were accepted by English law. "Attainder of treason" means that the traitor's estate is forfeited to the government. "Corruption of blood" means that the traitor's heirs would not inherit land from him, claim title to land they had already obtained from the traitor nor, in turn, will the land to their own descendants.

Article Four

This ARTICLE deals with relationships among the states, admission of new states to the Union, territorial governments and the responsibilities of the federal government to the states.

SECTION 1

Full Faith and Credit shall be given in each State to the public Acts, Records, and judicial Proceedings of every other State. And the Congress may by general Laws prescribe the Manner in which such Acts, Records and Proceedings shall be proved, and the Effect thereof.

This is known as the "full faith and credit" clause. All states must give recognition to the laws made and the judicial decrees rendered in other states.

Examples

1. Marriages legally contracted in one state are valid in all others.[1]

2. A child legally adopted in one state is the legitimate child of his adoptive parents in all states.[2]

3. A is sued by B for breach of contract. A has promised to sell B his car and accepts B's money, but drives off in the car and does not deliver it to B. B sues him and obtains a judgment for damages, but A goes to another state with the car and B's money. Instead of having to go to the other state and sue A again, B sends his judgment to a court where A is and they will make A pay.

Courts do not have to recognize decrees granted by courts in foreign countries, but they do have to recognize all state laws and court decrees within this country. If, for example, a person is a legal resident of one state, his divorce must be upheld in all states. A student away at school or a member of the Armed Forces can usually obtain a divorce in either his home state or the state in which he is currently living.

Because child custody decrees are not "final," in the sense that they can be changed if the child's circumstances change and the present arrangements are not in the child's best interests, custody rulings were not considered covered by full faith and credit guarantees. This often meant that a parent without custody would take the visiting child to a new state and seek to obtain custody there, often creating years of litigation and turmoil. Congress enacted the Parental Kidnapping Prevention Act,[3] which, in effect, gives a custody decree awarded in the child's home state the same full faith and credit protection that other court decrees have.[4]

Example

A divorce decree provided that a father would continue to pay child support until the child of the marriage finished college, even though she would become an adult before she graduated. The father moved to Florida, which does not require child support after a child reaches the age of majority. When the father refused to pay after his daughter became an adult, the girl's mother sued. The Florida court held that full faith and credit applied and ordered the father to pay.[5]

SECTION 2

1 The Citizens of each State shall be entitled to all Privileges and Immunities of Citizens in the several States.

2 A Person charged in any State with Treason, Felony, or other Crime, who shall flee from Justice, and be found in another State, shall on Demand

of the executive Authority of the State from which he fled, be delivered up, to be removed to the State having Jurisdiction of the Crime.

3 [No Person held to Service or Labour in one State, under the Laws thereof, escaping into another, shall, in Consequence of any Law or Regulation therein, be discharged from such Service or Labour, but shall be delivered up on Claim of the Party to whom such Service or Labour may be due.]

CLAUSE 1 A state may not discriminate against citizens of another state temporarily within its jurisdiction. All citizens of all states are entitled to protection by the government of any state in which they are physically present.[6]

Example

A state law that provided that the police would not answer calls from out of state citizens temporarily in their state would violate this section.

All citizens have the right to acquire property in any state.[7]

Example

A state law that stated that citizens of another state could not buy summer homes in that state would violate this clause.

A physician or lawyer licensed in one state is not automatically licensed in all states, since licenses to practice are neither statutes nor decrees of courts. However, if the applicant for a state license can pass the requisite examinations and meet other qualifications (such as graduation from an accredited school or other training requirements), the state may not refuse to license her or him solely on the basis that she or he is a nonresident. To do so is to deny the physician or attorney the privileges and immunities of the state's residents who are practicing law or medicine.[8]

Reasonable restrictions on qualifications that apply to everyone, regardless of the state in which they live, do not violate the privileges and immunities clause.

Example

One state permitted graduates of a nonaccredited law school in the state to take its bar exam. A man who graduated from the school took and passed the bar exam and was licensed to practice law in the state. He applied for a job as an attorney with the Internal Revenue Service and his application was denied because a requirement for the job was graduation from an accredited school as well as a license to practice. The lawyer claimed that this rule violated the privileges and immunities clause.

The Court held that because lawyers from other states who also graduated from unaccredited schools in their states were also disqualified, there was no violation of privileges and immunities.[9]

Citizens of every state have the right to travel through all the other states.[10] The federal government, of course, controls the right of people in this country to travel abroad. While most people who are United States citizens may get passports without problems and go practically anywhere they wish, the government does have the right to forbid travel to some countries for foreign policy or safety reasons.

Citizens also have the right to writs of habeas corpus, and any state tax laws imposing higher taxes on nonresidents than on residents violate this clause. However, in matters relating to its own government, such as prescribing residency requirements for voter registration, a state may make reasonable rules.[11]

The Voting Rights Act,[12] however, provides that any person who is registered to vote in his home state and who moves to another state at least 30 days prior to a presidential election must be allowed to vote for president and vice-president even though they have not met residency requirements to vote for any other office. The voter in these circumstances may alternatively elect to vote absentee in his former home state. All states are now required by the same act to permit absentee voting in presidential elections. This provision was upheld by the Supreme Court in *Oregon v. Mitchell.*[13]

State residency requirements for voting in state and local elections may not be longer than the minimum period that may be reasonably required to permit the voter to become knowledgeable about the candidates for office.[14] Fifty days, for example, has been upheld by the Supreme Court as reasonable.[15] Further, a state may still make reasonable, non-discriminatory restrictions on who may vote. Absentee ballots, for example, do not have to be provided to those detained in jail awaiting trial.[16]

CLAUSE 2 Each governor has a duty to extradite (return) a fugitive in his or her state wanted by another state. Until 1987, if a governor thought that the legal or prison systems of the requesting state were inhumane, he or she could refuse to extradite. In 1987, the Supreme Court ruled that a federal court could force a governor to extradite a wanted person without reference to the character of the crime or the policy or laws of the state from which the fugitive had fled.[17]

There are, after that decision, only four grounds on which a governor may refuse to extradite: (1) the documentation in the request is deficient; (2) the person has not been charged with a crime; (3) the person is not the person sought; and (4) the person is not a fugitive. The governor may no longer refuse to extradite because he or she has cause to believe that the state requesting the extradition has a prison system "with a wretched history and a present demeanor violative of international standards of treatment of prisoners, including the barbaric 'discipline' of the chain gang."[18]

CLAUSE 3 This clause became obsolete when slavery was abolished.

SECTION 3

1 New States may be admitted by the Congress into this Union; but no new State shall be formed or erected within the Jurisdiction of any other State; nor any State be formed by the Junction of two or more States, or Parts of States, without the Consent of the Legislatures of the States concerned as well as of the Congress.

2 The Congress shall have Power to dispose of and make all needful Rules and Regulations respecting the Territory or other Property belonging to the United States; and nothing in this Constitution shall be so construed as to Prejudice any Claims of the United States, or of any particular State.

CLAUSE 1 The admission of new states into the Union is a legislative, not executive matter.

CLAUSE 2 Congress makes all laws, including rules of criminal procedure, for all United States territories.

Example

The state of Nevada, its governor, both senators, and all its members of the House of Representatives sued the secretary of energy to review the decision of the secretary to investigate the use of federal land in Nevada as a site for the only national depository for high-level radioactive waste. The federal court of appeals held that the authority that Congress has over public lands allows it to control the use and occupancy of those lands. A state's objection to Congress's decision about federal lands within that state's borders is irrelevant. The Court held, moreover, that challenges to legislation based on this clause are not judiciable because they are political questions.[19]

SECTION 4

The United States shall guarantee to every State in this Union a Republican Form of Government, and shall protect each of them against Invasion; and on Application of the Legislature, or of the Executive (when the Legislature cannot be convened) against domestic Violence.

A state bears the primary responsibility for establishing its own form of republican government, defined as a government by representatives chosen by the people.[13]

Example

State legislators in Wisconsin (of the political party opposing the governor) brought a suit seeking a declaration that the partial veto provision of the state's constitution violated the constitutional guarantee of a republican form of government. The court said: "In analogizing the Governor of Wisconsin to the Kings of England and the legislature of Wisconsin to the Parliaments that struggled against royal prerogative in the Eighteenth Century, the plaintiffs merely give analogy a bad name." The Court advised these unhappy legislators to work to amend the state constitution and dismissed the suit.[21]

If a governor dissolved the legislature and had himself crowned emperor for life, the federal government would have the obligation to intervene. The federal government would also have the right to intervene against an elected government that devoted itself to sedition or violent overthrow of the federal government.[22]

The president may send federal troops or federalize and dispatch the National Guard to quell a domestic disturbance at the request of the governor. This was a fairly common "strike-breaking" practice during the 1920s and 30s. The president's duty is to execute the laws passed by Congress and to enforce the decrees of the federal courts and to carry out his duty, he has full authority to dispatch troops into a state *without* the consent of and over the objections of the governor.

Article Five

The Congress, whenever two-thirds of both Houses shall deem it necessary, shall propose Amendments to this Constitution, or, on the Application of the Legislatures of two-thirds of the several States, shall call a Convention for proposing Amendments, which, in either Case, shall be valid to all Intents and Purposes, as Part of this Constitution, when ratified by the Legislatures of three-fourths of the several States, or by Conventions in three-fourths thereof, as the one or the other Mode of Ratification may be proposed by the Congress: Provided that no Amendment which may be made prior to the Year One Thousand eight hundred and eight shall in any Manner affect the first and fourth Clauses in the Nineth Section of the first Article; and that no State, without its Consent, shall be deprived of its equal Suffrage in the Senate.

THIS ARTICLE deals with the procedures for amendment of the Constitution. It should be noted that the power to amend is strictly a legislative power. Unlike ordinary acts of Congress that require the signature or veto of the president, the president has nothing to do with the amendment of the Constitution.[1] The proposed amendment, once adopted by Congress, is sent directly to the state legislatures.

An amendment has never been proposed by conventions called by the state legislatures.

Example

The residents of Montana attempted to put an initiative on the ballot that would have directed the Montana legislature to apply to Congress to call a Constitutional Convention to consider a balanced budget amendment. The required number of signatures was obtained to put the initiative on the ballot in November, 1984. The state government asked the Supreme Court of Montana to rule on the initiative.

The court held that this was invalid under this Article of the Constitution. The court held that a legislative call for a constitutional amendment must be initiated by a deliberate, representative assembly (the legislature) acting in the absence of any external restrictions or limitations.[2]

The usual method of amending the Constitution is that a proposal is made by two-thirds of a quorum in both houses of Congress and it is then sent to the state legislatures for ratification. When three-fourths of the legislatures have ratified it, it becomes part of the Constitution without further action.

Most proposed amendments incorporate a clause giving a time limit for ratification.

Article Six

1 All Debts contracted and Engagements entered into, before the Adoption of this Constitution, shall be as valid against the United States under this Constitution, as under the Confederation.

2 This Constitution, and the Laws of the United States which shall be made in Pursuance thereof; and all Treaties made, or which shall be made, under the Authority of the United States, shall be the supreme Law of the Land; and the Judges in every State shall be bound thereby, any Thing in the Constitution or Laws of any State to the Contrary notwithstanding.

3 The Senators and Representatives before mentioned, and the Members of the several State Legislatures, and all executive and judicial Officers, both of the United States and of the several States, shall be bound by Oath or Affirmation, to support this Constitution; but no religious Test shall ever be required as a Qualification to any Office or public Trust under the United States.

CLAUSE 1 This clause is now obsolete. It was originally designed to assure the creditors of the states under the Articles of Confederation that they would be paid.

CLAUSE 2 The United States government has authority extending over all states of the Union and over all federal territory. The authority of the federal government acts upon all the states and all the people of the states. The powers of the federal government are restricted by the Constitution, but as far as its powers extend, they are supreme. The Constitution, federal laws enacted under it, and the Supreme Court's interpretation of them are the supreme law of the land.

Any law of any state, so far as it conflicts with any federal law, is null and void.

Example

The Postal Service leased land on which to build a post office in Greenwich, Connecticut. The town of Greenwich refused to issue a building permit until the local authorities determined that the plans were in compliance with the local building code, and the town wished to charge a fee for the inspection by local authorities. The Postal Service claimed that it had its own inspection procedures. The town further objected to some aspects of the design for the new post office and demanded a building permit fee of $43,470 before construction could begin. The Postal Service brought suit against the town. The judge held that under the Supremacy Clause, federal activities are shielded from state or local regulations.[1]

Decisions of the Supreme Court, where relevant, are binding on all state courts, even if they conflict with state laws. In short, the duty rests on all courts, state and federal, to guard, protect, and enforce every right guaranteed by the United States Constitution.[2]

Example

A group of citizens in Oklahoma filed a petition to put an initiative on the ballot. The initiative would have criminalized and absolutely prohibited most abortions. The Supreme Court of Oklahoma held that the initiative would have restricted the constitutional right to abortion that had been established by the United States Supreme Court and that under Article VI, the state courts were required to comply with federal constitutional law. The opinion said: "Because the United States Supreme Court has spoken, this court will uphold the law of the land, whatever it may be."[3]

CLAUSE 3 All members of Congress, all federal judges, the president, all governors, all state judges, and all state legislators take oaths when they assume their offices that they will support, protect, and defend the Constitution of the United States. This is the first duty they assume.[4]

When, notwithstanding the oaths they have taken, state officials fail to obey the commands of the Constitution, it is the duty of the federal courts to secure the rights of those to whom the officials have denied them.[5]

Example

A group of persons with mental retardation brought suit against the governor of Ohio, alleging that their civil rights under the Constitution and the Americans with Disabilities Act were being violated. They claimed that the state had refused to comply with provisions of federal law requiring them to be placed in community housing instead of in large institutions and they also claimed that other services were not provided as required by federal regulations. The Court held that the plaintiffs' rights would be enforced because the federal courts can require state officials to cease interference with federal rights.[6]

Article VI of the Constitution has always been, and remains, the foundation of our system of federal government.

Article Seven

The Ratification of the Conventions of nine States, shall be sufficient for the Establishment of this Constitution between the States so ratifying the Same. DONE in Convention by the Unanimous Consent of the States present the Seventeenth Day of September in the Year of our Lord one thousand seven hundred and Eighty seven and of the Independence of the United States of America the Twelfth. IN WITNESS whereof We have hereunto subscribed our Names.

THE FINAL ARTICLE of the Constitution provided for the original ratification by the states. March 4, 1789 was the day fixed for commencing operation of the new government under the Constitution, but because George Washington was late in arriving to assume his duties as president, the Articles of Confederation continued in effect until he was finally inaugurated on April 30, 1789.

The Bill of Rights

THE BILL OF RIGHTS consists of the first ten Amendments to the Constitution. Many citizens of the newly formed United States remembered too vividly for comfort the power of the king of England and urged their states not to ratify the Constitution until some provisions were made to limit the power of the central government against the rights of the individual citizen. The first ten amendments, along with two more that were not ratified, were proposed to the legislatures of the states by the first Congress in September, 1789 and declared to be ratified in 1791.

Many of the provisions in the Bill of Rights concern the rights of a person accused of crime. When the Constitution and these amendments were written, a conscious decision was made that where an individual's rights conflict with protection of society from criminal activity, the individual is more important. Our system of justice is predicated on the idea that it is better to let a guilty person go free than to convict an innocent one. A person charged with a crime is presumed to be innocent until he is convicted by a jury. It is not up to him to prove that he didn't do it. It is up to the government to prove that he did. The basic difference between a democracy and a totalitarian state is that in a democracy individuals are free of compulsion to agree with governmental actions that they think are wrong, Because we are free to speak, write, and vote as we please, changes in our government arise from the ballot box, not by revolution. A state in which the right to dissent is abridged is not a democratic state although it may be a benevolent dictatorship. From time to time well-meaning citizens wish to restrict the right of others to disagree with the government and claim that certain beliefs are "un-American." The American nation was founded on a theory of respect for the dignity of all people and consequently for their views, however absurd or repugnant they may be. If we refuse to let a person with whom we disagree speak his mind (as long as he is not inciting a specific criminal act), we have, basically, denied the fundamental principles of democracy and substituted a totalitarian method of requiring obedience to the government. The difference, therefore, between a democracy and a totalitarian state is a basic respect for the rights of all people and not just those with whom we happen to agree. There is an old saying that "a chain is only as strong as its weakest link" and this is never more true than in the relationship between government and citizens. When the rights of all people, no matter how annoying some of them may be to the majority, are not protected, and when the most ridiculous view is not protected as much as the most sensible, our system of law and our basic philosophy of human rights have broken down. If the government is empowered to pass a law today that makes it a crime to worship the sun, tomorrow it may well be a crime to be an orthodox Protestant. When infringements of fair play are accepted in some cases—denial of a fair trial to a "notorious criminal," in which case people may say "he got what he deserved," the next step may be transgressions of our basic principles against whomever the government chooses to persecute at the moment. Our legal system is not set up to guarantee rights to the "nice people." It is set up by this Constitution and these amendments to protect the rights of *all* the people.

Amendment One

Congress shall make no law respecting an establishment of religion, or prohibiting the free exercise thereof, or abridging the freedom of speech, or of the press, or the right of the people peaceably to assemble, and to petition the Government for a redress of grievances.

ALTHOUGH in early colonial times, some settlers had fled from Europe for *freedom to worship* as they pleased and then required the other members of their colonies to worship with them, as settlement progressed it was more important to have help with Indians, farming, and other problems than it was to maintain religious conformity. By 1787 when the Constitution was written, the framers knew that it was necessary to build a wall between church and state. Tolerance was a matter of necessity. They did not intend the government to be opposed to either religious practice or to religion itself, but they meant to make it quite clear that religion is none of the government's business.[1] This clause prohibits the federal government and, construed with the 14th Amendment, the state governments, from dictating what a person must believe about religion, what forms of religious exercise he may practice, or that he must believe in religion at all. The only restraint permitted any branch of the government is that it may prohibit religious practices that endanger the physical health of the citizens. It may not restrict or require any religious or antireligious belief, however unorthodox it may be.[2]

Examples

1. A child may not be required to salute the flag at school if this violates the religious beliefs of his parents. The community health and safety are not threatened by a refusal to salute the flag.

2. A religious group that handles dangerous snakes as part of its worship may be ordered to cease the practice. This is a justifiable prohibition to protect the health of the community of which the church members are a part.

3. Public schools may not include religious activities within the academic program. A public school was prohibited from broadcasting morning prayers over the intercom and allowing student-led prayers in class during the school day.[3]

4. Prayers at high school football games or at high school graduation ceremonies given by students, not by adults (either faculty or clergy persons), are permissible.[4]

5. A high school that permits student clubs to meet after school must permit student religious groups to meet on the same basis as other clubs.[5]

6. A court may order medical treatment of a seriously ill child even if parents' religious beliefs do not allow such treatment. The health of the child is more important than the parent's right to a particular belief.[6]

7. A competent adult, however, may refuse medical care on any basis, religious or other, even if the result of the refusal is that he or she will almost certainly die.[7]

In all cases where restrictions on religious practices have been held constitutional, there was a clear and immediate danger to some vital aspect of the community's life.[8]

Example

A person may be prosecuted for driving without a license even if he or she claims that such a requirement violates his religious beliefs. Requiring drivers' licenses is a reasonable means of protecting the public safety.[9]

For example, zoning regulations may not be used to forbid church activities. If a church in a residential neighborhood operates a soup kitchen for the homeless, some of the neighbors might prefer that these persons go elsewhere. Feeding the poor, however, is a valid exercise of religious convictions, and the zoning regulations do not apply.[10]

Children whose Amish parents objected, for religious reasons, to education beyond the eighth grade were held by the Supreme Court to have a valid exemption from state compulsory education laws. The Court held that a high school education was not so vital to a child's well-being that the state could require it over parental objections based on religion.[11]

If a child is in public school, parents do not have any right to require that the standard secular curriculum (such as the books the children read) reflect their own religious beliefs.[12] If children are taught at home, whether the home schooling is undertaken for religious or other reasons, the state may enforce reasonable requirements, such as requiring the parent or other teacher to have a college degree.[13]

Since the 14th Amendment makes the right of freedom of and from religion applicable to the state governments, no state may engage in any activity that infringes upon a citizen's right to believe or disbelieve as he chooses. The famous "School Prayer" cases have held that a public school may not require a student to participate in any religious observances. Private schools may, of course, teach any religious beliefs they wish.

Example

A teacher paid by the Ministerial Association in a community came into the public school classroom and taught religious education classes. Although children whose parents did not wish them to participate could be excused, the Supreme Court held that such instruction in a public building was lending the force of the state and the school to the beliefs of the teacher and to permit such instruction violated the 1st Amendment.[14]

The theory behind this decision was that the matter of religious education is a matter for the home, not the school. A parent whose child is in public school should not have his child taught something about religion in which the parent does not believe and does not wish the child to believe. It is perfectly acceptable to teach the Bible from a literary instead of a theological viewpoint, since knowledge of its contents is important to a well-rounded education, but the line is drawn at the point where any conversion of a student could result.[15]

Cadets at the United States service academies may not be required to attend church or compulsory chapel services.[16] The Armed Forces may, however, restrict some aspects of religious freedom among military personnel. For example, the Supreme Court held that it was not a violation of his right of religious freedom for the Air Force to refuse to let an officer who was an Orthodox Jew wear his yarmulke indoors while he was required to be in uniform.[17] Uniform regulations forbid any headwear indoors.

The government supports religion in any number of perfectly constitutional ways.[18] Chaplains in the Armed Forces are commissioned officers and are paid by the government. State legislatures and Congress have chaplains.[19] Prison chaplains are also paid by the states. To eliminate chaplains would constitute "prohibiting the free exercise of religion." An ordinary citizen is free to go to church or to stay home, as he chooses. This is not true of a serviceman or of a prisoner. If a person is in jail or on patrol in the jungle, the church must come to him if he is to worship.

Tax exemptions are granted to churches as well as to nonreligious charitable organizations such as colleges and hospitals. The question of tax exemptions for church-owned property was upheld by the Supreme Court in 1970.[20] Questions of tax exemptions for property owned by churches, hospitals, and universities usually do not involve issues about levying taxes on the church or classroom buildings themselves, but rather on income-producing property owned by the church or other organization.

Example

The Faithful Church receives ownership of a girdle factory by the will of its former owner, Mr. Snap. The church does not pay either income or property taxes on either the factory or the profits that it derives from the sale of its girdles. Across the street from the church's Hold Tight factory, there is a Skinny Look girdle factory owned by Mr. Pop, who has to pay all the usual taxes on his factory and his sales. The church's girdles can, therefore, be sold at a lower price than Mr. Pop's girdles. The question involved in these cases is, therefore, the fairness of this exemption to other taxpayers, particularly to competitors in the same business.

It is, however, clear that the workers in profit-making businesses owned by religious organizations must receive minimum wages, overtime pay, and all other employment benefits that accrue to workers employed by any other corporation.[21]

State aid to parochial education has been the subject of many Supreme Court decisions.

In 1971, the Supreme Court developed a three-part test to determine if state action relating to religious schools is constitutional. If the state action (1) has a primary secular purpose, (2) does not have the principal effect of either advancing or inhibiting religion and (3) does not create excessive governmental entanglement with religion, it is constitutional.[22] In applying these guidelines, the Supreme Court has refused to allow state aid to parochial schools in the form of state maintenance and repair grants[23] or tuition reimbursement.[24] It is also unconstitutional for public school teachers to spend parts of their days teaching at parochial schools even if they provide remedial education otherwise unavailable in the parochial school.[25] The Supreme Court has felt that all of these activities created a symbolic link between government and religion and directly promoted religion.

The test is more easily satisfied in cases involving higher education. The Higher Education Facilities Act of 1963[26] that provided federal construction grants for secular-use facilities in church-related colleges was held constitutional in *Tilton v. Richardson*.[27] The Court reasoned that there was less likely to be religious involvement in secular subjects at the college level than in elementary and secondary schools. Furthermore, the college grants were for construction, not continuing aid to the colleges' programs and operating budgets. Grants to college students are also permissible even if the student is attending a church-related college. For example, state aid to a blind college undergraduate studying for the ministry at a church-related college did not violate provisions against the establishment of religion because aid to blind students was available regardless of where they enrolled or what they studied.[28]

In essence, unless religious activities are dangerous to the health of the community, no part of the state or federal government may stop anyone from practicing his religion, or from believing whatever he wishes, and it may not make him go to church at all. State universities, for example, may not constitutionally ban worship on their campuses any more than they may require it.[29] However, if a person is under the control of the government in some way, the government must assure him or her the right to worship if he or she chooses.

Freedom of speech means that we have a right to advocate ideas. This guarantee is not confined to an expression of ideas that are conventional or shared by the majority. Freedom of speech and of the press permit us to exchange ideas for bringing about political and social changes desired by the people and to keep the people fully informed about the acts or misconduct of public officials. All ideas must be protected, no matter how unpopular they may be. An unorthodox or controversial idea is entitled to as much protection as any other, unless it conflicts

directly and immediately with vital national interests.[30] All persons living under our legal system have the right to hold, express, teach, or advocate any opinion, and to join with others to express it, although the opinion may be repugnant to the vast majority of the citizens.

Examples

1. A city ordinance banned all residential political signs "to minimize clutter." A woman displayed a sign at her home that said "For Peace In The Gulf" during the Gulf War. The local government objected. The Supreme Court held that the ordinance violated the woman's rights of free speech.[31]

2. The Ku Klux Klan had the free speech right to erect a cross in a public square near a state capitol during the Christmas season. The Supreme Court said that "Where an area is a traditional public forum for expression of opinion, the government may not distinguish among opinions."[32]

3. A city park in Portland, Oregon had a "public speech area" where anyone who wished to make public statements could go and talk about practically anything he or she wished, make music, or otherwise perform. One could not, however, address the public or perform anywhere else in the immediate area. The speech or performance could only last a maximum of two 30-minute segments, and then there was a 15-minute silent period. A "street preacher" was prohibited from preaching on nearby sidewalks, but he refused to go to that area. The Court held that the ordinance was too restrictive of free speech.[33]

As was true of the freedom of religious practice, however, this right is not an absolute right. The amendment does not give anyone the right to speak or write in a way that injures another person or his property, that corrupts public morals, that incites criminal activity, or that advocates a specific action for overthrowing the government by force.[34]

As we saw, under Article I, a member of Congress cannot be sued for slander for anything he or she says on the floor of Congress. All other persons who defame another person may be sued and damages may be recovered from them. Even if what one publishes is true, it may not be the business of the press to report on all activities of private citizens (as opposed to public figures). Even true reports may invade a person's privacy.

Example

A newspaper in Detroit ran a "public interest" article about love relationships involving people's former spouses. The paper had run an ad inviting people to submit material. A woman's former husband gave them material that led to a report of abortions, spouse-swapping, a surrogate child, and other salacious material. The people involved in the story were identified only by their first names. The woman had remarried and her current husband knew nothing about these alleged activities, and neither did her employer. She sued the paper and, after deciding whether the stories were true or not was irrelevant because she was not a public figure, the court held that her privacy had been invaded and she was entitled to damages.[35]

If the person defamed is a public official, the Supreme Court has held that criticism of public officials is so vital to the prevention of tyranny that the official must show that the defamation was made with knowledge of its falsity and actuated by deliberate malice.[38]

Examples

1. Mrs. Doe tells Mrs. Roe that her next door neighbor, Mrs. Jones, is a crook. Mrs. Jones may recover damages from Mrs. Doe for slander unless Mrs. Doe can prove that she said is true.

2. Mrs. Doe makes a speech in which she says that Richard Roe, the governor of her state, is stupid and a crook. Before Roe may collect damages, he must prove (1) that Mrs. Doe was acting for malicious reasons, (2) that he is neither stupid nor a crook, and (3) that Mrs. Doe knew that he was smart and honest at the time she made her speech.

The Supreme Court has decided several cases under the "public official" doctrine. In one the court decided that for this purpose, a candidate for public office was a "public official." He, therefore, must prove actual malice.[37] Actual malice is considered to be a knowing disregard of the truth and not just an honest mistake of fact.

Examples

1. A magazine carried an article indicating that a policeman had been charged with brutality in criminal court. In fact, the policeman had been sued for damages in a civil case. The Supreme Court held that this error did not constitute "actual malice."[38]

2. The mayor of a city was alleged in a newspaper story to have been charged with perjury. The person actually charged was his brother. The Court held that no actual malice existed.[39]

3. Two politicians in South Carolina charged the publisher of a newspaper with violating the state's criminal libel statute. The publisher was charged with publishing false statements about the politicians with malicious intent. The article to which they objected came out shortly before Election Day. The newspaperman was arrested and spent two nights in jail. He was then indicted by the grand jury. The two politicians (who had been re-elected by the time that the grand jury met) then dropped the charges. The federal court found the criminal libel statute unconstitutional because it did not require proof that the story was written when the newspaper knew or should have known that it was false or was written "in reckless disregard" of whether it was true or false.[40]

Although a person may express any political theory he wishes, speech or writing that incites others to acts of violence is not protected by the Constitution if it is likely that violence will result.[41] Speech of this type is known as "seditious speech" if the desired result is violence against the government. However, the advocated act must be specific and immediate in order to constitute sedition.[42]

Examples

1. Henry Hoe stands on the street corner and makes a speech objecting to our government's policy in Latin America. He says that the president is a nitwit. This is permissible, because freedom of speech is designed to protect anyone's right to criticize the actions of the government.

2. Joe also stands on the corner and also makes a speech protesting the government's activities in Latin America. He says that the way to end the problem is to shoot everyone who works for the National Security Council. This speech is also not seditious because Joe has not advocated any immediate and specific act of violence.

3. In the example above, Joe continues by saying that he has guns and ammunition at his house on the corner and that his listeners must come with him, get the guns, and be off on his bus to Washington. He says that they will be on their way in half an hour to kill everyone who works for the National Security Council. Joe may be arrested for sedition.

In order for speech to be restricted in the national interest, there must be a "clear and present danger" to an interest the government must protect, such as defense of the country, and it must be shown that the speech would have incited direct and illegal action.

A student in a public school also has a right to freedom of speech and expression. He may not be punished for wearing symbols protesting governmental action or other noninflammatory, nonobscene expressions of opinion.[43]

Example

A high school student distributed religious literature at school. The school had a rule that literature could not be handed out. The Court held that "students do not shed their right of freedom of expression at the school house door," although the right to free speech at school is not as extensive as it is outside. The Court held that the distribution could not be banned unless the school could demonstrate a reasonable belief that the student would cause interference with the work at the high school.[44]

Schools may prohibit behavior or expression of opinion, even if legal for an adult, that would interfere with other students' work or cause disorder. It is, for example, permissible to suspend a high school student who makes a sexually suggestive but nonobscene speech in assembly.[45] There are, however, limitations on the school's right to restrict free speech and free press rights of public school students. A school board, for example, does not have unlimited discretion to remove books from school libraries because new members of the board decide that they do not like the ideas expressed in those books.[46]

College newspapers, with very few exceptions, have all of the 1st Amendment rights guaranteed to other newspapers.[47]

Example

The University of Virginia denied funds to a student religious organization that published a Christian newspaper. The university's position was that, as a state institution, it could not promote religion. The Supreme Court held that the university could not deny funding to all religious groups in order to maintain a "policy of neutrality." Such a denial was held to be an abridgment of the students' right to free speech.[48]

College students, generally, have the same rights of free speech as other adults do.

Example

The University of Michigan wished to curb what its Regents saw as a rising tide of racial intolerance on campus. The university instituted a policy forbidding speech stigmatizing anyone or any group on grounds of race, sex, sexual orientation, religion, or other status. A graduate student asked the Court to enjoin this policy. The graduate student taught biopsychology, and he said that the policy could be used to chill his ability to teach about biologically based differences between the sexes or among races. The Court held that an antidiscrimination policy that prohibits speech because the institution disagrees with the ideas expressed violated the students' and faculty's 1st Amendment rights. The Court concluded: "While the Court is sympathetic to the University's obligation to ensure equal educational opportunities for all of its students, such efforts must not be at the expense of free speech."[49]

Freedom of the press, however, does not include immunity from legal investigation. A newspaper reporter does not have a right to refuse to answer grand jury questions concerning the identity of the reporter's informants. Even if the reporter was given the information in confidence, the Supreme Court has ruled that such information must be revealed if it is linked to the commission of a criminal act.[50]

The 1st Amendment also involves books, newspapers, television, and radio programs. Obscene speech or writing is not protected by the 1st Amendment.[51] However, the problem is the definition of obscenity. The Supreme Court decided that it must be the final arbiter of obscenity and judge each book on its own merits.[52]

Example

Several performance artists applied for grants to the National Endowment for the Arts (NEA). The review panel approved awards for the applications but the chairperson apparently vetoed the grants. Their grants were denied because, after substantial criticism by some congressmen about grants awarded to other artists, the NEA statute was amended to state that grants be given only for works that met "general standards of decency and respect for the diverse beliefs and values of the American public." The artists sued, claiming that their applications had been denied on impermissible political grounds. The Court found that "The right of artists to challenge conventional wisdom and values is a cornerstone of artistic and academic freedom, no less than the rights of scientists funded by the National Institutes of Health." The

Court thus held that the "decency clause" was too vague and broad and violated the artists' 1st Amendment rights.[53]

The Supreme Court defines[54] obscenity as something that (1) appeals to prurient interests; (2) portrays, in a patently offensive way, sexual conduct specifically denied by an applicable state statute; and (3) taken as a whole, does not have serious literary, political, or social value. The standards to be applied are those of the "average person applying the contemporary community standard." This definition means that violence, no matter how revolting, cannot be defined as obscene if it is not sexual, and it also means that a book or movie that is perfectly acceptable in some parts of the country may be considered obscene and those selling it prosecuted and sent to jail in other parts of the country.

Statutes that differentiate between what may be sold to minors as opposed to adults and that create a criminal offense of selling obscene material to minors have been upheld.[55] However, an adult's possession of obscene material for his or her own use cannot be made a criminal offense.[56] This right of privacy, however, does not extend to the right of an adult to view obscene films in public theaters.[57] Ordinances, for example, that ban adult movie theaters within a certain distance of churches, schools, or homes are constitutional.[58] Statutes allowing criminal prosecution of persons selling films showing children engaging in sexual activities also do not violate the 1st Amendment.[59]

The only reason a book may be removed from a store is that it is either seditious or obscene.

Radio and television broadcasting fall into a different category. There is a basic right to read a book, but there is no right to broadcast.[60] Licenses for radio and television stations are issued by the Federal Communications Commission and may be revoked if the station is not broadcasting "in the public interest," which is much more restrictive than merely prohibiting seditious or obscene material. If a radio station broadcasts a number of bogus news bulletins, for example, its license could be revoked.

The Supreme Court protects advertising as "commercial speech."[61] Although it may be regulated, advertising by professionals is permitted. State statutes that defined advertising by pharmacists[62] and attorneys[63] as "unprofessional conduct" were found by the Supreme Court to be unconstitutional.

The clause of the 1st Amendment pertaining to *peaceable assembly* protects the right to picket, a right that has been exercised in political, labor management, and civil rights disputes.[64]

A Chicago ordinance prohibited peaceful picketing for any reason other than a labor dispute within a certain distance of a school. The Supreme Court held that differentiating between peaceful picketing based on the substance of the picket violated the Equal Protection Clause of the 14th Amendment.[65] An ordinance prohibiting noise from pickets so close to a school that a disruption occurred was, however, constitutional.[66]

During the civil rights demonstrations of the 1960s, many cities required parade permits before a demonstration could be "legal." They then used the ordinances to prohibit demonstrations of which city officials disapproved. The Supreme Court, however, held that such ordinances were unconstitutional and that protesters were free to ignore them.[67] Reasonable traffic restrictions may, however, be enforced against demonstrators.[68]

In general, picketing is protected when it is for a lawful purpose—to publicize a grievance—and is conducted in an orderly manner. Disorder or violence by pickets, however, does not have to be tolerated.[69] Although many anti-abortion protestors are polite and respectful when they picket clinics where abortions are performed, some have been both physically and verbally abusive and sometimes quite dangerous. In 1994, Congress enacted the Freedom of Access to Clinic Entrances Act,[70] which makes it a federal crime to use force or threaten to use force or to use physical obstruction to injure or to intimidate anyone who is attempting to obtain or to provide reproductive health services. This statute has been upheld as constitutional by the Supreme Court and many lower federal courts.[71]

Although the 1st Amendment does not exist only for the expression of popular views, whatever cause one wishes to advocate, one must not use violence or the threat of violence to achieve it.

A privately owned shopping center has the right to bar political leaflets that have no relation to business conducted there.[72] However, where the leaflets concern matters involving any of the businesses within it, distribution cannot be prohibited.[73]

In short, there is a national commitment to the idea that debates on public issues must be uninhibited and our right to criticize cannot be denied. A government in a democracy must accept the fact that discussions of its policies are not always complimentary.

The right of *freedom of association* gives one the right to belong to any group he chooses and assures the citizen that he has the right to belong to any organization that agrees with him.[74]

An organization that discriminates in choosing its members, however, may not enjoy non-profit tax status or other benefits of clubs or other organizations that select their members from all qualified candidates.

Example

Burning Tree Country Club, in the Maryland suburbs of Washington, D.C., refused to admit women members. A Maryland statute provided that private country clubs that maintained their land as open spaces would receive a favorable assessment of this land for property tax purposes. This statute was amended to provide that the favorable assessments would not apply to benefit clubs that discriminated in granting membership on the basis of race, color, creed, sex, or national origin of the prospective member. The Burning Tree Country Club was notified that it would be assessed at its full value because it refused to admit women members and, in fact, would not permit them to play golf as the guests of male members. The Court of Appeals of Maryland ruled that this law did not violate the club members' right of association.[75]

Many cities, in an attempt to prevent juvenile crime, especially in the evenings, enacted curfew ordinances that provide that juveniles under a certain age had to be off the streets (and presumably at home) after a certain hour. Many of these ordinances have been declared unconstitutional as a denial of the young peoples' right of association.[76] In one such case, the judge wrote: "The right to walk the streets, or to meet publicly with one's friends for a noble purpose or for no purpose at all—and to do so whenever one pleases—is an integral component of life in a free and ordered society."[77]

A public college cannot, for example, refuse to recognize a student organization because the administration disagrees with its philosophy.[78] Only groups that are genuinely disruptive to activities of other students may be prohibited. A college newspaper may not be subject to censorship that cannot be applied to other newspapers.[79]

Freedom of association may also impose an obligation to associate. For example, many states require all lawyers who wish to practice there to belong to the state bar association in order to maintain professional standards. As long as dues are not used for political purposes, this is constitutionally permissible.[80]

The *right of petition* is exemplified by the Declaration of Independence, a statement to the world explaining our rebellion against King George III. Petitions, marches, and appeals to the state, local, or national authorities are protected by this amendment and petitioners may not be arrested simply because the governmental official disagrees with them.

Amendment Two

A well regulated Militia, being necessary to the security of a free State, the
right of the people to keep and bear Arms, shall not be infringed.

THIS AMENDMENT is not applicable to the states, which are free to regulate use and sale of firearms as they see fit.[1]

One part of the "common law" or basic legal system that we inherited from England was the right to self-protection, which implies the right to own and bear arms. However, this right is not guaranteed to all citizens by the Constitution. Congress may place heavy restrictions on the interstate sale of weapons. For example, Congress enacted legislation forbidding the manufacture, transfer, or possession of machine guns, and this statute was upheld as constitutional.[2]

The purpose of this amendment is to provide for the effectiveness of the militia, which would presumably protect the citizen against unconstitutional usurpation of power by the federal government.[3] This amendment alone does not give all citizens the right to own weapons to use for duck-hunting if Congress wishes to restrict that right. It merely prevents the federal government from disarming the members of the National Guard. Courts have consistently held that the 2nd Amendment only confers a *collective* right of keeping and bearing arms, which must bear a "reasonable relationship to the preservation or efficiency of a well-regulated militia."[4]

Example

A man was convicted of possessing an unregistered machine gun. He contended that he was subject to enrollment in the state militia (the National Guard) and that therefore he had a fundamental right under the 2nd Amendment to possess the gun. The Court held that the 2nd Amendment guarantees a collective, rather than an individual right to bear arms, which does not give any individual a personal right to own a machine gun.[5]

The 1968 Crime Control Act[6] provides that transportation of firearms in interstate commerce without compliance with certain regulations applicable to gun dealers only is a criminal offense. Transportation of weapons for sale without such a license, which only dealers may obtain, is a crime. The Supreme Court held in *United States v. Bass*[4] that the statute would be construed to mean that one violates the act only if the firearm was moving in interstate commerce or was on an interstate carrier such as an airplane, at the time it was discovered.

The "Brady Bill" of 1993[8] provides for background checks and a five day waiting period for those persons who wish to purchase weapons. Until a federal mechanism for checking the possible criminal backgrounds of those wishing to buy guns is in place by November 30, 1998, the act provided that local law enforcement personnel would perform the checks. At least one federal circuit court of appeal has ruled that the federal government does not have the authority to require local authorities to do such checks, and the Supreme Court agreed with that view. All courts, however, have held that the waiting period is constitutional.[9]

Mandatory sentences for possession of a firearm during commission of a felony do not violate due process rights, the right to a jury trial, or any rights under this amendment.[10]

Amendment Three

No Soldier shall, in time of peace be quartered in any house, without the consent of the Owner, nor in time of war, but in a manner to be prescribed by law.

THIS AMENDMENT has never been the subject of construction by the courts and has been unimportant since its adoption.

Amendment Four

The right of the people to be secure in their persons, houses, papers and effects, against unreasonable searches and seizures, shall not be violated, and no Warrants shall issue, but upon probable cause, supported by Oath or affirmation and particularly describing the place to be searched, and the persons or things to be seized.

NO MATTER how important society's right to be protected from criminal behavior may be, the means used to restrict criminal activity must be lawful and constitutional. No one, no matter how obnoxious or dangerous, may be "railroaded" to jail without protection of his basic rights.

The right to go to our homes and be let alone by the government is a very precious freedom.

The rights of privacy and personal security protected by this amendment are regarded as essential to liberty.[1] Protection of one's privacy and possessions must be extended to all by both the states and the federal government.[2]

Usually, no one may be arrested without a warrant, an order signed by a judicial officer to arrest a named individual for a specified crime. A warrant may issue if a reasonable person would believe that the crime has, in fact, been committed and that the individual to be arrested has been involved in its commission.[3] In two situations, however, an arrest may take place without a warrant. In case of a serious crime, known as a felony, if there is no time to obtain a warrant, a policeman may arrest someone if he believes that a crime has been committed and that the person is involved. Shortly after such an arrest, a judge must determine that there is probable cause to continue to hold the person arrested.[4]

Examples

1. A man had an argument with a friend while he was standing on the second-floor balcony of his apartment house and the friend was outside, standing underneath the balcony. The man went into his apartment and came back out on the balcony with a gun, which he pointed at his friend. She left and found two policemen, to whom she reported the incident. The policemen went with her to the man's apartment building and he came out onto the balcony to speak to them. They asked him if they could come into the apartment and he refused. He came and went from the balcony to inside his apartment while the policemen were there. They were afraid he might bring the gun out on the balcony and endanger them, the woman, and anyone else in the vicinity, so they called additional officers to the scene. One officer climbed up a pipe on the side of the building and onto the balcony. He then let the other officers into the apartment. The man was arrested and handcuffed and, without a warrant, his apartment was searched. Illegal weapons were found. There was no search warrant. The court held that it was constitutional to arrest the man without a warrant, although the circumstances did not support the search without a warrant, because the man was in custody and no longer a danger.[5]

2. Officer Smith, a policeman, is walking past Mrs. Jones's store when she rushes out screaming "Help! Police!" She tells him that she has been robbed by a bandit who had a gun and took her cash register with him. She describes the man. Smith looks up and sees a man answering that description running and carrying a cash register. He may arrest the man.

3. In the same example, Smith does not see anyone, so he takes Mrs. Jones to the police station where she identifies the robber from a picture. A warrant is necessary before Smith may go to the man's house and arrest him.

An arrest without a warrant may also be made in the case of a minor infraction of criminal law, known as a misdemeanor, but usually only if the offense is committed in the presence of the arresting policeman. If the policeman is told about a misdemeanor and goes to the person's house without a warrant to arrest him, the arrest is invalid.[6]

Examples

1. Throwing paper on the street is usually a misdemeanor in most cities. If Officer Smith sees Dan Dumb throw a candy bar wrapper on the sidewalk, he may make an arrest.

2. If Ned Nasty comes up to Officer Smith and tells him that he saw Dan throw the candy wrapper on the sidewalk around the corner, Officer Smith may not arrest Dan without a warrant.

If a policeman without a warrant stops someone on the street to check his identity, it is not an "arrest" and is permissible if the reason for the inquiry is that the person looks like a picture on a wanted poster.[7]

This amendment prohibits police use of deadly force in the course of arresting someone unless the person poses a threat of death or serious injury to the policemen or others. For example, a man was escaping from a burglary when the officers arrived. He did not appear to be armed. A policeman shot and killed him. His father sued and the Supreme Court upheld the award of damages the jury had given.[8]

If a person is lawfully arrested, he may be searched at the police station and any evidence found may be used against him even if it is unrelated to the crime for which he was arrested.[9]

Example

Fred Foolish is arrested for being drunk and disorderly. When he is taken to the police station, he is searched and narcotics are found in his pocket. He may be arrested for possession of narcotics.

Only reasonable searches are allowed. For example, police officers may not hold a suspect down and pump out his stomach if they believe that he swallowed narcotics.[10]

The Supreme Court held that when a suspect is subject to valid arrest, although his person and the area immediately around him (such as the room in which he was found) may be searched, his entire house may not be searched unless the police have a search warrant as well as an arrest warrant.[11] If a person is arrested in the yard of his home, it is unconstitutional to go into the house without a search warrant[12]

Examples

1. A woman sold narcotics at her house to a police informer. The two arranged to meet at another place for another drug transaction. The police obtained a warrant to search her house and to arrest her. They came to her house, opened an unlocked door, and announced themselves. They did not knock first and announce their intent to search. The Supreme Court held that an unannounced entry may be an unreasonable search.[13]

2. A man was suspected of being the driver of a getaway car used in a murder. The actual murderer was arrested almost immediately after the crime was committed. The police surrounded the home of two women where they thought the suspect might be staying. With guns drawn, they entered the home, found the man in a closet, and arrested him. The Supreme Court held that a warrant had been required in order to enter, even if it were not the man's actual residence. The Court held that a houseguest has a reasonable expectation of privacy and pointed out that all the police would have had to do was to wait for him to come outside.[14]

Fingerprinting is constitutionally permissible only if it is undertaken pursuant to an arrest warrant based on reasonable cause to believe that the person whom the police wish to fingerprint has had something to do with the crime.[15]

Example

A suspect was arrested without probable cause and taken to the police station and fingerprinted. The fingerprints matched those found at the scene of a rape. The Supreme Court held that the fingerprints were not admissible as evidence because use of them violated the man's rights under the 4th Amendment.[16]

At the time of a lawful arrest, and in some other circumstances, a vehicle may be searched without a warrant if the searchers believe that it might contain evidence of a crime.[17]

Examples

1. A car was stopped for speeding. The policeman noticed that a passenger seemed extremely nervous. He told the passenger to get out of the car. When he did so, a bag of cocaine fell out of his lap. He claimed that the arrest was illegal because the policeman had no authority to order him to stand up, thus to allow the cocaine to become visible. The Supreme Court held that passengers may be ordered out of a car to prevent danger to a policeman.[18]

2. A policeman overheard a man on a public telephone making what appeared to be an appointment to sell drugs. He followed the man and stopped his car for a traffic violation. The man consented to a search of the car. On the floorboard in the front seat was a paper bag with

cocaine in it. The Supreme Court held that it was reasonable of the policeman to believe that consent to search the car included consent to search a container in plain view. [19]

Obviously, if the searchers had to leave the car in order to go get a warrant, the car would not be there when they got back.

Any search except of an arrested person or of a vehicle must be conducted under a search warrant. A valid warrant must specify the location to be searched, the crime involved, and the evidence that the police believe they will find. If, however, either the arrest or the search has been conducted unconstitutionally, the evidence cannot be used against the accused. [20] A search must have been legal from the outset and valuable evidence found in the course of an unconstitutional search is still inadmissible in court.

Example

A woman killed her husband and tried to kill herself. She became frightened after she had swallowed what she believed to be a lethal dose of sleeping pills and called her daughter for help. The daughter called the police, who rushed to the home and found the woman unconscious and her husband's dead body. The woman was sent to the hospital and one-half hour later, detectives searched her house without a warrant. Based on such things as letters they found, she was charged with second-degree murder. The Supreme Court held that the warrantless search violated her rights and the evidence was inadmissible. [21]

Restrictions on searches without warrants apply to law enforcement officers and situations that may lead to criminal proceedings. There may be other situations in which other persons, such as teachers, are entitled to conduct noncriminal searches without need for a warrant.

Examples

1. A teacher discovered a fourteen-year-old girl smoking in the school bathroom. The student was sent to the principal's office, where she denied that she had been smoking. The assistant principal opened her purse and found cigarettes, marijuana, and letters indicating that she was a drug dealer. She was reported to the juvenile authorities and the Supreme Court held that the search was legal. [22]

2. A sixteen-year-old student was outside the school building, which was against the rules. A teacher thought he saw a bulge in the boy's clothes and thought he might have drugs on his person. The teacher called the boy's mother for permission to search him and she refused. Notwithstanding that refusal, two male teachers took him into a locker room and made him take off his clothes. No drugs or other contraband was found. The boy sued for damages and the Court held that the search was unreasonable. A "strip search" of a student is warranted only if the student's conduct is such that a reasonable suspicion is created that a law has been violated. [23]

3. Two seventh-grade students reported that $4.50 was missing after their gym class. Three teachers searched the lockers and book bags of all the girls in the class and made them take off their shoes. No money was found. The teachers then thought that the girls might have hidden the money in their underwear, so they were required to take off their shirts and shake out the rest of their clothes. The principal called all the parents and apologized later. The court held that strip searches could not be justified to look for money, although it might be permissible if the search was for guns. [24]

4. Two eight-year-old girls were accused by a classmate of stealing money. The classmate said that they put it in the book bag of one of the girls. The teacher searched the book bag and found nothing. The teacher took the girls into the bathroom and told them to pull down their underpants so she could see if money was hidden there. They left the bathroom and she took them back and made them take off all of their clothes. Another child's mother, who heard the girls weeping, investigated and stopped the situation. The girls and their families sued the teacher and the school. The Court held that the teacher had violated the girls' constitutional rights. She had made no effort to investigate the claim that the money was missing, and the search was certainly a violation of the little girls' rights. The Court held that a physical search of a child may be made in school only if there is a serious threat of immediate physical harm. [25]

5. A school district authorized random drug testing of all students who wished to play on athletic teams. Written consent to testing was required from both parents and students before they were allowed to participate in the athletic program. A boy and his parents refused to consent and he was not allowed to be on the football team. The Supreme Court pointed out that a school may exert supervision over students that would not be allowed over adults. The Court held that the drug

testing program was not unreasonable and that the privacy interests involved were negligible.[26]

Similarly, a case worker's home visit to a family on public assistance is not considered to be a "search" and no warrant is necessary. A state statute providing that benefits may be terminated if the welfare recipient refuses to allow the social worker into the house is constitutional as long as the visit is made within reasonable hours and contains no elements of harassment.[27]

Searches of a defendant's body, such as removal of a bullet, present 4th Amendment questions as well. While these may be permissible if there is no risk to the arrestee,[28] the state may not compel major surgery—one that requires general anesthesia, for example—to remove a bullet to be used in evidence.[29] A legal search, with or without a warrant, may result in discovery of evidence of an unrelated crime. The Supreme Court has upheld seizure of the evidence as long as it was in plain view during the legal search.[30] The discovery must be genuinely accidental, however. When police lawfully enter a home (for example, when a resident consents to their coming in) and evidence of a crime is in plain view, they do not need a warrant to seize it.

Example

A college policeman observed a student walking on campus with an open bottle of gin. The student appeared to be younger than the legal age for drinking, so the policeman asked the student for his ID. The student said that he had left it in his dorm room and the policeman went with him to get it. When the student opened the door to his room, the policeman, standing out in the hall, saw marijuana and a pipe on top of a desk. When asked, the student's roommate, who was already in the room, handed over a quantity of marijuana. All of the drugs were seized and the seizure was upheld.[32]

No warrant is necessary for the police to look for something outside of a building or a private yard. For example, no warrant is necessary if the police fly over an open field,[33] observe marijuana growing there, and come back later and seize the plants.[34] There is no right of privacy outside except in the yard of a home. Even within a private yard, moreover, police may seize and use as evidence objects in plain view.[35]

A "plain view" search cannot be used as an excuse to find something the police suspect is on the premises but for which they have insufficient evidence to obtain a search warrant.[37]

Examples

1. A proper search warrant is obtained to search Joe Dumb's house for narcotics. While looking in a drawer in the kitchen, a reasonable place for narcotics to be hidden, the police find stolen jewelry. They may seize the jewelry and use it in evidence against Joe.

2. The police have a warrant to look in Joe's garage for a stolen car. The car is not there, but they look in a tool box and find the jewelry. Since the car could not have been hidden in the tool box, the jewelry may not be used in evidence against Joe.

Amendment Five

No person shall be held to answer for a capital, or otherwise infamous crime, unless on a presentment or indictment of a Grand Jury, except in cases arising in the land or naval forces, or in the Militia, when in actual service in time of War or public danger; nor shall any person be subject for the same offence to be twice put in jeopardy of life or limb; nor shall be compelled in any criminal case to be a witness against himself; nor be deprived of life, liberty, or property, without due process of law; nor shall private property be taken for public use, without just compensation.

THE 5TH AMENDMENT guarantees the right to indictment by a grand jury in federal criminal cases, prohibits double jeopardy, protects against compulsory self-incrimination, guarantees due process of law in the federal courts, and establishes the requirement that the government pay for property taken under the right of eminent domain.

The purpose of the *grand jury* is to limit the power of the federal government to prosecute citizens. A grand jury is a group of citizens selected to hear evidence of criminal activity and to determine if the person charged with the crime should be held for trial. They do not determine the guilt or innocence of the accused, the function of the trial or petit jury, but decide whether or not the evidence against him is strong enough to present to the petit jury. This portion of the 5th Amendment has not been made applicable to the states through the 14th Amendment and so many states do not have grand juries. In those that do not, the office of the district attorney issues the charges, called indictments. There has been discussion to the effect that grand juries are no longer useful and merely prolong the legal process, since the district attorney presents the evidence against defendants to them and the grand jury simply "rubber stamps" his decisions. However, unless the Constitution is amended to eliminate them, all felony indictments in the federal courts will still be issued by grand juries. Where states do use grand juries, however, selection of members of the grand jury must be on a racially non-discriminatory basis.[1]

The right to a grand jury indictment or a trial in the regular courts does not apply to service personnel on active duty. If a serviceman transgresses a military law, he or she is *court-martialed*.

The Supreme Court held in the case of *O'Callahan v. Parker*[2] that a serviceman may not be court-martialed for a crime committed off his or her base in the United States against a civilian. The Court held that in case of such an offense, he or she may be tried only by the regular civilian courts as if he were an ordinary civilian and he or she may not be court-martialed either instead of or in addition to the civilian trial. Court-martial for a non-service-connected offense instead of a civilian trial by jury was held to violate the serviceperson's rights under numerous provisions of the Bill of Rights as well as under general principles of due process of law.

A civilian employee or a dependent on a base may not be court-martialed, since the military has no jurisdiction over them.[3] If the crime is committed on an American base either here or overseas, the employee or dependent is returned for trial in the ordinary federal courts.

When United States service personnel are stationed outside of this country, treaties with the host countries provide whether military personnel will be tried in the courts of that country if they commit crimes off their base. In most cases, if the court system of the host country meets minimal standards of fairness, they will try service personnel. In almost no situation can the United States government intervene if a civilian employee or dependent is charged by the host country with committing a crime.

Examples

1. Private Jane Doe and her husband, who is living with her on her base in England, hold up the post exchange on the base. Private Doe would be court martialed and her husband returned to the United States for trial in a federal court.

2. Private Doe and her husband hold up a store in London. They would be tried by the British courts.

3. Several servicemen were charged with rape of a teenager in Okinawa, where they were stationed. The victim was a Japanese girl who lived with her family in Okinawa. The servicemen were tried in a Japanese court and convicted, and are serving their sentences in a Japanese prison.

The *double jeopardy* clause in the 5th Amendment prevents either state or federal authorities from bringing the same person to trial more than once for the same offense after he has been acquitted by a jury. It is designed to prevent unfair harassment of a person by repeated attempts to convict him of a crime of which he has already been found not guilty.

Example

Nathan Nasty is tried for murdering his wife. The jury renders a verdict of not guilty. Once the verdict is given Nasty may write a book about how he did it and no further criminal proceedings may be taken against him.

If a defendant is convicted, appeals his conviction, and the appellate court finds a legal error and orders a new trial, the defendant may not plead double jeopardy.[4] In this case, he is the one who initiated the appeal.

If the defendant has been convicted of a lesser charge at his first trial, however, he may only be tried for that crime at his second. For example, if someone is charged with murder and convicted of manslaughter, appeals that conviction, and is awarded a new trial, he may only be charged with manslaughter at the second trial.[5]

A single trial on two counts charging different crimes arising out of the same events that results in a finding of guilty on both is grounds for the judge giving two consecutive, not concurrent, sentences. This does not violate the defendant's right against double jeopardy.[6]

If the members of the jury cannot reach a verdict and the judge declares a mistrial, the defendant's rights against double jeopardy are not violated if he is tried again.[7] If, however, the judge dismisses the charges because of defects in the prosecution's case, the defendant may not be tried again.[8]

One act may constitute violations of both state and federal law. If so, the courts have held that two sovereign powers are involved and that each level of government may try the defendant and no double jeopardy has occurred.[9]

Example

John Criminal robs a bank. This is a crime under both state and federal law. He is tried in state court.

Regardless of the outcome of that trial, he may also be tried in federal court. He has not been tried in the same court twice.

Double jeopardy also does not prohibit trials in two states if one event involved both of them.[10]

Example

A woman is kidnapped at gunpoint from the parking lot of a shopping center in State A. Eighteen hours later, her body is found in a ditch in State B, thirty miles from the shopping center. Medical evidence establishes that she was killed where she was found. State A arrests a suspect and he is tried and convicted of kidnapping. State B may try him for murder and his right against double jeopardy has not been violated.

A city, county, or municipal court is not, however, considered to be separate from a state court. Thus a person may not be tried twice in two different courts if both are instrumentalities of the same government.[11]

Example

A member of the Navajo tribe was convicted in a tribal court and served his punishment. He was then tried for the same offense in federal court. The Supreme Court said that the second trial was not double jeopardy because the two were different jurisdictions.[12]

One act may also constitute more than one crime under state law or under federal law.[13] Two prosecutions in the same court for different offenses do not constitute double jeopardy.

Example

If more than one person is murdered in a shooting spree, separate trials for each murder do not constitute double jeopardy.[14]

Where, however, the evidence to be presented at the trial of the second offense is the same used in the first, the second trial violates the defendant's rights.

Example

A defendant was charged with committing a murder in the course of a robbery. He was tried for both murder and robbery and acquitted. He was brought to a second trial for robbery alone. The Supreme Court held that his right against double jeopardy had been violated.[15]

The guarantees against double jeopardy apply only to criminal proceedings.

Example

The federal government began proceedings to seize a house in which it was alleged that drug transactions had taken place. Before that issue was resolved, the owner of the house was arrested and charged with violation of the drug statutes. The Supreme Court held that it was not a violation of the man's rights against double jeopardy to both punish a person and to require forfeiture of his property for the same offense in a separate civil proceeding. The court held that forfeitures are not "punishment" nor criminal proceedings for purposes of the double jeopardy clause.[16]

The philosophy behind the clause of the 5th Amendment that prohibits compulsory *self-incrimination* is that the state and federal government must establish guilt of criminal acts by independent evidence, since no one should be required to testify against himself.[17] This right is designed to protect against the force of the courts themselves. This right is an absolute one and may not be abridged for any reason. Again we see the principle that in our legal system, the end does not justify the means. The operative word, however, is "compulsory." If a witness makes voluntary disclosures instead of claiming the right to remain silent, the government has not compelled him to incriminate himself.

If a person is involved in any sort of investigation by law enforcement officials, he has the right to invoke this privilege. He must, however, claim that he would be incriminated by answering questions—that what he said would link him to a criminal act.[18]

There may be information that might but does not necessarily incriminate someone and in some cases, the right against self-incrimination does not apply.

Example

An infant was removed from his mother's custody after a finding of child abuse. He was later returned to her on condition that she engage in therapy and take parenting classes. When she did not comply with the court's order, the Child Protective Agency got another custody order from the court to put the baby in a foster home. When they went to get the child, he could not be found. The mother refused to tell them where he was, although she began by telling them that he was with other relatives, who, when contacted, said that they had not seen the child. She was put in jail for contempt of the family court, for refusing to obey the order to surrender her baby. She claimed that her rights against self-incrimination were vio-

lated, because child abuse is a crime. The Supreme Court held that this was not self-incrimination, because the state had an interest in the welfare of the child and proceedings to protect him are civil, not criminal. The Court noted that the mother could not, if he were found, claim the right against self-incrimination as to any evidence of abuse that might be found if the child were examined. The Court held that the 5th Amendment privilege may not be invoked to resist compliance with a regulatory scheme (in this case, the protection of children) unrelated to the enforcement of the criminal law.[19]

Refusal to answer cannot be based on a statement that it would be embarrassing or that it would ruin one's reputation. Also, the only person one may refuse to incriminate is one's self.[20]

The privilege against self-incrimination applies only to compelled oral or written testimony. It does not apply, for example, to statements made to an informant in the same jail cell, as long as the cellmate just listens to what the accused says and does not question him.[21] It does not apply to statements volunteered to a policeman prior to an arrest.[22] For example, if a person walks up to a policeman on the street, tells him that God has told him to confess and that he would like the policeman to know that he murdered someone and buried the body under a tree, if the body is found under the tree and the person is tried, the statement may be admitted in evidence.

The privilege does not apply to books or records, whether they are in the hands of the person being investigated[23] or his or her accountant.[24] The privilege protects us from coerced testimony, not from volunteered testimony and not from coercion to produce existing evidence.[25]

Evidence obtained by forcible stomach pumping, blood tests, or physical examinations may violate the 4th Amendment provisions restricting searches and seizures, but they do not constitute 5th Amendment self-incrimination.[26] For that reason, if a person who has been arrested for driving under the influence of alcohol refuses to take a blood alcohol test, submission of that refusal into evidence at his trial is permitted and does not violate his right against self-incrimination.[27]

Rights under the 5th Amendment begin when a person is questioned.[28] No influence may be used to induce admission of criminal behavior or commission of a crime. The person may not be frightened or threatened or promised a lighter sentence if he confesses. He must be advised by the police that he has a right to remain silent and that if he wishes to make a statement, it will be used in evidence at his trial.

A suspect must be advised that he has the right to confer with an attorney and that if he wishes to do so, he has the right to appointed counsel if he cannot afford one.[29]

Example

A man was arrested and questioned by federal agents about two murders. When he asked for a lawyer, they stopped questioning him. He was provided with counsel and met with his lawyer two or three times while being held in jail. The county sheriff told him that he could not refuse to talk to him. He confessed, was convicted of two counts of murder, and sentenced to death. He appealed and the Supreme Court held that his rights had been violated. The Court held that once a person has a lawyer, he may not be questioned unless his lawyer is present.[30]

If a suspect says that he would like to speak to a lawyer, questioning must stop and if it does not, any subsequent statements are inadmissible in evidence.[31] If a suspect remains silent, however, failure to tell him that his lawyer is trying to contact him does not violate this right.[32]

If a confession is completely voluntary, it may be used in evidence at trial, but if it has been coerced, not only may the confession not be used, but any information the police received by coercing a prisoner is also inadmissible.[33]

Example

Joe is held in jail for three days and beaten by the police. They are trying to get him to admit involvement in a robbery. Joe finally tells them that he did it and the loot is buried under his back steps. Since the police would not have found the loot except by the use of unconstitutional activities, neither the confession nor the goods may be used in evidence at Joe's trial.

If a defendant does not make a statement or elects not to testify in his own behalf at his trial, a prosecutor may not comment on his refusals. Since one has the constitutional right to remain silent, adverse comment upon its exercise would make it worthless.[34]

During an investigation, the prosecutor or a congressional committee may grant the witness "immunity."[35] This means that he will not be prosecuted for any criminal acts disclosed by answering questions. At this point, the self-incrimination privilege no longer applies and the witness must answer.[36]

If one person who has been accused of a crime is offered immunity in return for an agreement to testify against a co-defendant, failure to inform the jury of that fact violates the co-defendant's rights, since it affects the believability of the testimony given against him.[37]

If the acts under investigation constitute a crime under both federal and state law, granting immunity only under one will not end the privilege.[38]

"Privilege," which is a matter of the rules of evidence, not of constitutional law, is the right of a person who occupies a confidential relationship to the accused to refuse to answer questions about him or his business. Normally, this right exists as to a defendant's physician, attorney, religious advisor, and spouse.

Example

A policeman shot and killed a man. The dead man's family sued the policeman and the village that employed him. The policeman had sought counseling from a female psychiatric social worker after the event. The dead man's family demanded that her notes be produced to use in evidence and she refused. The Supreme Court held that communications to psychotherapists are privileged, because effective psychotherapy depends on an atmosphere of trust, and if the patient were concerned about the possibility of disclosure of information, the development of the relationship necessary for successful treatment might be impeded.[39]

Usually, the only time any of those persons may be required to testify either to a prosecutor who wants a statement from them or to a grand jury or jury is where the defendant himself wishes to offer testimony by the privileged person. The Supreme Court has held in the case of *Branzburg v. Hayes*[40] that a newspaper reporter does not have either common law privilege or a right under the 1st Amendment guarantees of freedom of the press to refuse to answer grand jury questions about confidential news sources. He also may not refuse to disclose information from news stories that he did not publish. Even if the source of the news item was considered confidential information, the Supreme Court has held that he is obliged to reveal it if it is evidence of a criminal act. An accountant also has no privilege and must testify about a taxpayer's records he has prepared.[41]

The clause in the 5th Amendment pertaining to deprivation of life, liberty, or property without due process of law applies only to the federal government but there is a parallel clause requiring application of due process by the states in the 14th Amendment. Due process of law does not grant any specific rights such as the right to counsel. It means that the law must "play fair." It requires compliance not only with the outward forms of the law but with all that is meant by the ideas of liberty and justice for all.

There are two aspects of due process. Substantive due process means that laws that create rights, define crimes, or regulate behavior must be reasonable and not arbitrary. A law that makes some conduct illegal and provides for a fine or prison sentence for commission of some act must be restricting a truly anti-social act. The purpose of the law is, therefore, involved in determination of substantive due process.

Examples

1. A law that made it a crime to have red hair would be an unreasonably arbitrary law. Having red hair is not an antisocial act. This law would violate substantive due process.

2. Laws that provide penalties for murder are designed to prevent a genuinely anti-social act. Laws making murder a crime do not violate substantive due process.

Procedural due process, on the other hand, prescribes the method of enforcing or obtaining rights under the law. Procedural due process means that the process through which the law moves (the arrest, indictment, trial, verdict, and sentence in a criminal case) must be fair.

Example

Using torture to extract a confession violates fundamental principles of fairness and justice and therefore violates the idea of procedural due process.

Due process, then, means that the law sets forth upon a course of action according to those rules and principles that have been established in our legal system for the protection of private rights.[42]

Our rights under due process are far more extensive than those we have with what we perceive to be relationships with "the legal system." Interactions with state institutions or private institutions receiving federal funds must also be governed by fairness. For example, a severely retarded patient in a state institution has the due process right to adequate training to ensure his safety and freedom from restraint.[43]

In the context of civil litigation, due process also encompasses a requirement of fundamental fairness. For example, the father of an illegitimate child who supports the child and has a "significant relationship" with him or her has the right to be heard when the child's mother's husband wishes to adopt the child.[44] In child-abuse cases, if the state wishes to terminate

permanently the parents' rights to the children, the state must prove the charges by a fair preponderance of the evidence.[45] Anything less violates the parents' right to due process of law.

In summary, requirements for substantive due process demand that the federal government (or states, under the 14th Amendment) or the institutions they support may not deprive any person (not just citizens) of life, liberty, or property without good reason and in a fair manner. In our complex society, questions of governmental fairness are around us every day.

Examples

1. Does an elderly person who has lived in a nursing home for years and whose care is paid by the federal government have any right to complain if a social worker decides he should be moved to a different facility that is cheaper?

2. Does a man who will die if he stops kidney dialysis, financed by the federal government, have any right to be heard about cut-backs in funding that will exclude him from coverage unless he can pay for it himself, where the nature of the disease means that he cannot work?

3. A widowed mother with two babies is entirely dependent on Aid to Families with Dependent Children. Does she have any rights not to give the name of a man with whom the welfare worker suspects she is having a relationship, since the man has no legal obligation whatever to support her children?

The last clause in the 5th Amendment restricts the federal government's right of *eminent domain*, which is the power to acquire private property for public use, by requiring that the owner be paid the fair value of the property taken.[46] State governments also have the right of eminent domain, but the same restrictions apply. Cities and states may put restrictions on land use, such as enacting zoning laws that prohibit certain types of land use in residential areas without invoking the power of eminent domain.[47] Eminent domain only applies when the governmental agency seeks to remove ownership of the property to itself from private landowners or to transfer ownership for some public purpose.[48]

The property taken must be used in some manner that benefits the public and the owner must be paid its fair value. Determination of price is made in many ways, but it always requires some form of judicial process.

Examples

1. A city planning commission approved a woman's application for a building permit to expand her store and pave her parking lot conditioned on her compliance with a requirement that she dedicate some of her land for a public greenway and for a public bicycle pathway. The Supreme Court held that this constituted uncompensated taking of property in violation of her rights under eminent domain.[49]

2. A man bought two building lots on a South Carolina barrier island. He intended to build a house on each lot and sell them. A few years later, the state legislature enacted the Beachfront Management Act to preserve the area from over-building. The legislature specifically found that new construction in the area was a threat to a valuable public resource. Under the new act, he could not build anything on those lots. The man sued, claiming that this was a "taking" of his property, for which he should be paid. The Supreme Court held that total deprivation of the right to use property is the equivalent of physical appropriation of the property, so the landowner was entitled to compensation.[50]

Amendment Six

In all criminal prosecutions, the accused shall enjoy the right to a speedy and public trial, by an impartial jury of the State and district wherein the crime shall have been committed, which district shall have been previously ascertained by law, and to be informed of the nature and cause of the accusation, to be confronted with the witnesses against him, to have compulsory process for obtaining Witnesses in his favor, and to have the Assistance of Counsel for his defence.

THIS AMENDMENT specifies procedural rights granted to persons charged with federal crimes, all of which have been made applicable through the 14th Amendment to state court proceedings.

The requirement of a *speedy trial* is designed to prevent indefinite imprisonment before trial. If not so restricted, the government could dispose of its critics by holding them in jail for years "awaiting trial" on ridiculous charges. This provision means only that the state or federal government may not purposefully and deliberately hold a person awaiting trial for an unnecessarily long time. The Federal Speedy Trial Act[1] provides that any federal prisoner must be indicted or charged within 30 days of arrest and this right cannot be waived by the defendant.[2] In many areas the dockets of the criminal courts are very crowded and a defendant who is tried in his proper turn may not complain of denial of his right. The right is only abridged when the prosecuting authority either deliberately or negligently delays a trial.

Example

A man was indicted on February 22, 1980 for various drug offenses. When federal officers went to his mother's home to arrest him, she told them that he had left the country. His name was put on the federal "wanted persons" computer system, but somehow was deleted in error. In 1982 he came back to the United States, went to college, got married, and was working. Apparently, no federal agent was looking for him. On September 5, 1988, he was arrested. The Supreme Court held that the government's negligence violated his right to a speedy trial and the charges were dismissed.[3]

In the case of *Klopfer v. North Carolina*,[2] the Supreme Court held that the right to a speedy trial applied to state courts through the due process clause of the 14th Amendment. However, the Court reiterated its position that as long as a defendant was tried in his turn, mere delay in reaching trial due to an overcrowded court docket was not a violation of his constitutional rights.[5]

If a person is questioned about a crime but no further action is taken for several years, at which time the person is arrested, the right to a speedy trial is inapplicable. This right does not apply during a period in which a defendant is not under indictment or restraint.[6]

Example

A military physician was charged by the Army with the murder of his wife and two small daughters in their home on the base. After preliminary hearings, those charges were dismissed. Four years later, largely due to the efforts of his dead wife's parents, he was indicted for the murders by the ordinary civilian authorities. The jury convicted him and he appealed. The Supreme Court held that the four-year-delay was not a violation of his right to a speedy trial, because during that time he had no constraints on his freedom and no criminal charges were pending.[7]

Secret inquisitions by any branch of the government are repugnant to our judicial system. The right to a *public trial* assures that justice must be carried out under the eye of the citizens. The right to a public trial also includes the right of the press to attend pretrial hearings[8] and questioning of prospective jurors.[7] Although normally reporters and other spectators are allowed to observe all trials, many courts have refused to allow television or movie cameras in the courtrooms. This policy has been upheld by the Supreme Court on the grounds that a trial is not a sideshow and the equipment necessary for picture-taking can prove very distracting to those involved.[10] A defendant who wishes the court to be cleared of spectators may ask the judge to do so. In some cases, where a witness is obliged to testify to events that are very embarrassing and about which privacy should be assured, the judge may also clear the courtroom.[11] This is very often done when the prosecuting witness is called to testify in a case involving a sexual assault.

Example

A defendant was convicted of the sexual assault of a six-year-old girl. He appealed on the ground that his right to a public trial had been violated because the courtroom had been closed to nonessential persons while she was testifying. The Court held that closing a court to safeguard the well-being of a small child is a compelling state interest, and the right to a public trial is not absolute.[12]

The verdict in all federal criminal trials must be rendered by a *jury* unless the defendant himself requests that he be tried by the judge alone. In federal courts, however, one is not entitled to a jury trial for a "petty offense," usually defined as a misdemeanor, the maximum sentence of which cannot exceed six months.[13] This is the case even if one is charged with more than one misdemeanor, thus the possible sentence may, in total, exceed six months.[14]

Juries in federal courts when they are conducting criminal trials are always composed of twelve people and most states require twelve-person juries in cases involving serious crimes. However certain traffic violations and other minor crimes are frequently tried in traffic courts by six-man juries in many states and some state constitutions provide for less than twelve persons in all cases. The Supreme Court has held that in those states, having fewer than twelve persons on a jury does not violate the defendant's rights.[15] State laws in most states also require a unanimous verdict to convict a defendant, as is true of all federal juries. The Supreme Court has held that state statutes that allow jury verdicts of guilt by nine of twelve jurors are constitutional,[16] although a jury of less than six would deprive the defendant of a constitutional right.[17] The Court has also decided that lack of unanimous jury verdicts in those states that do not require them does not deprive defendants of due process of law or to trial by jury.[18] The Court did, however, draw the line at nonunanimous six-member juries and found them unconstitutional in trials for serious offenses.[19] Unanimous verdicts are still required, however, in all federal trials and in those states whose laws provide for them, and if the jury can-

not agree, the judge usually orders a "mistrial" and the defendant may be tried again. The jury must be impartial, which eliminates those with any special knowledge of the case, any relationship to any of the parties involved, or those with any special interests.

The 6th amendment right to trial by jury in all criminal cases that would constitute jury matters in federal court is now applicable to all state trials, regardless of any state constitutional provision to the contrary, through this amendment and the due process clause of the 14th Amendment.[20] The Supreme Court has held that a jury trial must be allowed in any case where there is a possibility of imprisonment for more than six months.[21] Except for some very minor misdemeanor charges, therefore, a state's failure to provide a defendant with the opportunity for trial by jury is considered to be a denial of due process of law and is therefore unconstitutional.

The Supreme Court has held in many cases that racial or sexual discrimination in the selection of jurors is unconstitutional.[22]

In any case where the death penalty is sought by the prosecution, because the jury must be impartial, potential jurors who are unalterably in favor of or unalterably opposed to the death penalty may not serve. To do otherwise would violate the defendant's right to fairness.[23]

One problem arising in jury trials is the question of prior knowledge by a prospective juror who has read about the case in the newspapers. There may be a distinct collision between 1st Amendment rights to freedom of the press and the defendant's right to a fair trial. If a newspaper has indulged in lurid reporting of a particularly revolting crime and keeps up sensational coverage day after day, it is quite likely that jurors who are called to hear the case may have arrived at firm opinions. Since only the evidence presented in court may be used as the basis of a verdict, this obviously affects the defendant's right to a fair trial.

The defendant is tried in the district where the crime is committed. Before the American Revolution, colonists charged with political crimes against the British authorities were taken to England for trial. This, of course, meant that the jurors were more sympathetic to the Crown, and was the basis for this provision of the Constitution. If local feeling in a sensational case is, however, running strongly against the defendant and he believes that he will be unfairly convicted, he may ask for a "change of venue," which is removal of the trial to another area. The right of change of venue belongs only to the defendant and may not be exercised by the government. A right to change of venue exists even in a misdemeanor case which is to be tried before a jury.[24]

One of the fundamental principles of criminal law is that the defendant must know why he is being tried or, as the Constitution terms it *"to be informed of the nature and cause of the accusation."* This prevents imprisonment for noncriminal acts such as criticism of government policy. In order to prepare his defense properly, a defendant is entitled to know exactly with what he is charged and the circumstances under which he is supposed to have done it.

In all criminal proceedings, the prosecution has the burden of proving criminal intent. A defendant never has to bear the burden of convincing a jury that he or she "didn't mean to."[25]

Example

John Smith is in jail for murder. The state must furnish him with the following information: (1) the crime with which he is charged—murder; (2) the name of the person killed; (3) when and where the murder occurred; and (4) by what means he is charged with committing it.

A prosecutor must also disclose to the defense prior to trial all material evidence favorable to the accused.[26]

The *right to confront and cross-examine* witnesses gives the defendant the right to rebut their testimony. This right is guaranteed in all federal and state criminal trials[27] but is not guaranteed in legislative investigations.

The one constitutionally permissible exception to the defendant's right to confront and cross-examine witnesses against him or her is a situation (usually involving sexual assault) where the victim is a small child who would be traumatized by seeing the defendant. In those situations, courts have adopted a variety of methods to protect the child and to preserve the rights of the defendants. In some cases, the child is allowed to testify on closed-circuit television, with the defendant's counsel present; in others, the child is in the courtroom but the defendant is sitting where the victim cannot see him or her.[28]

While a defendant ordinarily has the right to be present in the courtroom throughout his trial and in most cases no proceedings can continue in his absence, if he is disruptive of the orderly processes of the court, he may be removed and the trial continued.[29]

Compulsory process is a subpoena to compel the attendance of the defendant's witnesses. If he had no way to force people to come to his defense unless they wished to do so, he might well be unable to produce an alibi or other defense at his trial. The prosecution has always had the power of subpoena. The defendant's right to compulsory process in order to obtain witnesses on his behalf is now applicable to state courts through the 14th Amendment. In the case of *Washington v. Texas*,[30] the Supreme Court held that a state statute that denied the defendant the right to subpoena a confederate in the alleged crime to testify on his behalf was unconstitutional for this reason.

Example

Bertie Bad and Attila Awful were arrested together, but tried separately, for the murder of Dora Dead. Bertie knows Attila did it by himself. It would be unconstitutional not to permit Bertie to subpoena Attila as a witness for the defense at Bertie's trial.

Since 1963 and the famous *Gideon*[31] decision, all persons charged with felonies are entitled to have a free, court-appointed *attorney*, if they cannot afford their own, in state as well as federal trials. The right to counsel extends in federal courts to "petty offenses" as well as to felonies,[32] although the Supreme Court has held that states are not required to provide counsel for petty offenses unless the defendant could be sent to jail.[33] Prior to that decision, a defendant in a state court was automatically granted counsel only in a capital case or if he were illiterate, very young, or otherwise unusually unable to defend himself. In 1965 the Court handed down the *Escobedo*[34] decision that held that a person has the right to counsel at the time of his arrest if the charge is a serious one, in order to avail himself of legal advice on such subjects as his rights against self-incrimination and bail.

The right to counsel is also granted in some situations other than criminal trials. Persons who have been convicted of a crime and placed on parole or probation, for example, have the right to counsel at a hearing to revoke their parole.[35] Those persons charged with a crime who are committed to a mental hospital instead of being tried have the right to legal representation at the commitment hearing.[36] A person on public assistance whose welfare benefits are being terminated has the right to a hearing on the matter and to have counsel if desired, although the Supreme Court has not held that counsel must be provided for a welfare hearing.[37] Counsel must be provided in immigration and naturalization hearings if there is a possibility that an alien could be deported.[38]

Counsel, moreover, must prepare and present an adequate defense. Inattentive or negligent representation of a client is not "effective assistance of counsel" and a defendant therefore is entitled to a new trial.[39] There are, however, limitations on what an attorney may do in representing a client. Firstly, an attorney is an officer of the court and secondly an advocate for her or his client. Therefore, no client, civil or criminal, may ever require unethical conduct from a lawyer even if it would result in a favorable verdict. For example, an attorney may not present testimony at a trial that he or she knows to be perjured.[40] Likewise, if a defendant is convicted and wishes to appeal, the attorney does not have a constitutional duty to present every issue on appeal that the client wants, if the attorney believes the claim to be frivolous or unsupported by the record.[41]

If a defendant wishes to represent herself, she may do so, but if she is being tried for a serious crime, most judges appoint a "stand-by counsel" in case the defendant needs help in compliance with courtroom protocol and procedures. As long as the stand-by counsel participates but does not interfere, the defendant's rights have not been violated.[42]

In addition to court-appointed counsel, if a defendant's sanity is an issue in the trial or if the prosecution introduces psychiatric evidence, the defendant is entitled to the services of a psychiatrist at public expense to assist in defense of the charges.[43]

Basic rights of procedural due process also apply to children who have been brought before a juvenile court. The theory behind the juvenile court system is that a child should not be branded as a criminal or imprisoned and that he should be rehabilitated instead of punished. For this reason, a judgment of delinquency in a juvenile court has never been a "criminal conviction" and confining a child to a reform school is not a "sentence of imprisonment." Because the juvenile courts are not criminal courts, for many years they were not required to extend any specific constitutional rights to the children before them, although the child was entitled to a fair hearing. In the 1967 *Gault*[44] case, however, the Supreme Court decided that the right to counsel, the right to confront and cross-examine witnesses against him, the right to have notice of the charges against him, and the privilege against self-incrimination must be accorded a child in a juvenile court. The Court based its decision on the theory that a child in reform school has been deprived of his liberty to the same extent as an adult in a penitentiary and that he should be no less protected by the Constitution.

A juvenile does not have the right to trial by jury, however.[45] His conviction must be by the same basis of "guilt beyond a reasonable doubt" that is required to convict an adult of a criminal offense.[46] Since children have a right not to be held in detention except for very serious offenses, the question of the right of a child to bail has never been decided by the Supreme Court although there are numerous state and lower federal court decisions allowing it. Generally speaking, courts will release children without requiring money bonds prior to a juvenile hearing unless the child is considered dangerous, and therefore the question is rarely presented squarely to a court. Most authorities, however, think that a child who is detained because his parents are too poor to provide bail would have an excellent case on denial of due process of law. Unless the child or the home situation to which he would return is dangerous, he should not be incarcerated prior to a determination of guilt.

"Status offenses" are acts, such as truancy, running away from home, "being incorrigible," "being idle," or "smoking a cigarette in public" that are offenses if done by minors but that are not crimes if done by adults. In many states, a child can be sentenced to reform school for these offenses. Although the Supreme Court has never ruled on the constitutionality of the practice, in an increasing number of states, such children are either sent home or placed in foster care.[47]

Examples

1. A fifteen-year-old girl was adjudicated delinquent on grounds of incorrigibility and sentenced to six months in the state reformatory for girls. The state supreme court held that a juvenile taken into custody for a status offense cannot be placed in detention unless all less restrictive alternatives have failed in the past. The Court vacated the sentence.[48]

2. A boy was found to be a neglected child and placed in state protection. He was placed by the state in a residential school and ran away and went home. When he was located, he was placed in a foster home and then charged with the crime of escape. The Court found that he had not committed an offense because he had not been detained as a delinquent at the time he went home.[49]

Amendment Seven

In Suits at common law, where the value in controversy shall exceed twenty dollars, the right of trial by jury shall be preserved, and no fact tried by a jury, shall be otherwise re-examined in any Court of the United States, than according to the rules of the common law.

THIS AMENDMENT gives a right to a jury trial for monetary damages in federal court, but the Constitution does not require state courts to have juries in civil cases.

This right exists for claims "originating in the common law." The common law consists of decrees and decisions of the British courts, some of which date back to the earliest days of the English court system, and legal customs, which go back to antiquity. The English common law that existed at the time of American independence is still the theoretical basis of our law (and of the legal systems in almost all of the countries in the British Commonwealth) except where Congress or the state legislatures have created rights purely by statute. For example, adoption was not known in common law, so resolution of all issues involving adoption are dependent on interpretation of the adoption statutes in the states where disputes arise, and in most states, trials on these issues do not involve a jury. Cases in which the plaintiff wants an injunction (an order to force someone to do something or to stop doing something) usually do not involve juries, since no monetary damages are sought. This amendment, then, involves civil law suits in federal courts that are based on something other than a specific right created exclusively by an act of Congress and in which monetary damages are sought.

Examples

1. An automobile accident case between citizens of different states is tried by a federal court jury, because it is a common law claim for monetary damages and is not derived from legislation.

2. An employee was completely disabled in an off-duty automobile accident. After a certain period of time, her employee benefit plan was canceled. She sued her employer and the insurance company, and the Court held that she had a right to a jury trial under this amendment.[1]

3. Ringling Brothers Circus has a registered trademark: "The Greatest Show on Earth." The state of Utah uses the trademark "The Greatest Snow on Earth." The circus sued Utah to make them stop "confusing" the trademarks. Ringling Brothers was not entitled to a jury trial under this amendment because they were not asking for monetary damages.[2]

Only rarely are claims that properly belong in federal court and seek money damages outside the scope of this amendment.[3]

Active duty military personnel have no right to sue the government for damages, whether for personal injuries[4] (such as medical malpractice in a service hospital) or violation of their constitutional rights.[5]

Amendment Eight

Excessive bail shall not be required, nor excessive fines imposed, nor cruel and unusual punishments inflicted.

THIS AMENDMENT, made applicable to the states through the 14th Amendment, permits a person to be free from detention between the time of his arrest and the time of trial, allowing him to prepare his defense more effectively than if he were in jail. Bail is an amount of money that the accused agrees to forfeit if he does not appear at the time specified by the court for the trial of his case. The only reason money is required is to ensure the defendant's presence, and if it is set higher than an amount reasonably necessary for that purpose, it is "excessive." Bail is set by the judge, who considers such factors as the financial situation of the defendant, the gravity of the offense charged, character, and previous record. In cases where the death penalty may be imposed, bail may be denied, because no amount of money is sufficient to assure a person's presence at a trial in which he or she may be sentenced to death.[1]

Where a crime may be punished by a fine, an order of restitution to the victim, or by a prison sentence, it is cruel and unusual punishment to send an indigent to jail.[2] The Supreme Court has found that such an arrangement constitutes discrimination based on ability to pay. The court must allow him to pay in installments or make other arrangements to collect the money. Only those persons who can pay a fine and refuse to do so may be imprisoned in these cases.

Cruel and unusual punishments are those that are shocking to the conscience of the civilized world. They include inhumane, barbaric, or degrading acts.[3] Conditions in prisons need not be comfortable, but they may not be inhumane.[4] The Federal Civil Rights of Institutionalized Persons Act of 1980[5] allows the attorney general of the United States to intervene if state institutions—prisons or hospitals for the mentally ill or retarded—where people are kept against their will are systematically denying basic human rights to inmates or patients.[6] Prison conditions must, over time, reflect the "evolving standards of decency that mark the progress of a maturing society."[7]

Examples of behaviors that have been outlawed by the courts are beatings by guards when prisoners are shackled, even if the prisoner is not seriously injured,[8] shackling women prisoners during labor and while they are delivering their babies,[9] sending prisoners outside in an Iowa winter without allowing them to wear hats and gloves,[10] or failing to protect a prisoner from foreseeable assaults by other prisoners.[11] In one case, not allowing a prisoner to be moved from a cell where he was constantly subjected to secondhand smoke from his cellmates was considered to be cruel and unusual punishment.[12] The legal standard applied is whether those in charge of the prisoners are "obdurately and deliberately indifferent" to the prisoners' well-being and/or if their conduct is "wanton, malicious, and sadistic."[13] For example, in these times where a "get tough" attitude toward prisoners instead of any interest in rehabilitating them seems to be sweeping the country, there are thoughts in some states of returning, after decades of prohibiting it, to use of the "chain gang" where prisoners are shacked to each other in a line and forced to work for hours. Threats by advocacy groups to challenge chain gangs on grounds that they are barbaric have begun to stop the few instances where it has been begun.[14]

It is a violation of a prisoner's rights against cruel and unusual punishment to deny him medical treatment of serious problems.[15] If the treatment is provided but is provided so negligently that it constitutes malpractice, however, there is no constitutional violation.[16] If a physician orders medication or other treatment for a prisoner and the ordered therapy is not provided, in order for the prisoner to prevail in an action for violation of his Constitutional rights, he must be able to demonstrate that prison authorities acted with deliberate indifference to his medical needs.[17]

A person charged with an offense who wishes to raise the issue of insanity at trial is entitled to the services of a psychiatrist paid by the state in the preparation of his defense.[18] Prisoners who are so mentally ill that they cannot assist their counsel at trial may be committed to mental institutions, but they are entitled to counsel at judicial hearings on the question of their sanity.[19] A prisoner is considered competent to stand trial if he "has sufficient present ability to consult with his lawyer with a reasonable degree of rational understanding."[20] A prisoner who is sent to a mental hospital instead of to trial may not be held indefinitely without some determination of whether he or she committed the crime charged.[21]

Example

A defendant who was deaf and unable to speak was charged with robbery. He could not communicate with his lawyer, so he could not participate in his defense. The trial judge committed him to a mental hospital (with no indication of any psychiatric disorder) for an indefinite period. Because his condition was not capable of improvement, his rights under the 8th Amendment were violated.[22] Incidentally, this case arose years before the Americans with Disabilities Act became law, and today this defendant would have a right to sign-language interpreters.

If sent to a mental hospital instead of to trial, or if hospitalized after conviction, a prisoner has the right to be treated, not merely to be "warehoused."

A prisoner who is mentally ill has the right to a judicial hearing before he is forcibly medicated with anti-psychotic medications against his will.[23] Only if the prisoner is dangerous to himself or others may he be forced to take psychiatric drugs. A prison warden may not decide to make life easier for staff by "drugging prisoners into submission" or medicating them during trial, which would lead the jury to skepticism regarding a plea that the defendant was insane when the crime was committed.[24]

The death penalty is not considered "cruel and unusual punishment" although the United States is virtually alone in the industrialized world in permitting it. Except for conviction of treason in time of declared war, for all practical purposes in this country, a person may not be put to death for any crime that does not cause the death of another person. For example, the death penalty clause of the federal kidnapping act was declared unconstitutional.[25] An insane person may not be executed.[26] Psychiatrists who work with prisoners are, therefore, often asked to make people better so that they may be killed, and many have refused to do so. When lethal injections are the method of carrying out the death penalty, most physicians believe that they would violate their professional responsibilities to kill anyone, but on the other hand, if a nonphysician whose skills are deficient gives the drug, the prisoner may suffer agony before his death.

Executions must be "humane." A prisoner may not be tortured to death. Currently permissible means of execution are electrocution, gas, firing squad, or lethal injection.[27]

Amendment Nine

The enumeration in the Constitution, of certain rights, shall not be construed
to deny or disparage others retained by the people.

THIS AMENDMENT reiterates the view of the nature of man and the government expressed in the Declaration of Independence and the Preamble to the Constitution. This philosophy is based on the idea that all human beings have certain rights with which they are "endowed by their Creator" and that they possess simply because they are human beings. Some of these rights, such as freedom of worship, are enumerated in the Constitution while others, such as "life, liberty and the pursuit of happiness" are not. This amendment, rather than enunciating any particular affirmative right, serves to protect other fundamental rights that are not set forth in the Constitution.[1] The amendment is designed to protect the rights of the minority from the will of the majority. Individuals who believe certain things cannot be persecuted by those who would impose other values upon them, even if almost all of the population despises what the individual believes. Since it was difficult to determine what, if any rights, exist under natural law in addition to the ones guaranteed by other amendments, only recently has this amendment been frequently used as a basis for court decisions. In 1947, the Supreme Court held that a right to engage in political activity was protected by this amendment.[2]

The modern use of the 9th Amendment as a protection of one of our basic freedoms, the right of personal, bodily privacy, began in 1965. In that year, the Supreme Court struck down as an unconstitutional violation of this amendment and of the 4th and 5th Amendments as well, a Connecticut statute forbidding the dissemination of contraceptive devices or medications. The Court held that a married couple has a "right of privacy" that may not be transgressed by the government.[3] In 1972, the Court extended the right to access to contraception to unmarried adults, since it found that statutes restricting that right were in violation of both this amendment and the equal protection clause of the 14th Amendment.[4] In 1977, the Supreme Court held that statutes making it a criminal offense to sell non-prescription contraceptives to minors were unconstitutional, since

minors as well as adults had a right of privacy.[5] In 1978, Congress amended Title X of the Public Health Service Act of 1970[6] to provide that no federally funded family planning clinic could deny access to contraceptives to adolescents.

The Supreme Court has also used this amendment to strike down state statutes restricting interracial marriage, holding that the right to marry is a "natural right."[7]

In beginning a series of cases that are without doubt the most controversial Supreme Court decisions in the latter part of the 20th century, on January 22, 1973 the Court held that state laws restricting the right of a woman to have an abortion violated her right of privacy and the right of her physician to treat his or her patient as his or her best medical judgment indicated. In Roe v. Wade[8] and Doe v. Bolton,[9] the Supreme Court found that statutory restrictions on the right of a woman to control her own body, at least in the first two trimesters of pregnancy, were unconstitutional. During the third trimester, when the fetus may be viable, the state may lawfully restrict abortion except where the mother's life or health would be endangered by continuing the pregnancy, and the state may lawfully require that certain restrictions, such as waiting periods, be observed as long as these restrictions do not constitute "undue burdens" on the woman's right to choose to terminate her pregnancy. The Court has recognized that a woman's right to choose contraception or abortion is "central to personal dignity and autonomy" and has noted that "the destiny of the woman must be shaped to a large extent on her own conceptions of her spiritual imperatives and her place in society."[10]

Many states, following the abortion decisions, enacted statutes requiring a married woman to obtain her husband's consent before she could have an abortion, but the Supreme Court declared that these restrictions were an unconstitutional interference with the woman's right to make this decision, because she, and not he, was the one who was pregnant, so if the two could not agree, the decision was hers to make.[11] Many states have tried to enact statutes requiring minors to obtain parental consent to have an abortion, although many of those same states have statutes permitting minors of the same age to consent to any other medical or surgical procedure. The Supreme Court has held that a state may require either parental consent or a finding by a judge that the girl is sufficiently mature to make the decision on her own.[12]

In 1986 the Supreme Court refused to extend privacy rights to homosexual relationships and held that there was no right to bodily privacy even if both parties were consenting adults and the acts were performed in private. Thus the Georgia statute making homosexual acts (and some heterosexual ones) a criminal offense was constitutional.[13] Homosexuals, however, may not be deliberately discriminated against by the body politic.

Example

Various cities in Colorado banned discrimination based on sexual orientation. An amendment to the state constitution, initiated by those who objected to the antidiscrimination provisions, prohibited governmental protection of the status of persons based on sexual orientation. The Supreme Court found this amendment to violate the United States Constitution because it imposes a broad disability on homosexuals who would, by this amendment, be forbidden to seek legal protection from discrimination. The Court found that the amendment was motivated by status-based animosity, which is forbidden under equal protection of the laws. The Court held that "If the Constitutional conception of equal protection of the laws means anything, it must at the very least mean that a base desire to harm a politically unpopular group cannot constitute a legitimate governmental interest."[14]

This amendment was added because Alexander Hamilton believed the Bill of Rights to be dangerous. He took the position that listing certain rights throughout the other amendments and giving them specific protection would leave the government free to transgress any that had not been so enumerated.

Amendment Ten

The powers not delegated to the United States by the Constitution, nor prohibited by it to the States, are reserved to the States respectively, or to the people.

THIS AMENDMENT neither adds to nor subtracts from the powers of the federal government as described in the body of the Constitution and was merely designed to reduce fears that the new national government might someday seek to exceed its proper powers.[1]

As we have seen, the powers of the federal government are limited to those specifically enumerated in the Constitution or powers that may reasonably be implied from them. This amendment does not diminish the authority of the federal government to resort to appropriate action to carry out an otherwise constitutional power, regardless of the extent to which the use of that power might conflict with state power.[2] It merely reiterates the relationships already established between the states and the federal government. This amendment has been the cornerstone of states' rights thought, but it is clear that the words "to the people" mean, as the Preamble says "*We* the people," all the people of the United States.

Examples

1. The voters of Arkansas wished to have term limits on their federal representatives. They amended the state constitution to provide that no one could be on the ballot (although he or she could be a write-in candidate) if he or she had served more than three terms in the House of Representatives or two in the Senate. This amendment was challenged by the League of Women Voters and other citizens. The Supreme Court held that states have no authority to change, add, or diminish the qualifications for Congress set forth in Article I. The Court held that establishing qualifications for Congress was not one of the original powers of the states and that the 10th Amendment involves powers reserved at the time the Constitution was adopted. Article I made members of the Congress officers of the national union, not of the states.

Furthermore, the Court held that this amendment would impose a restriction that is contrary to the fundamental principle of representative democracy: the people may choose whom they please to represent them.[3]

2. The federal Individuals with Disabilities Education Act (IDEA) provides federal funds to the states to help with the expenses of educating disabled children. A specific provision said that if a disabled child were expelled or suspended from school for misbehavior, alternative educational resources were required. Under Virginia law, children whose behavior was unrelated to their disability could be suspended or expelled on the same basis as nondisabled children. The secretary of education informed Virginia that if this provision was not changed, all IDEA funds would be withheld. The federal appellate court held that there was no violation of the state's authority under the 10th Amendment, because the state could run its schools as it pleased by forgoing federal funds.[4]

3. Medicare, the federal program that pays physicians and hospitals for the medical care of those over age 65, undertook cost-containment measures that provided restrictions on how much physicians would be paid for taking care of Medicare patients. A group of physicians sued to challenge the constitutionality of these regulations. They argued that the states, not the federal government, have the authority to control the practice of medicine and that, therefore, these regulations encroached on powers reserved to the states by the 10th Amendment. The Court held that Medicare does not regulate the practice of medicine, it just regulates how much will be paid for it, and that, in any case, the 10th Amendment does not bar legislation that is intended to be national in scope.[5]

Amendment Eleven

The Judicial power of the United States shall not be construed to extend to any suit in law or equity, commenced or prosecuted against one of the United States by Citizens of another State, or by Citizens or Subjects of any Foreign State.

THIS AMENDMENT was proposed by Congress to the state legislatures in 1794 and was ratified in 1798. It amended Section 2 of Article II, which seemed to provide that a state could be sued in federal court by citizens of its own state or citizens of a different state. The amendment prohibits anyone from suing a state in federal courts without the state's consent. The original impetus for the amendment was the fear among all the states that the federal courts would force them to pay their Revolutionary War debts, which would have bankrupted most, if not all, of them.[1] Even when the Constitution vests in Congress complete federal authority over a particular area, if Congress wishes to abrogate the states' immunities under this amendment in order to permit enforcement of rights guaranteed under the 14th Amendment, it must provide a "clear legislative statement" of such an intention.[2] This amendment applies only to suits brought by individuals. It does not affect the right of the federal government to sue a state or one state to sue another. The privilege of immunity from suit in federal court also does not apply to political subdivisions of the state.[3] Thus, a citizen may sue a city, county, school board, or other municipal entity.

Examples

1. A student at a state university was taking a course in marine life. The boat on which diving operations were conducted as part of the course was owned by the university. The student vanished and was presumed drowned during a dive. His parents brought suit for negligence and wrongful death against the university and against the professor who was in charge of the course and supervised the diving. The federal court held that the suit was barred by the 11th Amendment, and the only recourse open to the parents was to bring an action in the state's court of claims.[4]

2. A man who was owed a workers' compensation payment sued the New York state insurance fund. The Court dismissed the action because the state agency was immune from suit on 11th Amendment grounds.[5]

3. A student at a state university was taking the course Introduction to Political Theory. He withdrew from school and filed suit, claiming that he was unlawfully required to read profane language as part of the course. He sought damages from the professor. The Court held that the professor was acting within the proper scope of his employment when he made the assignments in the course; thus, the suit was barred by the 11th Amendment.[6]

4. A child who had learning disabilities was enrolled in a public school. Her parents objected to the program for her presented by the school and enrolled her in a private school. When the state educational authority approved the public school's plan, the parents sued the school district. The parents claimed that the district had breached its duty under the Individuals with Disabilities Education Act (IDEA), and they sought reimbursement for her tuition. The Supreme Court held that IDEA requires states to reimburse for private school placements if the school system fails to meet the child's needs in public schools.[7] Congress specifically abrogated the states' immunities from suit under the 11th Amendment when it enacted IDEA.[8]

Amendment Twelve

The Electors shall meet in their respective states and vote by ballot for President and Vice-President, one of whom, at least, shall not be an inhabitant of the same state with themselves; they shall name in their ballots the person voted for as President, and in distinct ballots the person voted for as Vice-President, and they shall make distinct lists of all persons voted for as President, and of all persons voted for as Vice-President, and of the number of votes for each, which lists they shall sign and certify, and transmit sealed to the seat of the government of the United States, directed to the president of the Senate;—The President of the Senate shall, in presence of the Senate and House of Representatives, open all the certificates and the votes shall then be counted;—The person having the greatest number of votes for President, shall be the President, if such number be a majority of the whole number of Electors appointed; and if no person have such majority, then from the persons having the highest numbers not exceeding three on the list of those voted for as President, the House of Representatives shall choose immediately, by ballot, the President. But in choosing the President, the votes shall be taken by states, the representation from each state having one vote; a quorum for this purpose shall consist of a member or members from two-thirds of the states, and a majority of all the states shall be necessary to a choice. [And if the House of Representatives shall not choose a President whenever the right of choice shall devolve upon them, before the fourth day of March next following, then the Vice-President shall act as President, as in the case of the death or other constitutional disability of the President.] The person having the greatest number of votes as Vice-President, shall be the Vice-President, if such number be a majority of the whole number of Electors appointed, and if no person have a majority, then from the two highest numbers on the list, the Senate shall choose the Vice-President; a quorum for the purpose shall consist of two-thirds of the whole number of Senators, and a majority of the whole number shall be necessary to a choice. But no person constitutionally ineligible to the office of President shall be eligible to that of Vice-President of the United States.

THIS AMENDMENT was proposed in 1803 and declared by the secretary of state to be ratified in 1804. It supersedes Article II, Section 1, Clause 3. The bracketed portions have been superseded by Section 3 of Amendment Twenty.

In a presidential election, a voter casts his ballot not for candidates for president and vice-president but for a slate of presidential electors selected by the various parties in his state. Each state has the same number of electors as the total number of its senators and representatives.

Once the election returns have been counted, the electors with the majority of the state's popular vote are entitled to cast *all* of the state's electoral vote.

If a candidate received two votes less than his opponent, he would not receive any electoral votes, since "the winner takes all." For this reason it is possible for a president to be elected by a minority of the popular vote and a majority of the electoral vote.

Example

Mr. Smith and Mr. Jones are the Republican and Democratic presidential candidates.

	SMITH (R)	JONES (D)
South Carolina 8 Electoral Votes	170,000	150,000
North Carolina 13 Electoral Votes	243,000	245,000
	413,000	395,000

Mr. Jones receives 13 electoral votes and Mr. Smith receives 8.

The electors meet in each state at a time specified by Congress—the first Monday after the second Wednesday in December—and cast their ballots. Their sealed votes are then sent to the vice president, in his capacity as president of the senate. He assembles the House and Senate on January 6 and in their presence opens and counts the electoral votes and then declares the new president officially elected.

If there are more than two major candidates for either the presidency or vice-presidency, it is possible that none will receive a clear majority of the electoral vote. In this situation, the House of Representatives elects the president from the top three candidates. Two thirds of the members constitute a quorum for this purpose and each state has one vote. A simple majority vote in the House is required for election. If the same situation occurs in the vice-presidential election, the Senate elects him from the top two vote-getters, again by majority vote with one vote for each senator, with a quorum being two thirds of the Senate.

As a result of this method, it is quite possible that the House would not be able to break a deadlock. It is assumed in such a case that the vice-president would serve as president until the House could decide. This assumption was made explicit in Amendment Twenty.

If the president should die or become disabled between the time of the popular election and determination of the electoral vote, the vice-president would become president, just as he would if the president died during his term of office.

Twice in our history a president has been elected with a minority of the popular vote. The first time, in 1876, Hayes won over Tilden with a minority vote. In 1888 Cleveland, with a majority, lost the presidency to Harrison. There has been, from time to time, discussion about amendment of the 12th Amendment to ensure that this cannot happen again. The usual proposal is that the electoral vote be counted in proportion to the popular vote instead of the current practice. In that case, in a state with 10 electoral votes, if Mr. X received 60 percent of the popular vote, he would receive 6 electoral votes and his opponent 4.

Amendment Thirteen

SECTION 1

Neither slavery nor involuntary servitude, except as a punishment for crime whereof the party shall have been duly convicted, shall exist within the United States, or any place subject to their jurisdiction.

THIS AMENDMENT was proposed and ratified following the Civil War in 1865. The first section of the amendment outlaws slavery, which is the ownership of one person by another. Whereas, of course, the original prohibitions against slavery were to protect African-Americans who had been slaves until Emancipation, even in modern times the question may be raised in other contexts.

Example

During litigation of a case about "surrogate motherhood," in which a woman is paid to be artificially inseminated with a husband's sperm and to bear a child for a couple in which the wife is infertile, one issue raised was whether the couple was "buying" the baby from her and, if so, whether this would constitute slavery for the child. The courts resolved the issue on other grounds, however, and this question was never answered.[1]

The amendment also outlaws peonage, in which a debtor is held by his creditor to work out a debt, and involuntary servitude, in which one is compelled by force to work for another, even if the worker is paid.

Examples

1. Several men were arrested and convicted of violating the peonage laws. They induced poor, non-English-speaking Indonesians to come to the United States by paying for their tickets. Once they arrived, they confiscated the workers' passports and return tickets and made them "work off" without any pay the debts resulting from the costs of their transportation.[2]

2. A Kuwaiti family moved to the United States and brought their female servant, a native of Sri Lanka, with them. Her passport was confiscated and she was not allowed outside alone; she was not permitted to use the phone or the mails; and she was not allowed to speak to anyone but the couple. The couple's child became ill, and the woman told the visiting nurse who came to the house about her situation. The nurse got her out of the house and to the police. The couple was charged with violating the criminal laws against involuntary servitude and the husband was convicted and sentenced to prison.[3]

There are other required activities, however, that do not constitute involuntary servitude. Being drafted, for example, is not involuntary servitude,[4] nor is requiring welfare recipients to work,[5] or requiring a restaurant owner to serve all races.[6]

Medical students may receive federal loans from the National Health Service Corps (NHSC) to pay for their school expenses, and upon completion of their training are required to spend a year of service in a medically underserved area for every year for which they have received a scholarship. Several young physicians have decided that "payback time" constituted involuntary servitude when they were ordered to areas where they did not want to go. The courts uniformly reject this notion and require the physicians to serve or to pay a penalty of three times the amount of scholarship money they received.[7] Lawyers in many states are required to represent indigent people who cannot afford counsel when they are charged with crimes. Attempts to avoid this responsibility by claiming that it is involuntary servitude are uniformly unsuccessful.[8] The courts invariably note that the medical students did not have to take the NHSC funding and lawyers are not required to practice law.

Many public high schools now require some form of community service activity as a prerequisite to graduation. Many students and their families have objected, claiming that altruism is a value in which the family does not believe, and, thus, these programs violate the students' rights under the 1st Amendment and also subject the students to involuntary servitude. All courts that have considered this matter have rejected this claim, and have upheld the concept that community service is a valuable learning experience for the students.[9]

SECTION 2

Congress shall have power to enforce this article by appropriate legislation.

Congress has enacted many statutes under this amendment guaranteeing the civil rights of all Americans. People in this country, regardless of race, have the right to access to equal employment opportunities, equal housing, equal educational benefits, and equality in other aspects of living in this country. Although prejudice, racial and of other sorts, is certainly still present in this country, the 1964[10] and 1968 Civil Rights Acts,[11] have done a great deal to deliver on the promise of a just society that is the basis of American life.

Amendment Fourteen

SECTION 1

1 All persons born or naturalized in the United States, and subject to the jurisdiction thereof, are citizens of the United States and of the State wherein they reside.

2 No State shall make or enforce any law which shall abridge the privileges or immunities of citizens of the United States;

3 nor shall any State deprive any person of life, liberty, or property, without due process of law;

4 nor deny to any person within its jurisdiction the equal protection of the laws.

THIS AMENDMENT was proposed in 1866 and ratified in 1868.

CLAUSE 1 In 1857 the Supreme Court held in the *Dred Scott*[1] decision that if Negroes were not citizens of the states in which they live, neither were they citizens of the United States, since one must be a citizen of a state to possess national citizenship. This amendment was passed as a result of that decision. It creates a national citizenship independent of state citizenship and confers all rights arising from it on all people born or naturalized in this country and on all those subject to the laws of the United States.

Except for children born here to enemy aliens in wartime and children of foreign diplomats, all babies born in the United States including those whose parents are illegal aliens have American citizenship. Children who are born to foreign nationals in this country usually have dual citizenship.

Children born to American citizens abroad are also American citizens by birth and may usually claim dual citizenship. A child who is born abroad of an American citizen and an alien is considered a natural born citizen. Persons who were born in the Philippines while it was a United States territory of Philippine parents are not, however, United States citizens.[2] At one time, children born abroad to American citizen mothers and noncitizen fathers were not considered American citizens, but Congress amended this statute in 1934. Persons in that category who were born before 1934 have been admitted to citizenship by the courts, on the theory that to do otherwise would violate their rights to equal protection of the laws.[3] Illegitimate children of American citizen fathers and noncitizen mothers, however, do not have United States citizenship unless the citizen-father acknowledges paternity prior to the child's becoming an adult.[4] Children born outside this country to American diplomats are solely United States citizens.

Examples

1. Baby Doe, born to an illegal immigrant, is born in New York. He is an American citizen.

2. Baby Doe, born in this country to an ambassador from another country, is not an American citizen.

3. Baby Doe, whose father is a member of the United States Air Force, is born in Paris. He has dual French and American citizenship.

A child born to aliens on a foreign ship in American waters is not an American citizen, but Congress has defined the United States to include Guam, Puerto Rico, the Virgin Islands, and the Northern Marianas.

Although a native-born American's citizenship cannot be revoked for any reason, if a naturalized citizen commits fraud or lies on his or her citizenship application, he or she can be denaturalized and deported to the country of origin. This has happened in many instances where men concealed their pasts as Nazi concentration camp guards and lied on their applications when they became citizens.[5]

CLAUSE 2 The "privileges and immunities" clause of this amendment means that rights that owe their existence to United States citizenship—that is those that are entirely derived from this Constitution or federal laws—may not be abridged by the states in any way. These rights, which are few in number, have been held by the Supreme Court to include the right to travel between states,[6] the right to vote in national elections[7], and the right to engage in interstate commerce.[8] Most of our rights consist of those that we hold as citizens of the states in which we live—the right to trial by jury, for example. This clause merely protects some of the basic rights that are more particularly described by another portion of the Constitution.

For example, the Supreme Court held that a state statute requiring lawyers who wished to practice within New Hampshire to be residents of the state was an unconstitutional violation of their rights under the privileges and immunities clause. The woman who sought to be admitted to practice lived immediately across the state line in Vermont. She was closer to the city in New Hampshire where she wished to practice than she was to a city in Vermont.[8] This section forbids transgression of these rights by an action of the state, but is not involved in a transgression of the Constitution or federal law by a private individual.[8]

CLAUSE 3 As we saw in Amendment Five, in regard to actions of the federal government, due process of law means that the law must not be arbitrary in its subject matter and that it must be conducted with fairness in its procedure. Criminal laws, in particular, must not be vague or indefinite. This clause of the 14th Amendment, known as the "due process" clause, requires state actions to meet these requirements. Due process at the state level exists when laws operate equally and fairly on all citizens.

This clause has been the subject of more Supreme Court cases than any other. The Supreme Court, during its recent history, has greatly expanded the meaning of this clause.

Because the rights covered by this clause are basic and fundamental parts of the rights of man, they are protected by the federal Constitution against abuse or transgression by a state. The procedural rights protected by this clause include the right to a fair trial, the right to counsel,[11] the right to a public trial,[12] protection against unreasonable search and seizure,[13] the right of confrontation of witnesses,[14] and the right against self-incrimination.[15]

Example

Under Oklahoma law, a criminal defendant is presumed to be mentally competent to stand trial unless he proves that he is incompetent by "clear and convincing evidence." The Supreme Court held that this was a violation of defendants' rights to due process of law. The Court held that criminal trial of an incompetent defendant violates due process and that the "clear and convincing evidence"

standard of incompetency is not adequate to protect a defendant's rights.[16]

Laws that violate the freedom of worship, speech, press, and assembly violate the basic principles of substantive due process that must be guaranteed by the states.[17] A judge must be impartial in order not to violate a defendant's right to due process. In short, the rights guaranteed by this Constitution under Amendments One, Four, Five (except for the grand jury provision), Six, and Eight are so basic that they are protected by this clause against state transgression.

Due process also applies to other forms of legal action that are not directly covered by the Bill of Rights.

Example

A psychiatric patient, while heavily medicated, signed forms requesting "voluntary admission" to a state mental hospital. He remained there for five months without access to a lawyer or to a judicial hearing to determine if hospitalization was necessary. After his release, he sued and claimed that his due process rights had been violated because the hospital staff knew or should have known that he was too ill to consent to being admitted and that their failure to ask a court to commit him as an involuntary patient denied him the constitutional safeguards of which he was deprived when he was deprived of his liberty.

The Supreme Court held that "such a person is thus in danger of being confined indefinitely without benefit of the procedural safeguards of the involuntary placement process, a process specifically designed to protect persons incapable of looking after their own interests."[18]

For example, the Supreme Court has held that due process required a fair hearing prior to revocation of parole.[19] A person who receives public welfare assistance is also entitled to a fair hearing before benefits can be terminated,[20] but when the loss of assistance is not life threatening, as with disability payments, the assistance may be terminated prior to a hearing as long as there is eventually a meaningful, fair review process.[21] In both cases, the person is entitled to notice of the hearing, the right to counsel, the right to confront and cross examine witnesses and to testify and present evidence on his own behalf.

Students in public schools are also entitled to due process in academic and disciplinary hearings. Before a high school student may be suspended or expelled, she or he is entitled at least to an informal hearing where the school authorities listen to the facts with open-mindedness and hear what the student has to say.[22] College or professional school students have a right to due process before they are dismissed for either academic failure or for conduct, such as cheating, prohibited by the school.

Examples

1. A law student was dismissed from school for failing to maintain an acceptable average grade. Before he was dismissed, after being notified that he had failed to meet the school's standards, he met with the professor in one of his failed courses at least three times, appealed to the Law School Committee that had jurisdiction over academic problems, and had a hearing before that committee in which he presented his case to them. The Court held that the student had received review procedures that fully satisfied due process requirements and that there was no evidence that the faculty had acted in any way that could be considered arbitrary or capricious.[23]

2. A medical student failed the national examination required of all United States medical students and either failed or barely passed most of her medical school courses. School rules provided that if a student received unsatisfactory grades in two courses in any one term, she was subject to suspension or dismissal. The Performance Committee of the school, whose role was to evaluate students in academic difficulty, recommended that she be expelled. After she appealed, the committee met again, and again recommended her dismissal. She sued the medical school. The Court held that due process requirements are met by an informal review between the dismissing body and the student and that the school in this case had provided the student with numerous hearings. Due process requirements were satisfied.[24]

In some cases, civil courts must provide counsel and other help to litigants who cannot afford them and denial of such assistance violates the person's right to due process of law.

Example

A woman was divorced and her husband had custody of their two children. He remarried and wished to terminate the mother's rights to her children so his second wife could adopt them. The woman lost in the trial court and wished to appeal. State law required that she pay for the trial transcript before she could appeal. She did not have the $2,352.36 required to obtain the transcript, so her appeal was denied. The Supreme Court held that "Choices about marriage, family life, and the upbringing of children are among associational rights this Court has ranked as 'of basic importance in our society,' sheltered by the Fourteenth Amendment against the State's unwarranted usurpation, disregard, or disrespect." The state was ordered to provide the woman with the transcripts she needed, without charge.[25]

As was true of the privileges and immunities clause, this clause only involves state action, not action of private individuals.

Examples

1. As we have seen, denial of the right to a speedy trial is a violation of due process by a state.

2. Frank's next-door neighbor Hector gets mad at him and locks him in his basement for three weeks. This amendment has not been violated.

CLAUSE 4 The matter of primary concern to the authors of this clause was the prevention of state discriminatory actions against any group. It was originally designed to eliminate discrimination by race or color. It is designed to prevent any person or group of people from being singled out for hostile legislation or action by the state government and means that all persons in the same situation (school children, for example) must be dealt with alike by the state regardless of race or gender.

Probably the most important cases decided under this clause are the school segregation cases. *Brown v. Board of Education*[26] in 1954 overruled the Supreme Court's 1896 decision[27] that as long as segregated facilities were equal, black citizens were not denied constitutional rights. *Brown* and later decisions have held, in essence, that the segregation of children in public schools solely on the basis of race, even though the physical facilities and other tangible factors may be equal, deprives the children of a minority or special group of equal educational opportunities and therefore amounts to a deprivation of equal protection of the laws.

All public facilities operated on a segregated basis violate this clause. This means that public housing projects, municipal recreational facilities, and public transportation must be operated on an integrated basis.

Facilities such as public swimming pools may, however, be closed if a city does not wish to operate them on a racially integrated basis. As long as all pools are closed, unconstitutional discrimination will not be held to exist.[28]

Racial discrimination in marriage laws has also been found unconstitutional. In *Loving v. Virginia,*[29] the Supreme Court found state laws prohibiting interracial marriages to be unconstitutional. The same conclusion was reached as to state laws that made interracial cohabitation a separate offense unrelated to laws on fornication or adultery that applied to all citizens.[30]

The Supreme Court has held that race is simply not a permissible basis on which people may be classified. Thus a private university with racially discriminatory policies may lose its tax-exempt status.[31] A court may not remove custody of a child from a perfectly proper mother whose second husband happens to be black and give the child to the biological father on grounds that the judge disapproves of interracial marriage.[32]

Discrimination by race or gender in selection of either grand jury members or members of a trial jury is unconstitutional regardless of the race or gender of the person being tried.[33]

The most recent development in interpretation of the equal protection clause has been in court decisions involving the rights of women and girls, in their educational activities, their work, and their lives in general. As Justice Ruth Bader Ginsburg recently wrote:

"Inherent differences between men and women, we have come to appreciate, remain cause for celebration, not for denigration of the members of either sex or for artificial constraints on an individual's opportunity. Sex classifications may be used to compensate women for particular economic disabilities they have suffered, to promote equal employment opportunities, to advance full development of our Nation's people. But such classifications may not be used, as they once were, to create or perpetuate the legal, social, and economic inferiority of women."[34]

Discrimination in hiring or advancement in employment violates the equal employment section (known as Title VII) of the 1964 Civil Rights Act.[35]

Examples

1. An employer who produced automobile batteries barred all women who were not medically documented as being infertile from jobs involving exposure to lead, which could cause fetal defects. Even women who did not intend to become pregnant and were using contraception could not work there. The Supreme Court held that this rule created an unconstitutional classification based on gender. The Court noted that fertile women can make batteries as efficiently as anyone else and that decisions about the welfare of their future children (if any) were to be left to them, not decided by the company.[36]

2. A young woman with an excellent record in law school was hired as an associate by a large law firm. Several years later she was told that she was not going to be promoted to partner and was fired. She sued and demonstrated that only a few of the partners were women and that she had been denied a partnership on the basis of her gender, not on the basis of her abilities. The Supreme Court held that she had a right to bring a suit against the firm for their violation of Title VII.[37]

The Civil Rights Act of 1991[38] permits actions for monetary damages for violations of Title VII. Under this section, persons who have been sexually harassed at work or school can sue not only the harasser, but the organization that permitted the harassment to continue once its existence was reported. Although most sexual harassment suits have been brought by women, a few instances of harassment of men have been reported, and they are equally permitted to sue under this section.

Examples

1. A woman worked as a manager at an equipment rental company. The president of the company often insulted her because of her gender and made her the target of unwanted sexual innuendos. For example, he said: "You're a woman. What do you know?" He also engaged in sexually explicit behavior. The woman complained and the harassment continued. She resigned her position and sued the company, alleging that the president's behavior had created an abusive work environment for her because of her gender. The Supreme Court held that when the workplace is permeated with discriminatory intimidation, ridicule, and insult, an abusive work environment is created. The woman was allowed to prevail in the suit.[39]

2. A high school student filed an action for damages against her school district claiming that she had been subjected to continual sexual harassment and abuse by a male teacher. She said that the teacher engaged her in sexually oriented conversations, asking her about her sexual experiences with her boyfriend and whether she would have sex with an older man. He kissed her in the school parking lot and called her at home and asked her for a date. On three occasions, the teacher stopped class, took her to his office, and forced her to have sex with him. Although the other teachers and the administrators of the school were told about this, they did nothing but pressure the girl not to

file criminal charges against the teacher. The court held that she was entitled to recover from the school district.[40]

In the context of education, Title IX of the Civil Rights Act[41] prohibits discrimination by sex in any educational program, public or private, receiving federal funds. This protection applies to faculty as well as to students.[42] This means that neither men nor women may be denied access to education programs thought to be designed for one gender or the other. Athletic programs for women students, for example, must receive adequate funding, space, equipment, and faculty if male students' programs have them.[43]

Examples

1. A state university open only to women had a college level program in nursing leading to a B.S.N. degree. A male registered nurse, who worked in a hospital in the city wished to enroll in the degree program and was denied admission, although he was permitted to audit courses. To obtain a B.S.N. from any other school, he would have had to resign his job and move away. The Supreme Court held that single-sex public education violated the man's rights under the equal protection clause.[44]

2. The state of Virginia maintained a military college that admitted only male students. The Supreme Court found that its admissions policy violated the guarantee of equal protection of the laws for women who might wish to enroll.[45]

Private single-sex schools and colleges are permissible, even if they receive research grants, federal student loan funds, or have other federal involvement, because this amendment pertains only to state action.

A state that denied the right of appeal to persons who had been convicted of crimes but who did not have enough money to pay for the appeal has been held to violate equal protection of basic rights to the poor.[46] Transcripts must also be provided for those indigent persons who wish to appeal convictions of misdemeanors. The Supreme Court held in *Mayer v. Chicago*[47] that an Illinois Supreme Court rule providing for free transcripts only in felony cases was unconstitutional. State statutes requiring persons who wish to run for public office to pay large filing fees before their names could appear on the ballot denies equal protection of the laws to poor persons who are otherwise qualified political candidates.[48]

A tax exemption for churches and charitable organizations has been held valid although a taxpayer complained that he was denied equal protection.[49]

In the case of *Shapiro v. Thompson*[50] the Supreme Court held that state laws that established a requirement of a period of residency before persons could be eligible to receive public assistance were unconstitutional. The Court found that these laws unfairly restricted the basic right of individuals to travel from state to state as they might wish and that the laws violated the "equal protection" clause of the 14th Amendment by creating unreasonable classifications (residents and nonresidents) among poor people.

Example

Pauline Poor, living in Mississippi, with her two children, is sick and cannot work. Since her husband has recently died, she decides to go live with her mother in California. When she arrives there, she discovers that she and her children cannot receive public assistance until she has lived there for a year. Meanwhile, her children are hungry. However, her sister Paula, who is in identical difficulties, has always lived with her mother, so her children are eligible for assistance. The Court held that this denied equal protection of the laws to Pauline.

Equal protection of the laws also prohibits a state from withholding money from school districts that allow children who are illegal aliens to enroll. Since education is a fundamental interest, the children must be allowed to receive it.[51]

The Supreme Court has held, however, that where a state funds public education with both state supplements and district revenues, thus resulting in school districts with lower property valuations receiving less income, the equal protection clause has not been violated. As long as per-pupil expenditures are equal within each district, if one school district in a state spends twice as much per pupil as another, the child in the poorer district cannot complain that his right to an equal education has been denied.[52]

While state colleges and universities may constitutionally charge higher tuitions to out-of-state students than to students who are in-state residents, the criteria for determining what constitutes in-state residency may not be unreasonably restrictive.[53]

The rights of handicapped persons are also protected by federal legislation enacted under the authority of the equal protection clause. The Rehabilitation Act of 1973[54] was designed to allow handicapped persons access to federally funded educational and employment programs. In 1975 Congress enacted the Education for All Handicapped Children Act.[55] This act covers children ages 3 to 21 and provides that no handicapped child may be excluded from public education because of disability and that every handicapped child is entitled to a free, appropriate education regardless of the nature of his or her handicap. All supportive services required to allow the child to be at school, such as sign-language interpreters, teachers' aides, and the like are required.[56] If the school district cannot or will not provide an appropriate educational placement within the district for a handicapped child, the parent may place the child in an appropriate private school and the school district is responsible for the cost.[57]

The Americans with Disabilities Act (ADA) of 1990[58] further provided for access to education and employment for persons with handicaps, but it also required communities to assist the disabled by such simple matters as curb cuts on sidewalks to aid wheelchair travel, and the act established access standards for public accommodations. Whereas most of the cases arising under the ADA have revolved around such issues as how much accommodation an employer must make for a handicapped employee (such as special equipment), others have presented more complex issues.

Examples

1. A man had AIDS. His employer switched health insurance companies and the new company refused to provide insurance to the AIDS patient. The man sued and the courts held that if an employer does not provide all employees with equal access to group health insurance plans, if any insurance exists for any employees, the employer has violated the ADA. In other words, at present employers are not legally required to offer group health insurance for employees, but those that do must offer health plans that are available to all employees, regardless of handicap.[59]

2. A woman went to her regular dentist for a scheduled appointment. She told him that she had been diagnosed with HIV virus. The dentist examined her and found a cavity. He told the patient that he would not fill her cavity in his office, but he would admit her to a hospital (for which she would be charged) and fill the tooth there. The woman filed a complaint under the ADA. The Court found that the ADA "sends a clear message to those who operate places of public accommodation: you may not discriminate against individuals in the full and equal services on the basis of a disability." The dentist claimed that the patient would pose a threat to his health or safety (an exception to ADA requirements) but all medical evidence indicated that there was no meaningful risk to health care providers who treated patients with HIV disease as long as they observed precautions required by the Centers for Disease Control. Thus, the Court held that the dentist violated the patient's rights.[60]

Beginning in 1962, the Supreme Court decided the reapportionment cases, the first of which was *Baker v. Carr,* under this clause.[61] In states with a rapid growth in urban areas and in which apportionment of representatives on the statewide and congressional level had not been revised to keep pace with the growth, serious malapportionment occurred. It was possible for a county with a population of 1,000 to have the same number of votes in the state legislature as a county with a population of 100,000. This obviously meant that an urban vote was only one percent as effective as a rural vote. The Supreme Court held that unless all the voters have an equal voice in the election of those who make the laws, equal protection has been denied. The Court therefore ordered reapportionment of legislatures and congressional districts within a state in line with the "one man, one vote" rule. The reapportionment decisions overruled many previous cases that had held that the apportionment and composition of state or congressional legislative districts was a political question and as such would not be decided by a court.[62] These concepts continue to be applied in numerous reapportionment cases with the proviso that no plan for reapportionment is constitutionally permissible if it dilutes minority voting strength against the provisions of the 1965 Voting Rights Act.[63] Unless a proposed redistricting plan violates the Constitution or the Voting Rights Act, however, a federal judge must defer to the state legislature on reapportionment.[64] State legislatures continue to be reapportioned.[65] Local government has been realigned[66] and congressional districts have been readjusted.[67] School districts may no longer restrict the right to vote in school board elections to parents and property owners.[68] The Supreme Court held in two cases, however, that watershed district elections may properly be restricted to voters who are landowners.[69]

The Voting Rights Act was amended in 1982[70] to prohibit any electoral practice that had the *effect*, not merely the *intent*, of racial discrimination against minorities. Under the United States Department of Justice's interpretation of this new provision, a number of states were required to draw district lines for the House of Representatives and their state legislatures in such a way to maximize both the opportunities for minority candidates to be elected, and the number of such candidates who would be elected. These states were required to create districts containing a majority of minority voters, which were expected to elect minority candidates. In cases where more than one such district could be drawn, states were required to create as many "majority-minority" districts as possible. This requirement governed the redistricting process that took place following the 1990 census and was in effect beginning with the election of 1992. In the 1992 elections, five Southern states elected their first black member of the House of Representatives since the post-Civil War Reconstruction period; the number of black representatives from three other Southern states also increased.

However, in a series of decisions beginning in 1993, the Supreme Court struck down this practice, ruling that districts constructed with race as the dominant consideration violated the equal protection rights of the white voters in those districts.[71] As a result, many states were required to conduct their elections under new district lines beginning in 1994, 1996, or 1998. In the 1996 election, two black representatives from Georgia, who had originally been elected from majority-minority districts were reelected in newly drawn white-majority districts.

As of this writing, the Supreme Court continues to hear challenges to specific districting plans, but has not yet issued a definitive decision on this issue. There is no specific legal definition of a districting plan that maximizes opportunities for minority candidates and voters without discriminating against the white citizens in the same areas.

SECTION 2

Representatives shall be apportioned among the several States according to their respective numbers, counting the whole number of persons in each State, excluding Indians not taxed. But when the right to vote at any election for the choice of electors for President and Vice-President of the United States, Representatives in Congress, the Executive and Judicial officers of a State, or the members of the Legislature thereof, is denied to any of the male inhabitants of such State, being twenty-one years of age, and citizens of the United States, or in any way abridged, except for participation in rebellion, or other crime, the basis of representation therein shall be reduced in the proportion which the number of such male citizens shall bear to the whole number of male citizens twenty-one years of age in such State.

SECTION 3

No person shall be a Senator or Representative in Congress, or elector of President and Vice-President, or hold any office, civil or military, under the United States, or under any State, who, having previously taken an oath, as a member of Congress, or as an officer of the United States, or as a member of any State legislature, or as an executive or judicial officer of any State, to support the Constitution of the United States, shall have engaged in insurrection or rebellion against the same, or given aid or comfort to the enemies thereof. But Congress may by a vote of two-thirds of each House, remove such disability.

SECTION 4

The validity of the public debt of the United States, authorized by law, including debts incurred for payment of pensions and bounties for services in suppressing insurrection or rebellion, shall not be questioned. But neither the United States nor any State shall assume or pay any debt or obligation incurred in aid of insurrection or rebellion against the United States, or any claim for the loss or emancipation of any slave; but all such debts, obligations and claims shall be held illegal and void.

Sections 2, 3, and 4 of the 14th Amendment are now obsolete.

SECTION 5

The Congress shall have power to enforce, by appropriate legislation, the provisions of this article.

SECTION 5 was the constitutional authority under which the major portions of the Civil Rights Acts of the 1960s and subsequently have been enacted. The Civil Rights Act of 1964[72] outlawed racial discrimination in employment, public schools, public facilities, and private facilities engaged in interstate commerce, and provided federal court remedies for those denied the rights guaranteed by the act. The Civil Rights Act of 1968, [73] usually known as the Fair Housing Act, outlawed discrimination in the sale or rental of almost all residential real estate.

Amendment Fifteen

SECTION 1

The right of citizens of the United States to vote shall not be denied or abridged by the United States or by any State on account of race, color, or previous condition of servitude.

THIS AMENDMENT was proposed in 1869 and declared ratified by proclamation of the secretary of state in 1870.

Because the right to vote ensures a citizen that he has a voice in electing people who will ensure his other rights, the right to vote is the most important right of all.[1] This amendment forbids discrimination against citizens by denial of their right to vote on account of their race or color. The 19th Amendment gives women the right to vote.

This right applies to state and local as well as federal elections.[2] It applies to party primaries where the primaries are conducted under the authority of state laws.[3]

Article I, Section 2, gives the states the right to fix voter qualifications. This power, however, must not be used to deny the right to vote in contravention of this amendment or the 14th Amendment protections of equal protection of the laws and due process of law.[4] Reasonable qualifications imposed by the state for registration such as age and length of residence within the state are perfectly proper, but the courts have held for 94 years, since this amendment was ratified, that disqualification on the ground of race is not a proper classification.

Citizens of Puerto Rico brought an action charging that their inability to vote in presidential elections violated their constitutional rights under Article II, Amendment Five and this amendment. The court held that because the president is actually chosen by electors chosen by each state as the state legislators direct, only citizens residing in states may vote for electors and, thereby, indirectly for the president. The Court noted that the Constitution was amended specifically to permit residents of Washington, D.C. to vote for president. Thus, only a similar amendment or a grant of statehood to Puerto Rico could give these citizens the right to vote in the presidential election.[5]

SECTION 2

The Congress shall have power to enforce this article by appropriate legislation.

This section was the authority for the enactment by Congress in 1965 of the Voting Rights Act.[6] It provided criminal penalties for any official of a state or city who refused to permit a qualified voter to vote, for anyone who has intimidated a person who has or is going to exercise his right to vote, and provided further criminal penalties for destroying ballots already cast.

The act grants jurisdiction to the federal courts over the election practices of any states that violate this amendment. Congress took the position that if less than half the adults of a state were registered to vote, there was a reasonable assumption that discrimination was being practiced in some manner. If literacy tests were being unfairly used, Congress prohibited their use at all. In states or counties where less than 50 percent of the people of voting age were registered by November 1964 or had voted in the presidential election of that year, the federal courts are empowered to suspend literacy tests and require that prospective voters be registered without any determination at all of literacy. Under the Voting Rights Act as it has been amended and strengthened in 1975 and 1982, today no literacy tests at all may be given. The act now covers the entire nation. In particular, in any area in which 10 percent of the population does not use English as its first language, all provisions of the act now apply. Federal voting registrars may be sent by the federal courts to these states to register voters and supervise elections. The Supreme Court upheld the constitutionality of the original act in 1966 in a suit filed under the Court's original jurisdiction by the state of South Carolina.[7]

In the case of *Gaston County, North Carolina v. United States*,[8] the Supreme Court held that literacy tests are unconstitutional in states where a segregated school system had deprived blacks now of voting age of equal educational opportunity even if the test is not specifically designed to discriminate against prospective black voters. The Court held that in those areas where segregated schools had meant inferior educational opportunities for blacks, even equal application of literacy tests would abridge their 15th Amendment guarantees because their inferior educations in turn denied them an equal chance to pass the tests. Thus, even impartial administration of literacy tests in those areas where black citizens had been systematically deprived of the educational opportunities granted to whites violates the "equal protection" clause of the 14th Amendment, the 15th Amendment, and the Voting Rights Act of 1965.[9] The 1970 amendment to the 1965 Voting Rights Act,[10] however, abolished all literacy tests of any sort in any state. This provision was upheld by the Supreme Court in *Oregon v. Mitchell*.[11] The Supreme Court held in 1973 that reapportionment of state legislatures and congressional districts must be done in such a way that the votes of blacks or other minority groups are not diluted by the process.[12] In those states where judges are elected, judicial elections must also conform to the requirements of the Voting Rights Act, including, where indicated, supervision by the federal courts.[13]

Other irrelevant criteria for voter registration are also unconstitutional. For example, a state statute that prohibits persons convicted of misdemeanors—minor crimes, for which little or no jail sentence may be imposed—from voting was a violation of this amendment and of the equal protection provision of the 14th Amendment.[14]

Amendment Sixteen

The Congress shall have power to lay and collect taxes on incomes, from whatever source derived, without apportionment among the several States, and without regard to any census or enumeration.

THIS AMENDMENT was proposed to the state legislatures in 1909 and proclaimed ratified in 1913.

The Supreme Court in the *Pollock*[1] case in 1895 declared income taxes unconstitutionally in conflict with the "direct tax" provisions of Article I, Section 2, Clause 3, and Article I, Section 9, Clause 4. The Court held in that case that taxes on income must be apportioned among the states. This amendment, adopted to overcome that decision, permits the Congress to levy direct taxes on citizens' income from all sources.

Occasionally, people charged with criminal income tax evasion produce some interesting defenses, such as claims that they do not believe that the tax is constitutional,[2] or that paying money to the government violates some religious or moral belief,[3] or that paying taxes violates constitutional prohibitions on involuntary servitude by forcing one to work for the government.[4] Needless to say, none of these claims has ever been successful.

Amendment Seventeen

The Senate of the United States shall be composed of two Senators from each State, elected by the people thereof, for six years; and each Senator shall have one vote. The electors in each State shall have the qualifications requisite for electors of the most numerous branch of the State legislatures.

When vacancies happen in the representation of any State in the Senate, the executive authority of such State shall issue writs of election to fill such vacancies: Provided, That the legislature of any State may empower the executive thereof to make temporary appointments until the people fill the vacancies by election as the legislature may direct.

This amendment shall not be so construed as to affect the election or term of any Senator chosen before it becomes valid as part of the Constitution.

THIS AMENDMENT was proposed by Congress to the state legislatures in 1912 and proclaimed ratified in 1913.

This amendment supersedes the portion of Article I, Section 3, which provided for the election of United States senators by state legislatures. It establishes the direct election of senators in the same manner as the election of representatives. It also provides for an appointment until the next election of a senator by the governor of a state in which a Senate vacancy has occurred.

Amendment Eighteen

[**1** After one year from the ratification of this article the manufacture, sale, or transportation of intoxicating liquors within, the importation thereof into, or the exportation thereof from the United States and all territory subject to the jurisdiction thereof for beverage purposes is hereby prohibited.

[**2** The Congress and the several States shall have concurrent power to enforce this article by appropriate legislation.

[**3** This article shall be inoperative unless it shall have been ratified as an amendment to the Constitution by the legislatures of the several States, as provided in the Constitution, within seven years from the date of the submission hereof to the States by the Congress.]

THIS AMENDMENT was proposed in 1917 and declared ratified in 1919. It was repealed by the 21st Amendment in 1933.

Amendment Nineteen

The right of citizens of the United States to vote shall not be denied or abridged by the United States or by any State on account of sex.

Congress shall have power to enforce this article by appropriate legislation.

THIS AMENDMENT was proposed in 1919 and declared ratified in 1920. It was rejected by the states of Alabama, Georgia, Louisiana, Maryland, Mississippi, South Carolina, and Virginia.

This amendment gave women the right to vote subject to state voting requirements, which again could not transgress the 14th and 15th Amendments. A literacy test given to women but not to men was a violation of this amendment.[1] It did not give women the right to serve on juries,[2] and it also did not impose upon the states a requirement that women be eligible for public office.[3] All states, however, have now enacted their own legislation allowing women to serve on juries and, of course, to serve in public office.

The passage of the 19th Amendment was the first major accomplishment of the women's movement.

Amendment Twenty

SECTION 1

The terms of the President and Vice President shall end at noon on the 20th day of January, and the terms of Senators and Representatives at noon on the 3d day of January, of the years in which such terms would have ended if this article had not been ratified; and the terms of their successors shall then begin.

SECTION 2

The Congress shall assemble at least once in every year, and such meeting shall begin at noon on the 3d of January, unless they shall by law appoint a different day.

SECTION 3

If, at the time fixed for the beginning of the term of the President, the President elect shall have died, the Vice President elect shall become President. If a President shall not have been chosen before the time fixed for the beginning of his term, or if the President elect shall have failed to qualify, then the Vice President elect shall act as President until a President shall have qualified; and the Congress may by law provide for the case wherein neither a President elect nor a Vice President elect shall have qualified, declaring who shall then act as President, or the manner in which one who is to act shall be selected, and such person shall act accordingly until a President or Vice President shall have qualified.

SECTION 4

The Congress may by law provide for the case of the death of any of the persons from whom the House of Representatives may choose a President whenever the right of choice shall have devolved upon them, and for the case of the death of any of the persons from whom the Senate may choose a Vice President whenever the right of choice shall have devolved upon them.

SECTION 5

Sections 1 and 2 shall take effect on the 15th day of October following the ratification of this article.

SECTION 6

This article shall be inoperative unless it shall have been ratified as an amendment to the Constitution by the legislatures of three-fourths of the several States within seven years from the date of its submission.

THIS AMENDMENT was proposed in 1932 and declared ratified in 1933.

Until this amendment was ratified and superseded part of Article I, Section 4, a newly elected president and Congress did not assume their offices until March after the elections in November. Since Congress convened in December, this left defeated officials to carry out the legislative and executive business of the government. This was known as a "lame duck" session.

When the date for the assembly of Congress was changed to January, it meant that the new congressmen took their seats at once. Since the abolition of the December term of Congress, the old session now adjourns before the elections in November and the new session begins in January.

Section 3 was made necessary by a problem caused by Amendment Twelve. Since the names of the three top vote-getters in a presidential race were to be sent to the House in cases where no one was a majority winner in the Electoral College and each state was given only one vote, it was possible that none of the three could get a majority and a deadlock would occur. This section makes clear that in that situation, the vice president would serve until the House could finally elect someone by a majority.

Amendment Twenty-One

SECTION 1

The eighteenth article of amendment to the Constitution of the United States is hereby repealed.

> THIS AMENDMENT was proposed in 1933 and declared ratified the same year. It repealed the 18th Amendment and was rejected by South Carolina.

SECTION 2

The transportation or importation into any State, Territory, or possession of the United States for delivery or use therein of intoxicating liquors, in violation of the laws thereof, is hereby prohibited.

Section 2 of this amendment gives the states full powers to enact their own laws regarding the sale of alcohol within their own boundaries. A state is constitutionally empowered to forbid any sale of alcohol if it wishes.[1]

States and municipalities may regulate activities such as nude dancing in bars or other places where alcohol is served, even if the prohibited activity would be protected ordinarily by the 1st Amendment. Because the state may, if it wishes, ban alcohol entirely, it may ban sales where activities of which it disapproves take place.[2] On the other hand, under the authority of this amendment, Rhode Island banned publication of liquor prices in newspaper advertisements. In declaring such a law unconstitutional, the Supreme Court found that a state's authority to regulate alcohol did not empower it to ignore the 1st Amendment's guarantees of freedom of speech.[3]

SECTION 3

This article shall be inoperative unless it shall have been ratified as an amendment to the Constitution by conventions in the several States, as provided in the Constitution, within seven years from the date of the submission hereof to the States by the Congress.

> This is the only amendment that has ever been ratified by conventions instead of by the state legislatures.

Amendment Twenty-Two

SECTION 1

No person shall be elected to the office of the President more than twice, and no person who has held the office of President, or acted as President, for more than two years of a term to which some other person was elected President shall be elected to the office of the President more than once. But this Article shall not apply to any person holding the office of President when this Article was proposed by the Congress, and shall not prevent any person who may be holding the office of President, or acting as President, during the term within which this Article becomes operative from holding the office of President or acting as President during the remainder of such term.

SECTION 2

This article shall be inoperative unless it shall have been ratified as an amendment to the Constitution by the legislatures of three-fourths of the several states within seven years from the date of its submission to the States by the Congress.

THIS AMENDMENT was proposed in 1947 and declared ratified in 1951.

This amendment prevents election of anyone to the presidency for more than two terms. The only president who ever served more than two terms was Franklin D. Roosevelt, who died during his fourth term of office.

However, it is possible for a vice president who succeeds to the presidency as a result of the death of the president to serve as many as ten years, or two and one-half terms. If the vice president succeeds to the presidency for two years or less, he may then be elected for two terms.

Example

President Johnson served one year of President Kennedy's term. He was elected in 1964 and was eligible to run again in 1968. If he had chosen to run and had been reelected, he would, at the expiration of his second term, have served a total of nine years.

Amendment Twenty-Three

SECTION 1

The District constituting the seat of Government of the United States shall appoint in such manner as the Congress may direct:

A number of electors of President and Vice President equal to the whole number of Senators and Representatives in Congress to which the District would be entitled if it were a State, but in no event more than the least populous State; they shall be in addition to those appointed by the States, but they shall be considered, for the purposes of the election of President and Vice President, to be electors appointed by a State; and they shall meet in the District and perform such duties as provided by the twelfth article of amendment.

SECTION 2

The Congress shall have power to enforce this article by appropriate legislation.

THIS AMENDMENT, which was proposed in 1960 and ratified in 1961, gives residents of the District of Columbia the right to vote for the president and vice president. Congress has the power to establish voter requirements such as residency within the District, but these powers must be exercised in accordance with the various constitutional provisions protecting voting rights. The District has as many electoral votes as the state with the smallest population. Since all states have at least two senators and one representative, the District will always have at least three electoral votes.

Amendment Twenty-Four

SECTION 1

The right of citizens of the United States to vote in any primary or other election for President or Vice President, for electors for President or Vice President, or for Senator or Representative in Congress, shall not be denied or abridged by the United States or any State by reason of failure to pay any poll tax or other tax.

SECTION 2

The Congress shall have power to enforce this article by appropriate legislation.

THIS AMENDMENT was proposed in 1962 and ratified in 1964.

The purpose of the amendment was to prevent either the states or the federal government from impairing the right to vote in federal elections by requiring the payment of any tax.

Subsequent to the ratification of this amendment, although it did not affect poll tax requirements for state elections, the Supreme Court has declared any poll tax to be unconstitutional.[1] The Court held that the right to vote is so basic to our society that its exercise should never be made dependent on the payment of money. Such payments were held to violate the equal protection clause of the 14th Amendment.

Other fees involved with the political process, although not termed a "poll tax," may violate this amendment as well as constitute violations of the Voting Rights Acts.

Example

The Virginia Republican Party customarily nominates its choices to run for the United States Senate at party conventions. Prior to the convention of 1994, the party announced its intention to charge an entrance fee to delegates. Several persons who had wished to be delegates but refused to pay the fees brought suit. The Supreme Court held,[2] firstly, that primaries and nominating conventions are part of the electoral process covered by voting guarantees in federal statutes and by the Constitution, because the parties act under the authority of the state in these activities. Secondly, the Court found that charging fees limits opportunities for voters to participate in the process. The Court, finally, held that private individuals may bring suits to enforce the prohibition on poll taxes contained in this amendment, the 14th Amendment, and in other federal laws.

Amendment Twenty-Five

SECTION 1

In case of the removal of the President from office or of his death or resignation, the Vice President shall become President.

SECTION 2

Whenever there is a vacancy in the office of the Vice President, the President shall nominate a Vice President who shall take office upon confirmation by a majority vote of both Houses of Congress.

SECTION 3

Whenever the President transmits to the President pro tempore of the Senate and the Speaker of the House of Representatives his written declaration that he is unable to discharge the powers and duties of his office, and until he transmits to them a written declaration to the contrary, such powers and duties shall be discharged by the Vice President as Acting President.

SECTION 4

Whenever the Vice President and a majority of either the principal officers of the executive departments or of such other body as Congress may by law provide, transmit to the President pro tempore of the Senate and the Speaker of the House of Representatives their written declaration that the President is unable to discharge the powers and duties of his office, the Vice President shall immediately assume the powers and duties of the office as Acting President.

Thereafter, when the President transmits to the President pro tempore of the Senate and the Speaker of the House of Representatives his written declaration that no inability exists, he shall resume the powers and duties of his office unless the Vice President and a majority of either the principal officers of the executive department or of such other body as Congress may by law provide, transmit within four days to the President pro tempore of the Senate and the Speaker of the House of Representatives their written declaration that the President is unable to discharge the powers and duties of his office. Thereupon Congress shall decide the issue, assembling within forty-eight hours for that purpose if not in session. If the Congress, within twenty-one days after receipt of the latter written declaration, or if Congress is not in session, within twenty-one days after Congress is required to assemble, determines by two-thirds vote of both Houses that the President is unable to discharge the powers and duties of his office, the Vice President shall continue to discharge the same as Acting President; otherwise, the President shall resume the powers and duties of his office.

THIS AMENDMENT was proposed to the states in 1965 and ratified in 1967.

This amendment provides that a president who considers himself for any reason unable to perform his duties may notify the Speaker of the House and the president pro tempore of the Senate of his disability. The vice president would then become acting president until the president notifies the same officials of his recovery.

If the president is unwilling or unable to make such a notification and the vice president and the cabinet believe that he is unable to carry out his duties, they may notify the same officials of the situation, and the vice president again becomes acting president. When the president informs the Speaker and the president pro tem that he has recovered, he resumes his duties unless the vice president and a majority of the cabinet still feel that he is too ill. In that case, they make a declaration to that effect to the Speaker and the president pro tem and within 48 hours the question is submitted to Congress. Within 21 days Congress must decide whether or not the president has recovered, and a vote that the president is still disabled must be carried by a two-thirds majority vote of both Houses. If the two-thirds vote fails, the president automatically resumes his duties.

This amendment will fill the gap in constitutional law that occurs whenever a president is ill, and provides for the situation in which the president might be severely disabled, mentally or otherwise, but would refuse to acknowledge his impairment.

This does not remove the office or title of president from the elected official. The vice president serves as acting president only while discharging the presidential duties.

George Bush became the first "acting president" under this amendment when these provisions were invoked for a few hours during President Reagan's 1985 cancer surgery.

Section 2 provides that if the office of the vice president is vacated, either by succession to the presidency upon the death of the president or by the death or resignation of the vice president, the president may appoint a vice president whose nomination will be confirmed by a majority vote of both houses of Congress.

Amendment Twenty-Six

SECTION 1

The right of citizens of the United States, who are eighteen years of age or older, to vote shall not be denied or abridged by the United States or by any State on account of age.

SECTION 2

The Congress shall have power to enforce this article by appropriate legislation.

THE 1970 AMENDMENT to the Voting Rights Act of 1965[1] allowed eighteen year olds to vote in all elections. The Supreme Court, however, in *Oregon v. Mitchell*[2] declared that Congress was without authority to set the voting age in state or local elections by use of an ordinary statute. That section of the act permitting eighteen year olds to vote in federal elections was, however, upheld. The result was that eighteen year olds were enfranchised in some elections but not in others.

This amendment was introduced in Congress in January, 1971, almost immediately after the Supreme Court decision. It received approval of both House and Senate by March, 1971 and was ratified by the required number of states by the end of June 1971. This amendment was ratified in less time than any other in American history.

Eighteen year olds may now register and vote in any and all elections in this country.

Example

Shortly after this amendment was ratified, 113 students who lived in dormitories at Skidmore College applied to register as voters in Saratoga Springs, New York, the community in which Skidmore is located. The voter registration board turned them down because it found that they were not "residents." The students brought suit and the Court found that college students do have the right to qualify as "residents," register, and vote in the communities where they attend college instead of being required to register and vote in the place where their families live.[1]

Amendment Twenty-Seven

No law, varying the compensation for the services of the Senators and Representatives, shall take effect, until an election of Representatives shall have intervened.

THIS AMENDMENT was written by James Madison as part of the Bill of Rights, but was not ratified until 1992. Although it failed to achieve the approval of the necessary three quarters of the states (nine of the thirteen) at the same time as the first ten amendments, the Constitution places no limit on the time allowed for the ratification of an amendment. Congressional pay raises became an important political issue in the late 1980s, after Congress had enacted several increases that took effect immediately after their enactment. Interest in this issue resulted in a renewed effort for the ratification of this amendment and it was finally ratified by three quarters of the states (38 of 50) in 1992. The states that had originally voted to ratify the amendment in the late 1700s were counted for this purpose and did not have to ratify it again.

Cost of living adjustments to congressional salaries are not violative of this amendment.[1]

References

The Background of the Constitution

1. *Rochin v. California*, 342 U.S. 165 (1952).
2. *Griswold v. Connecticut*, 381 U.S. 479 (1965).

The Constitution in Our History

1. *Marbury v. Madison*, 1 Cranch. 137 (1803).
2. *McCulloch v. Maryland*, 4 Wheaton 316 (1819).
3. *Cohens v. Virginia*, 6 Wheaton 264 (1821).
4. *Gibbons v. Ogden*, 9 Wheaton 1 (1824).
5. *Dartmouth College v. Woodward*, 4 Wheaton 518 (1819).
6. *Charles River Bridge v. Warren Bridge*, 11 Peters 420 (1837).
7. *Dred Scott v. Sanford*, 19 Howard 393 (1857).
8. *Ex parte Merryman*, Fed. Cases, No. 9, 487 (1861).
9. *Ex parte Milligan*, 4 Wallace 2 (1866).
10. *Texas v. White*, 7 Wallace 700 (1869).
11. *Legal Tender Cases*, 12 Wallace 457 (1871).
12. Interstate Commerce Act, 49 U.S.C.A. § 1-29, 25-27, 301-312.
13. Sherman Antitrust Act, 15 U.S.C.A. § 1-7.
14. *Slaughterhouse Cases*, 16 Wallace 36 (1873).
15. *Munn v. Illinois*, 94 U.S. 113 (1877).
16. *Civil Rights Cases*, 109 U.S. 3 (1883).
17. *Wabash, St. Louis & Pacific Railway Co. v. Illinois*, 118 U.S. 557 (1886).
18. *Chicago, Milwaukee & St. Paul Railway Co. v. Minnesota*, 134 U.S. 418 (1890).
19. *In re Debs*, 158 U.S. 564 (1895).
20. Clayton Antitrust Act, 15 U.S.C.A. § 12-27.
21. *U.S. v. E. C. Knight Co.*, 156 U.S. 1 (1895).
22. *Pollock v. Farmer's Loan & Trust Co.*, 158 U.S. 601 (1895).
23. *Plessy v. Ferguson*, 163 U.S. 537 (1896).
24. *Cincinnati, New Orleans & Texas Pacific Ry. Co. v. ICC*, 162 U.S. 184 (1896).
25. *Champion v. Ames*, 188 U.S. 321 (1903).
26. *McCray v. U.S.*, 195 U.S. 27 (1904).
27. Elkins Act, 49 U.S.C.A. § 41-43.
28. Hepburn Act, 49 U.S.C.A. § 1, 6, 11, 14, 15, 16, 18, 20, 41.
29. Pure Food and Drug Act, 21 U.S.C.A. § 331, 352, 357.
30. Meat Inspection Act, 5 U.S.C.A. § 517, 537.
31. *Lochner v. New York*, 198 U.S. 45 (1905).
32. *Muller v. Oregon*, 208 U.S. 412 (1908).
33. *Northern Securities Co. v. U.S.*, 193 U.S. 197 (1904).
34. *Swift & Co. v. U.S.*, 196 U.S. 375 (1905).
35. *Illinois Central Ry. Co. v. ICC*, 206 U.S. 441 (1907).
36. *U.S. v. Atchison, Topeka & Santa Fe Railway Co.*, 234 U.S. 476 (1914).
37. *Standard Oil Co. v. U.S.*, 221 U.S. 1 (1911).
38. *Hipolite Egg Co. v. U.S.*, 220 U.S. 45 (1911).
39. Clayton Act, 15 U.S.C.A. § 12-27, 44.
40. Adamson Act, 45 U.S.C.A. § 65-66.
41. *Wilson v. New*, 243 U.S. 332 (1917).
42. *Hammer v. Dagenhart*, 247 U.S. 251 (1918).
43. *Schenck v. U.S.*, 249 U.S. 47 (1919).
44. *Missouri v. Holland*, 252 U.S. 416 (1920).
45. *Adkins v. Children's Hospital*, 261 U.S. 525 (1923).
46. *Hurtado v. California*, 110 U.S. 516 (1884).
47. *Myer v. Nebraska*, 262 U.S. 390 (1923).
48. *Pierce v. Society of Sisters*, 268 U.S. 510 (1925).
49. *Gitlow v. New York*, 268 U.S. 652 (1925).
50. *Near v. Minnesota*, 283 U.S. 697 (1931).
51. *Powell v. Alabama*, 287 U.S. 45 (1932).
52. *Myers v. U.S.*, 272 U.S. 52 (1926).
53. *Nebbia v. New York*, 291 U.S. 502 (1934).
54. *Humphrey's Executor v. U.S.*, 295 U.S. 602 (1935).
55. *Panama Refining Co. v. Ryan*, 293 U.S. 388 (1935).
56. *Schechter Poultry Co. v. U.S.*, 295 U.S. 495 (1935).
57. *Carter v. Carter Coal Co.*, 298 U.S. 238 (1936).
58. *West Coast Hotel Co. v. Parrish*, 300 U.S. 379 (1937).
59. *N.L.R.B. v. Jones & Laughlin Steel Corp.*, 301 U.S. 1 (1937).
60. Social Security Act, 42 U.S.C.A.
61. *U.S. v. Carolene Products Co.*, 304 U.S. 144 (1938).
62. Fair Labor Standards Act, 29 U.S.C.A. § 201-219.
63. *U.S. v. Darby Lumber Co.*, 312 U.S. 100 (1941).
64. *Mulford v. Smith*, 307 U.S. 38 (1939).
65. *Madden v. Kentucky*, 309 U.S. 83 (1940).
66. *Palko v. Connecticut*, 302 U.S. 319 (1937).
67. *DeJonge v. Oregon*, 299 U.S. 353 (1937).
68. *Herndon v. Lowry*, 301 U.S. 242 (1937).
69. *Senn v. Tile Layers' Union*, 301 U.S. 468 (1937).
70. *Hague v. C.I.O.*, 307 U.S. 496 (1939).
71. *Cantwell v. Connecticut*, 310 U.S. 296 (1940).
72. *Thornhill v. Alabama*, 310 U.S. 88 (1940).
73. *Lovell v. Griffin*, 303 U.S. 444 (1938).
74. *West Virginia State Bd. of Education v. Barnette*, 319 U.S. 624 (1943).
75. *Bridges v. California*, 314 U.S. 252 (1941).
76. *U.S. v. Lovett*, 328 U.S. 303 (1946).
77. *Brown v. Board of Education*, 347 U.S. 483 (1954).
78. *Missouri ex rel. Gaines v. Canada*, 305 U.S. 337 (1938).
79. *Sweatt v. Painter*, 339 U.S. 629 (1950).

80. *McLaurin v. Oklahoma State Regents,* 339 U.S. 637 (1950).

81. *Smith v. Allwright,* 321 U.S. 649 (1944).

82. *Mitchell v. U.S.,* 313 U.S. 80 (1941).

83. *Henderson v. U.S.,* 339 U.S. 816 (1950).

84. *Shelley v. Kraemer,* 334 U.S. 1 (1948).

85. *U.S. v. Curtiss-Wright Export Corp.,* 299 U.S. 304 (1936).

86. *Yakus v. U.S.,* 321 U.S. 414 (1944).

87. *Korematsu v. U.S.,* 323 U.S. 214 (1944).

88. *Ex parte Quirin,* 317 U.S. 1 (1942).

89. *In re Yamashita,* 327 U.S. 1 (1946).

90. *Cramer v. U.S.,* 325 U.S. 1 (1945).

91. *Haupt v. U.S.,* 330 U.S. 631 (1947).

92. *Youngstown Sheet & Tube Co. v. Sawyer* 343 U.S. 579 (1952).

93. Smith Act, 18 U.S.C.A. § 2385.

94. *American Communications Ass'n v. Douds,* 339 U.S. 382 (1950).

95. *Dennis v. U.S.,* 341 U.S. 494 (1951).

96. *Wieman v. Updegraff,* 344 U.S. 183 (1952).

97. *Terminiello v. Chicago,* 337 U.S. 1 (1949).

98. *Roth v. U.S.,* 354 U.S. 476 (1957).

99. *Burstyn v. Wilson,* 343 U.S. 195 (1952).

100. *Everson v. Board of Education,* 330 U.S. 1 (1947).

101. *McCollum v. Board of Education,* 333 U.S. 203 (1948).

The Preamble

1. *McCulloch v. Maryland,* 4 Wheat 316 (1819).

2. *Orleans Parish School Board v. Bush,* 188 F. Supp. 916 (1960), aff'd 365 U.S. 569 (1961).

3. *Jacobson v. Massachusetts,* 197 U.S. 11 (1905).

Article One

1. *Youngstown Sheet & Tube Co. v. Sawyer,* 343 U.S. 579 (1952).

2. *Bowsher v. Synar,* 478 U.S. 106 (1986).

3. *Wiley v. Sinkler,* 179 U.S. 58 (1900).

4. *Commonwealth ex rel Dummit v. O'Connell,* 298 Ky 44 (1944).

5. *Nixon v. U.S.,* 506 U.S. 224 (1993).

6. *Hastings v. U.S.,* 837 F. Supp 3, DC DC (1993).

7. *Powell v. McCormack,* 395 U.S. 486 (1969).

8. *Roudebush v. Hartke,* 405 U.S. 15 (1972).

8. *Shub v. Simpson,* 196 Md 177 (1950).

10. *Yellen v. U.S.,* 374 U.S. 109 (1963).

11. *U.S. v. Grumman,* 227 F. Supp 227 DC DC (1964).

12. *Senate Select Committee on Ethics v. Packwood,* 845 F. Supp 17, DC DC (1994).

13. *U.S. v. Johnson,* 383 U.S. 169 (1966).

14. *U.S. v. Brewster,* 408 U.S. 501 (1972).

15. *Chicago Tribune,* Page 1, Thursday, 5 October, 1995.

16. *U.S. v. Durenberger,* 48 F. 3d 1239, DC CA (1995).

17. *U.S. v. Rose,* 790 F. Supp 340, 28 F. 3d 181, DC CA (1994).

18. *U.S. v. Rostenkowski,* 59 F. 3d 129, DC CA (1995).

19. *Barsky v. U.S.,* 167 F. 2d 241, DC CA (1948).

20. *Yellin v. U.S.,* 374 U.S. 109 (1963).

21. *Skaggs v. Carle,* 898 F. Supp 1, DC DC (1995).

22. *Brown and Williamson v. Williams,* 62 F. 3d 408, DC CA (1995).

23. *Immigration and Naturalization Service v. Chada,* 462 U.S. 919 (1983).

24. *Rostker v. Goldberg,* 448 U.S. 1306 (1981).

25. *New York v. U.S.,* 326 U.S. 572 (1946).

26. *McCulloch v. Maryland,* 17 U.S. 316 (1819).

27. *First Agricultural National Bank v. State Tax Commission,* 392 U.S. 339 (1968).

28. *NLRB v. Carlisle Lumber Company,* 94 F. 2d 138, CCA 9 (1938).

29. *National Collegiate Athletic Association v. Miller,* 10 F. 3d 633, CCA 9 (1993).

30. *Pardin v. Terminal Railway of Alabama,* 377 U.S. 184 (1964).

31. *Hillsborough County v. Automated Medical Laboratories, Inc.,* 471 U.S. 307 (1985).

32. *Hisao Murata v. Acheson,* 99 F. Supp 591, DC Hawaii (1951).

33. *Harper and Row Publishers, Inc. v. Nation Enterprises,* 471 U.S. 539 (1985).

34. *Sony Corporation of America v. Universal City Studios,* 464 U.S. 417 (1984).

35. *Ex parte White,* 66 F. Supp 982, DC Hawaii (1944).

36. *Schueller v. Drum,* 51 F. Supp 383, DC Pa (1943).

37. *Knox v. Lee,* 12 Wall 457 (1870).

38. *People ex rel Ostwald v. Craver,* 70 NYS 2d 513 (1946).

39. *Kimmelman v. Morrison,* 477 U.S. 365 (1986).

40. *Zimmerman v. Walker,* 132 F. 2d 442 (1942).

41. *Korematsu v. U.S.,* 323 U.S. 214 (1945).

42. *Owens v. Ivey,* 525 NYS 2d 508 (NY 1988).

43. *Selective Service System v. Minnesota Public Interest Research Group,* 468 U.S. 841 (1984).

44. *U.S. v. Johnson,* 845 F. Supp 864, DC Fla (1994).

45. *Bae v. Shalala,* 44 F. 3d 489, CA 7, 1995; U.S., 323 U.S. 214 (1945).

46. *People v. Rolling,* 575 NYS 2d 577 (NY 1991).

47. *Commonwealth v. Kelley,* 411 Mass 212, 581 NE 2d 472 (1992).

48. *South Carolina Public Service Authority v. The Citizens and South ern National Bank,* 300 SC 142, 386 SE 2d 775 (1989).

49. *American Republic Insurance Company v. Superintendent of Insurance,* 647 A 2d 1195 (Maine 1994).

50. *Bowman v. Chicago Railway Co.,* 125 U.S. 465 (1888).

51. *Louisiana Land and Exploration Co. v. Pilot Petroleum Company,* 900 F. 2d 816, CCA 5 (1990).

52. *Bode v. Barrett,* 344 U.S. 583 (1953).

53. *Safe Harbor Water Power Co. v. FPC,* 37 F. Supp 9, DC Pa (1944).

Article Two

1. *Youngstown Sheet and Tube Company v. Sawyer,* 343 U.S. 579 (1952).

2. *U.S. v. Nixon,* 418 U.S. 683 (1974).

3. *U.S. v. John Poindexter,* 732 F. Supp 142, DC DC (1990); 732 F. Supp 163, DC DC (1990).

4. *Nixon v. Fitzgerald,* 457 U.S. 731 (1982).

5. *Clinton v. Jones,* 117 S. Ct. 1636, 1997

6. *Ex parte Quirin,* 317 U.S. 1 (1942).

7. *Dellums v. Bush,* 752 F. Supp 1141 DC DC (1990).

8. *Perpick v. Department of Defense,* 436 U.S. 334 (1990).

9. *Pietsch v. Bush*, 755 F. Supp 62 DC NY (1990).

10. *Ange v. Bush*, 755 F. Supp 509, DC DC (1990).

11. *Knote v. U.S.*, 95 U.S. 442 (1877).

12. *In re Bochiaro*, 49 F. Supp 37 (1943).

13. *Murphy v. Ford*, 390 F. Supp 1372, DC Mich (1975).

14. *In re Oliver L. North*, 94 F. 3d 685, DC DC (1996); *In re Oliver L. North*, 62 F. 3d 1434, DC CA (1994).

15. *In re Marshalship*, etc., 20 F. 379 (1884).

16. *U.S. v. Noriega*, 808 F. Supp 791, DC Fla (1992).

17. *Earth Island Institute v. Christopher*, 6 F. 3d 648, CCA 9 (1993).

18. *Goldwater v. Carter*, 444 U.S. 996 (1979).

19. *In re Neagle*, 135 U.S. 1 (1890).

20. *Trial of Andrew Johnson*, 175.

Article Three

1. *Oldham v. The American Civil Liberties Union Foundation of Tennessee*, 849 F. Supp 611, DC Tenn (1994).

2. *Ashwander v. T.V.A.*, 297 U.S. 288 (1936).

3. 18 U.S.C.A. § 3731; 18 U.S.C.A. § 1252.

4. *Jefferson Parish Hospital District v. Hyde*, 466 U.S. 2 (1984).

5. *NCAA v. Board of Regents of the University of Oklahoma*, 468 U.S. 85 (1984).

6. 28 U.S.C.A. § 1253.

7. 28 U.S.C.A. § 1252.

8. 28 U.S.C.A. § 1254.

9. 28 U.S.C.A. § 1257.

10. *U.S. v. Virginia*, 116 S. Ct. 2264 (1996).

11. *Federal Republic of Yugoslavia v. Park-71st Corporation*, 913 F. Supp 191, DC NY (1995).

12. *Spence v. Clinton*, 942 F. Supp 32, DC DC (1996).

13. *Aketepe v. U.S.*, 925 F. Supp 731, DC Fla (1996).

14. *Atlantic States Legal Foundation v. Buffalo Envelope Co.*, 823 F. Supp 1965, DC NY (1993).

15. *Planned Parenthood Association of Missouri v. Danforth*, 428 U.S. 52 (1976).

16. *Pennsylvania v. West Virginia*, 262 U.S. 552 (1962).

17. *E.g., Louisiana v. Mississippi*, 466 U.S. 96 (1984); *Colorado v. New Mexico*, 467 U.S. 310 (1984); *Idaho v. Oregon*, 462 U.S. 1017 (1983); *Arizona v. California*, 460 U.S. 605 (1983).

18. *State of Illinois v. Commonwealth of Kentucky*, 500 U.S. 52 (1976).

19. *Ankenbrandt v. Richards*, 504 U.S. 689 (1992).

20. *South Carolina v. Katzenbach*, 383 U.S. 301 (1966).

21. *U.S. v. Miller*, 984 F. 2d 1028, CCA 9 (1993).

Article Four

1. *Loughran v. Loughran*, 292 U.S. 216 (1934); *Ram v. Ramharack*, 571 NYS 2d 190, NY (1991); *Teamsters Local 639 Employers' Pension Trust Fund v. Johnson*, 1992 WL 200075, DC DC (1992).

2. *Kupec v. Cooper*, 593 So 2d 1176, Fla (1992).

3. 28 U.S.C.A. § 1738A.

4. *Thompson v. Thompson*, 484 U.S. 174 (1988); *Shute v. Shute*, 158 Vt. 242, 607 A 2d 890 (1992).

5. *Elortegui v. Elortegui*, 616 So 2d 69, Fla App (1993).

6. *Corfield v. Coryell*, 6 Fed Cas. 3230 (1823).

7. *Ward v. Maryland*, 12 Wall 418 (1871).

8. *Barnard v. Thorstenn*, 489 U.S. 546 (1989); *Supreme Court of Virginia v. Friedman*, 487 U.S. 59 (1988); *Frazier v. Heebe*, 482 U.S. 641 (1987).

9. *Whittle v. U.S.*, 7 F. 3d 1259, CCA 6 (1993).

10. *Griffin v. Breckenridge*, 403 U.S. 88 (1971).

11. *Blake v. McClung*, 172 U.S. 239 (1898).

12. 42 U.S.C.A. § 1973 (aa-1).

13. *Oregon v. Mitchell*, 400 U.S. 12 (1970).

14. *Dunn v. Blumstein*, 405 U.S. 330 (1972).

15. *Marston v. Lewis*, 410 U.S. 679 (1973); *Burns v. Fortson*, 410 U.S. 686 (1973).

16. *McDonald v. Board of Elections*, 394 U.S. 802 (1969).

17. *Puerto Rico v. Brandsted*, 483 U.S. 219 (1987).

18. *Alabama v. Engler*, 85 F. 3d 1205, CCA 6 (1996).

19. *State of Nevada v. Watkins*, 914 F. 2d 1545, CCA 9 (1990).

20. *Duncan v. McCall*, 139 U.S. 449 (1891).

21. *Risser v. Thompson*, 930 F. 2d 549, CCA 7 (1991).

22. *Commissioner v. Nelson*, 350 U.S. 497 (1956).

Article Five

1. *Hollingsworth v. Virginia*, 3 Dall 378 (1798).

2. *State of Montana v. Waltermire*, 213 Mont. 425, 691 P 2d 826 (1984).

Article Six

1. *U.S. Postal Service v. Town of Greenwich*, 901 F. Supp 500, DC Ct (1995).

2. *Smith v. O'Grady*, 312 U.S. 329 (1941); *Gade v. National Solid Wastes Management Association*, 505 U.S. 88 (1992); *U.S. v. The City and County of Denver*, 916 F. Supp 1058, DC Colo (1996).

3. *In re Initiative Petition No. 349*, 838 P 2d 1, Okla (1992).

4. *Ableman v. Booth*, 21 How 506 (1859).

5. *Orleans Parish School Board v. Bush*, 365 U.S. 569 (1961); *U.S. v. Barnett*, 376 U.S. 681 (1964); *Elizabeth Blackwell Health Center for Women v. Knoll*, 61 F. 3d 170, CCA 3 (1995).

6. *Martin v. Voinovitch*, 840 F. Supp 1175, DC Ohio (1993).

Amendment One

1. *Board of Education of Kiryas Joel Village School District v. Grumet*, 512 U.S. 687 (1994).

2. *U.S. v. Ballard*, 322 U.S. 78 (1944).

3. *Herdahl v. Pontotoc County Board of Education*, 933 F. Supp 582, DC Miss (1996).

4. *Lee v. Weisman*, 505 U.S. 577 (1992); *Jager v. Douglas County School District*, 862 F. 2d 824, CCA 11 (1989); *Ingebretson v. Jackson Public School District*, 88 F. 3d 274, CCA 5 (1996); *Sands v. Morongo Unified School District*, 809 P 2d 809, Cal (1991).

5. *Board of Education v. Mergens*, 496 U.S. 226 (1990); *Hsu v. Roslyn Union Free School District*, 85 F. 3d 839, CCA 2 (1996).

6. *In the Matter of the Application of Long Island Jewish Medical Center*, 557 NYS 2d 239 (1990); *M.N. and V.N. v. Southern Baptist Hospital of Florida*, 648 So 2d 769, Fla (1994).

7. *Cruzan v. Director, Missouri Department of Public Health*, 497 U.S. 261 (1990); *The Stamford Hospital v. Vega*, 674 A 2d 821, Ct (1996); *In re Milton*, 505 NE 2d 255, Ohio (1987).

8. *Baxley v. U.S.*, 134 F. 2d 937, CCA 4 (1943).

9. *State of Missouri v. David*, 745 SW 2d 249, Mo (1988); *State of Idaho v. Crisman*, 123 Idaho 277, 846 P 2d 928 (1992).

10. *Western Presbyterian Church v. The Board of Zoning Adjustment*, 862 F. Supp 538, DC DC (1994).

11. *Wisconsin v. Yoder*, 406 U.S. 205 (1972).

12. *Curtis v. School Commission of Falmouth*, 420 Mass 749, 652 NE 2d 580 (1995); *Alfonso v. Fernandez*, 606 NYS 2d 259 (1993); *Parents United for Better Schools v. School District of Philadelphia Board of Education*, 646 A 2d 689, Pa (1994); *Fleischfresser v. Directors of School District 200*, 15 F. 3d 680, CCA 7 (1994).

13. *Crites v. Smith*, 826 SW 2d 459, Tenn (1992).

14. *McCollum v. Board of Education*, 333 U.S. 703 (1948).

15. *Abington Township v. Schempp*, 374 U.S. 203 (1963).

16. *Anderson v. Laird*, 466 F. 2d 283, CCA DC 1973, *cert den* 93 S Ct. 690 (1972).

17. *Goldman v. Weinberger*, 475 U.S. 106 (1986).

18. *Elliot v. White*, 23 F. 2d 997, DC CA (1928).

19. *Marsh v. Chambers*, 463 U.S. 783 (1983).

20. *Waltz v. Tax Commissioner of the City of New York*, 397 U.S. 664 (1970).

21. *Alamo Foundation v. Secretary of Labor*, 471 U.S. 290 (1985).

22. *Lemon v. Kurtzman*, 403 U.S. 602 (1971).

23. *Committee for Public Education v. Nyquist*, 413 U.S. 756 (1973).

24. *Sloan v. Lemon*, 413 U.S. 825 (1973).

25. *Aguilar v. Felton*, 473 U.S. 402 (1985).

26. Higher Education Facilities Act of 1963, 20 U.S.C. § 701 et seq.

27. *Tilton v. Richardson*, 403 U.S. 262 (1971).

28. *Witters v. Washington Department of Services to the Blind*, 474 U.S. 106 (1986).

29. *Widmar v. Vincent*, 454 U.S. 262 (1981).

30. *Dennis v. U.S.*, 341 U.S. 494 (1951).

31. *City of Ladue v. Gilleo*, 512 U.S. 43 (1994).

32. *Capitol Square Review and Advisory Board v. Pinette*, 115 S Ct. 2440 (1995).

33. *Rohman v. City of Portland*, 909 F. Supp 767, DC Ore (1995).

34. *Taylor v. Mississippi*, 319 U.S. 583 (1943).

35. *Winstead v. Sweeney*, 205 Mich App. 664, 517 NW 2d 874 (1994).

36. *New York Times v. Sullivan*, 376 U.S. 254 (1964).

37. *Monitor Patriot Co. v. Roy*, 401 U.S. 254 (1971).

38. *Time, Inc. v. Pape*, 401 U.S. 279 (1971).

39. *Ocala Star-Banner Co. v. Damron*, 401 U.S. 295 (1971).

40. *Fitts v. Kolb*, 779 F. Supp 1502, DC SC (1991).

41. *Dennis v. U.S.*, 341 U.S. 494 (1951).

42. *Bridges v. California*, 314 U.S. 252 (1941).

43. *Tinker v. Des Moines School District*, 393 U.S. 503 (1969).

44. *Slotterback v. Interboro School District*, 766 F. Supp 280, DC Pa (1991).

45. *Bethel School District v. Fraser*, 478 U.S. 106 (1986).

46. *Board of Education v. Pico*, 457 U.S. 853 (1982).

47. *Papish v. Board of Curators*, 410 U.S. 667 (1973).

48. *Rosenberger v. Rector and Visitors of the University of Virginia*, 115 S Ct. 2510 (1995).

49. *Doe v. University of Michigan*, 721 F. Supp 852, DC Mich (1989).

50. *Brazenburg v. Hayes*, 408 U.S. 665 (1972).

51. *Roth v. U.S.*, 354 U.S. 476 (1957); *Accara v. Cloud Books*, 478 U.S. 697 (1986), *New York v. P.J. Video, Inc*, 475 U.S. 868 (1986).

52. *Ginzburg v. U.S.*, 383 U.S. 15 (1973).

53. *Finley v. National Endowment for the Arts*, 795 F. Supp 1457, 100 F. 3d 671, CCA 9 (1996).

54. *Miller v. California*, 413 U.S. 15 (1973).

55. *Ginzberg v. New York*, 390 U.S. 629 (1968).

56. *Stanley v. Georgia*, 394 U.S. 557 (1969).

57. *Paris Adult Theaters v. Slaton*, 413 U.S. 49 (1973).

58. *Renton v. Playtime Theaters, Inc.* 475 U.S. 41 (1986).

59. *New York v. Ferber*, 458 U.S. 747 (1982).

60. *National Broadcasting Company v. U.S.*, 319 U.S. 190 (1943).

61. *Posadas de Puerto Rico Associates v. Tourism Council of Puerto Rico*, 478 U.S. 328 (1986).

62. *Virginia State Board of Pharmacy v. Virginia Citizens Consumer Council*, 425 U.S. 746 (1976).

63. *Bates v. State Bar of Arizona*, 433 U.S. 350 (1977); *Zauderer v. Office of Disciplinary Counsel of the Supreme Court*, 471 U.S. 626 (1985).

64. *May Stores v. National Labor Relations Board*, 326 U.S. 376 (1945).

65. *Police Department of Chicago v. Mosely*, 408 U.S. 92 (1972).

66. *Grayned v. Rockford*, 408 U.S. 104 (1972).

67. *Shuttlesworth v. Birmingham*, 394 U.S. 147 (1969).

68. *Cox v. New Hampshire*, 312 U.S. 596 (1941).

69. *Cox v. Louisiana*, 379 U.S. 536 (1965).

70. 18 U.S.C. § 248.

71. *Schenk v. Pro-Choice Network*, 1997 WL 65718, United States Supreme Court February 19, 1997; *American Life League v. Reno*, 855 F. Supp 137, DC Va (1994); *Terry v. Reno*, 101 F. 3d 1412, DC CA (1996); *U.S. v. Dinwiddie*, 76 F. 3d 913 (1996).

72. *Lloyd Corporation v. Tanner*, 407 U.S. 551 (1972).

73. *Central Hardware Company v. National Labor Relations Board*, 407 U.S. 539 (1972).

74. *NAACP v. Alabama*, 357 U.S. 449 (1958).

75. *State of Maryland v. Burning Tree Country Club, Inc.*, 315 Md 254, 554 A 2d 366 (1989).

76. *City of Maquoketa v. Russell*, 484 NW 2d 179, Iowa (1992).

77. *Waters v. Barry*, 711 F. Supp 1125, DC DC (1989).

78. *Healy v. James*, 408 U.S. 169 (1972).

79. *Papish v. Curators*, 410 U.S. 667 (1973).

80. *Keller v. State Bar of California*, 496 U.S. 1 (1990). *In the Matter of the Virgin Islands Bar Association*, 758 F. Supp 1088, DC VI (1991).

Amendment Two

1. *The State of Washington v. Hernandez-Mercado*, 124 Wash 2d 368, 879 P 2d 283 (1994).

2. *U.S. v. Rybar*, 103 F. 3d 273, CCA 3 (1996); *U.S. v. Hale*, 978 F. 2d 1016, CCA 8 (1992).

3. *U.S. v. Miller*, 307 U.S. 174 (1939).

4. *Love v. Pepersack*, 47 F. 3d 120, CCA 4 (1995); *Hickman v. Block*, 81 F. 3d 98, CCA 9 (1996); *U.S. v. Hale*, 978 F. 2d 1016, CA 8 (1992).

5. *U.S. v. Warin*, 530 F. 2d 106, *cert. den.* 426 U.S. 958 (1976).

6. Crime Control and Safe Streets Act, 18 U.S.C. § 1202 (a), 1968.

7. *U.S. v. Bass*, 404 U.S. 336 (1971).

8. Brady Handgun Violence Prevention Act, 18 U.S.C. § 922(s).

9. *Koog v. U.S.*, 79 F. 3d 452, CCA 5 (1996).

10. *McMillan v. Pennsylvania*, 477 U.S. 79 (1986).

Amendment Four

1. *Jones v. U.S.*, 357 U.S. 493 (1958).
2. *Stanford v. Texas*, 379 U.S. 476 (1965); *Mapp v. Ohio*, 367 U.S. 643 (1961).
3. *U.S. v. Leon*, 486 U.S. 897 (1984).
4. *Powell v. Nevada*, 114 S. Ct. 1280 (1994).
5. *U.S. v. Maiden*, 879 F. Supp 359, DC DC (1994).
6. *Welch v. Wisconsin*, 466 U.S. 740 (1984).
7. *U.S. v. Hensley*, 469 U.S. 221 (1985).
8. *Tennessee v. Garner*, 471 U.S. 1 (1985).
9. *Illinois v. Lafayette*, 462 U.S. 640 (1985).
10. *Rochin v. California*, 342 U.S. 165 (1952).
11. *U.S. v. Cucci*, 892 F. Supp 775, DC Va (1995).
12. *Vale v. Louisiana*, 399 U.S. 30 (1970).
13. *Wilson v. Arkansas*, 115 S. Ct. 1914 (1995).
14. *Minnesota v. Olson*, 495 U.S. 91 (1990).
15. *Davis v. Mississippi*, 394 U.S. 721 (1969).
16. *Hayes v. Florida*, 470 U.S. 811 (1985).
17. *Pennsylvania v. Labron*, 116 S. Ct. 2485 (1996).
18. *Maryland v. Wilson*, 117 S. Ct. 882, 1997.
19. *Florida v. Jimeno*, 500 U.S. 248 (1991).
20. *Mapp v. Ohio*, 367 U.S. 643 (1961).
21. *Thompson v. Louisiana*, 469 U.S. 17 (1984).
22. *New Jersey v. T.L.O.*, 469 U.S. 325 (1985).
23. *Cornfield v. Consolidated High School District No. 230*, 991 F. 2d 1316, CCA 7 (1993).
24. *Oliver v. McClung*, 919 F. Supp 1206, DC Ind. (1995).
25. *Jenkins v. Talladega City Board of Education*, 95 F. 3d 1036, CCA 11 (1996).
26. *Vernonia School District 47J v. Acton*, 115 S Ct. 2386 (1995). *See also, Bridgman v. New Trier Township High School*, 1997 WL 43222, DC Ill, January 27, 1997.
27. *Wyman v. James*, 400 U.S. 309 (1971).
28. *McFarland v. U.S.*, 150 F. 2d 593, DC CA (1945).
29. *Winston v. Lee*, 470 U.S. 753 (1985).
30. *Harris v. U.S.*, 390 U.S. 234 (1968).
31. *Horton v. California*, 496 U.S. 128 (1990); *Illinois v. Rodriguez*, 497 U.S. 177 (1990).
32. *Washington v. Chrisman*, 455 U.S. 1 (1982).
33. *California v. Ciraolo*, 476 U.S. 207 (1986); *Dow Chemical Company v. U.S.*, 476 U.S. 227 (1986).
34. *Oliver v. U.S.*, 466 U.S. 170 (1984).
35. *Michigan v. Clifford*, 464 U.S. 287 (1984).
36. *Coolidge v. New Hampshire*, 403 U.S. 443 (1971).

Amendment Five

1. *Alexander v. Louisiana*, 405 U.S. 625 (1972).
2. *O'Callahan v. Parker*, 395 U.S. 258 (1969).
3. *Kinsella v. U.S. ex rel Singleton*, 361 U.S. 234 (1960).
4. *Forman v. U.S.*, 361 U.S. 416 (1960).
5. *Price v. Georgia*, 398 U.S. 323 (1970); *Grady v. Corbin*, 495 U.S. 508 (1990).
6. *Missouri v. Hunter*, 459 U.S. 359 (1983).
7. *Richardson v. U.S.*, 468 U.S. 317 (1984).
8. *Smalis v. Pennsylvania*, 476 U.S. 140 (1986).
9. *Bartkus v. Illinois*, 359 U.S. 121 (1959).
10. *Heath v. Alabama*, 474 U.S. 82 (1985).
11. *Waller v. Florida*, 397 U.S. 387 (1970).
12. *U.S. v. Wheeler*, 435 U.S. 313 (1978).
13. *Ferina v. U.S.*, 340 F. 2d 837, CCA 8 (1965).
14. *Ciucci v. Illinois*, 356 U.S. 571 (1958).
15. *Turner v. Arkansas*, 407 U.S. 366 (1972).
16. *U.S. v. Ursery*, 116 S. Ct. 2135 (1996).
17. *Miranda v. Arizona*, 384 U.S. 436 (1966).
18. *Brown v. Walker*, 161 U.S. 591 (1896).
19. *Baltimore City Department of Social Services v. Bouknight*, 493 U.S. 549 (1990).
20. *Rogers v. U.S.*, 340 U.S. 367 (1951).
21. *Illinois v. Perkins*, 496 U.S. 292 (1990).
22. *Berkemer v. McCarty*, 468 U.S. 420 (1984).
23. *Andreson v. Maryland*, 427 U.S. 563 (1976).
24. *Couch v. U.S.*, 409 U.S. 322 (1973).
25. *Fisher v. U.S.*, 425 U.S. 391 (1976).
26. *McFarland v. U.S.*, 150 F. 2d 593, DC CA (1945).
27. *South Dakota v. Neville*, 459 U.S. 553 (1983).
28. *Escobedo v. Illinois*, 378 U.S. 478 (1964).
29. *Mueller v. Virginia*, 504 U.S. 1043 (1993).
30. *Minnick v. Mississippi*, 498 U.S. 146 (1990).
31. *Edwards v. Louisiana*, 451 U.S. 77 (1981); *Shea v. Louisiana*, 470 U.S. 51 (1985).
32. *Moran v. Burbine*, 475 U.S. 412 (1986).
33. *Mapp v. Ohio*, 367 U.S. 643 (1961).
34. *Wainwright v. Greenfield*, 474 U.S. 284 (1986).
35. *U.S. v. Poindexter*, 951 F. 2d 369, DC CA (1992).
36. *Smith v. U.S.*, 337 U.S. 137 (1949).
37. *Giglio v. U.S.*, 405 U.S. 150 (1972).
38. *Murphy v. New York Harbor Commission*, 378 U.S. 52 (1964).
39. *Jaffe v. Redmond*, 116 S Ct. 1923 (1996).
40. *Branzburg v. Hayes*, 408 U.S. 665 (1972).
41. *Couch v. U.S.*, 409 U.S. 322 (1973).
42. *McNabb v. U.S.*, 318 U.S. 332 (1943).
43. *Youngberg v. Romeo*, 457 U.S. 307 (1982).
44. *Lehr v. Robertson*, 463 U.S. 248 (1983).
45. *Santosky v. Kramer*, 455 U.S. 745 (1982).
46. *MacDonald, Sommer and Frates v. Yolo County*, 447 U.S. 340 (1986).
47. *Planning Commission v. Hamilton Bank*, 473 U.S. 172 (1985).
48. *Hawaii Housing Authority v. Midkiff*, 467 U.S. 22 (1984).
49. *Dolan v. City of Tigard*, 512 U.S. 374 (1994).
50. *Lucas v. South Carolina Coastal Council*, 505 U.S. 1003 (1992).

Amendment Six

1. 18 U.S.C. § 3161 (b).
2. *U.S. v. Saltzman*, 984 F. 2d 1087, CCA 10 (1993); *U.S. v. Upton*, 921 F. Supp 100, DC NY (1995).
3. *Doggett v. U.S.*, 505 U.S. 647 (1991).
4. *Klopfer v. North Carolina*, 386 U.S. 213 (1967).

5. *U.S. v. Ewell*, 383 U.S. 116 (1966).

6. *U.S. v. Hawk*, 474 U.S. 302 (1985).

7. *U.S. v. MacDonald*, 456 U.S. 1 (1982).

8. *El Vocero De Puerto Rico v. Puerto Rico*, 508 U.S. 147 (1993).

9. *Press-Enterprise Co. v. Superior Court of California*, 464 U.S. 501 (1984).

10. *Estes v. Texas*, 381 U.S. 532 (1965).

11. *Geise v. U.S.*, 262 F. 2d 151, CCA 9 (1958).

12. *Fayerweather v. Moran*, 1990 WL 40914, DC RI (1990).

13. *U.S. v. Nachtigal*, 507 U.S. 1 (1993).

14. *Lewis v. U.S.*, 116 S Ct. 2163 (1996).

15. *Williams v. Florida*, 399 U.S. 78 (1970).

16. *Johnson v. Louisiana*, 406 U.S. 356 (1972).

17. *Ballew v. Georgia*, 435 U.S. 223 (1978).

18. *Apodaca v. Oregon*, 406 U.S. 404 (1972).

19. *Burch v. Louisiana*, 441 U.S. 130 (1979).

20. *Duncan v. Louisiana*, 391 U.S. 145 (1968).

21. *Baldwin v. New York*, 399 U.S. 66 (1970).

22. *Hill v. Texas*, 316 U.S. 400 (1942); *Peters v. Kiff*, 407 U.S. 493 (1972); *Taylor v. Louisiana*, 419 U.S. 522 (1975); *Georgia v. McCollum*, 505 U.S. 42 (1992); *Powers v. Ohio*, 499 U.S. 400 (1991); *J.E.B. v. Alabama*, 511 U.S. 127 (1994).

23. *Morgan v. Illinois*, 504 U.S. 719 (1992).

24. *Groppi v. Wisconsin*, 400 U.S. 505 (1971).

25. *Francis v. Franklin*, 471 U.S. 307 (1985).

26. *U.S. v. Bagley*, 473 U.S. 667 (1985).

27. *Barber v. Page*, 390 U.S. 719 (1968).

28. *Maryland v. Craig*, 497 U.S. 836 (1990); *Idaho v. Wright*, 497 U.S. 805 (1990); *White v. Illinois*, 502 U.S. 346 (1991).

29. *Illinois v. Allen*, 397 U.S. 337 (1970).

30. *Washington v. Texas*, 388 U.S. 14 (1967).

31. *Gideon v. Wainwright*, 372 U.S. 355 (1963).

32. *U.S. v. Reilley*, 948 F. 2d 648, CCA 10 (1991).

33. *Scott v. Illinois*, 440 U.S. 367 (1979).

34. *Escobedo v. Illinois*, 378 U.S. 478 (1964).

35. *Mempa v. Rhay*, 389 U.S. 128 (1967).

36. *Specht v. Patterson*, 386 U.S. 605 (1967).

37. *Goldberg v. Kelley*, 397 U.S. 1 (1967).

38. *Montilla v. Immigration and Naturalization Service*, 926 F. 2d 162, CCA 2 (1991).

39. *Evitts v. Lucey*, 469 U.S. 387 (1985); *Smith v. Texas*, 1992 WL 323386, Tex App (1992); *Bonin v. California*, 494 U.S. 1039 (1990).

40. *Nix v. Whiteside*, 475 U.S. 157 (1986).

41. *Jones v. Barnes*, 463 U.S. 745 (1983).

42. *McKaskle v. Wiggins*, 465 U.S. 168 (1984).

43. *Ake v. Oklahoma*, 470 U.S. 68 (1985).

44. *In re Gault*, 387 U.S. 1 (1967).

45. *McKeiver v. Pennsylvania*, 403 U.S. 528 (1971).

46. *In re Winship*, 397 U.S. 358 (1970).

47. *Missouri ex rel K.R. v. Ryan*, 1990 WL 88976, Mo. App. (1990); *City of Covington v. Court of Justice*, 784 SW 2d 180, Ky (1990).

48. *In the Interest of Stacey R.*, 311 S.C. 312, 428 SE 2d 869 (1993).

49. *In the Interest of R.B.*, 424 Pa Super 57, 621 A 2d 1038 (1993).

Amendment Seven

1. *Vicinanzo v. Brunschwig & Fils, Inc.*, 739 F. Supp 882, DC NY (1990).

2. *Ringling Brothers-Barnum & Bailey Shows, Inc. v. Utah Division of Travel Development*, 955 F. Supp 598, DC Va 1997.

3. *Chauffeurs, Teamsters and Helpers, Local No 391 v. Terry*, 494 U.S. 558 (1990).

4. *Feres v. U.S.*, 340 U.S. 135 (1950).

5. *Chappell v. Wallace*, 462 U.S. 296 (1963).

Amendment Eight

1. *Rehman v. California*, 379 U.S. 930 (1964).

2. *Williams v. Illinois*, 399 U.S. 3235 (1970).

3. *McDougle v. Maxwell*, 1 Ohio St. 2d 68 (1964).

4. *Farmer v. Brennan*, 511 U.S. 825 (1994).

5. 42 U.S.C.A. § 1997 et seq.

6. *U.S. v. County of San Diego*, 1991 WL 642768, DC Cal (1991); *U.S. v. State of Massachusetts*, 1993 WL 122499, DC Mass (1993).

7. *LaGrand v. Lewis*, 883 F. Supp 469, DC Ariz (1995).

8. *Hudson v. McMillian*, 503 U.S. 1 (1992).

9. *Women Prisoners of the District of Columbia Department of Corrections v. District of Columbia*, 877 F. Supp 634, DC (1994); 93 F. 3d 910, CA DC (1996).

10. *Gordon v. Faber*, 800 F. Supp 793, DC Iowa (1991).

11. *Lewis v. Richards*, 107 F 3a 549 CA 7, 1997; *Farmer v. Brennan*, 511 U.S. 825 (1994).

12. *Helling v. McKinney*, 509 U.S. 25 (1993).

13. *Wilson v. Seiter*, 501 U.S. 294, (1991); *Keenan v. Hall*, 83 F. 3d 1083, CCA 9 (1996).

14. *Washington v. State*, 690 So. 2d 539, Ala. App. 1997.

15. *Estelle v. Gamble*, 429 U.S. 97 (1976).

16. *Medley v. Frame*, 1995 WL 141918, DC Pa (1995).

17. *Brewer v. Blackwell*, 836 F. Supp 631, DC Iowa (1993).

18. *Ake v. Oklahoma*, 470 U.S. 68 (1985).

19. *Furman v. Georgia*, 408 U.S. 238 (1972).

20. *Dusky v. U.S.*, 362 U.S. 402 (1960); *McCormack v. Maass*, 73 F. 3d 369, CCA 9 (1995).

21. *Foucha v. Louisiana*, 504 U.S. 71 (1992).

22. *Jackson v. Indiana*, 406 U.S. 715 (1972).

23. *Washington v. Harper*, 494 U.S. 210 (1994).

24. *Riggins v. Nevada*, 504 U.S. 127 (1992).

25. *U.S. v. Jackson*, 390 U.S. 570 (1968).

26. *Ford v. Wainwright*, 477 U.S. 399 (1986); *Rector v. Bryant*, 501 U.S. 1239 (1991).

27. *Campbell v. Wood*, 511 U.S. 119 (1994).

Amendment Nine

1. *U.S. v. Vital Health Products, Limited*, 786 F. Supp 761, DC Wisc (1992).

2. *United Public Workers v. Mitchell*, 370 U.S. 75 (1947).

3. *Griswold v. Connecticut*, 381 U.S. 479 (1965).

4. *Eisenstadt v. Baird*, 405 U.S. 438 (1972).

5. *Carey v. Population Services International*, 431 U.S. 678 (1977).

6. Public Health Service Act, 42 U.S.C. § 300–300a(8).

7. *Loving v. Virginia*, 388 U.S. 1 (1967).

8. *Roe v. Wade*, 410 U.S. 113 (1973).

9. *Doe v. Bolton*, 410 U.S. 179 (1973).

10. *Planned Parenthood v. Casey*, 505 U.S. 833 (1992).

11. *Planned Parenthood v. Danforth*, 428 U.S. 52 (1976).

12. *Planned Parenthood v. Ashcroft*, 462 U.S. 476 (1983).

13. *Bowers v. Hardwick*, 478 U.S. 686 (1986).

14. *Romer v. Evans*, 116 S Ct. 1620 (1996).

Amendment Ten

1. *U.S. v. Darby Lumber Co.*, 312 U.S. 100 (1941); *McCulloch v. Maryland*, 4 Wheat 316 (1819).

2. *Oklahoma ex rel Phillips v. Atkinson Co.*, 313 U.S. 508 (1941).

3. *U.S. Term Limits, Inc. v. Thornton*, 115 S. Ct. 1842 (1995).

4. *Commonwealth of Virginia v. Riley*, 86 F. 3d 1337, CCA 4 (1996).

5. *Metrolina Family Practice Group v. Sullivan*, 767 F. Supp 1314, DC NC (1989).

Amendment Eleven

1. *Hess v. Port Authority Trans-Hudson Corporation*, 115 S. Ct. 394 (1994).

2. *Seminole Tribe v. Florida*, 116 S. Ct. 1114 (1996).

3. *Hopkins v. Clemson College*, 221 U.S. 636 (1911).

4. *Harvis v. The Board of Trustees of the University of Illinois*, 744 F. Supp 825, DC Ill (1990).

5. *Lipofsky v. Steingut*, 86 F. 3d 315, CCA 2 (1996).

6. *Boles v. Gibbons*, 694 F. Supp 849, DC Fla (1988).

7. *Florence County School District Four v. Carter*, 510 U.S. 7 (1996).

8. *Straube v. Florida Union Free School District*, 778 F. Supp 774, DC NY (1991).

Amendment Thirteen

1. *In re Baby M.*, 109 NJ 396, 537 A 2d 1227 (1988).

2. *U.S. v. Mussry*, 726 F. 2d 1448, CCA 9 (1984).

3. *U.S. v. Alzanki*, 54 F. 3d 994, CCA 1 (1995).

4. *Holmes v. U.S.*, 391 U.S. 936 (1968).

5. *Brogan v. San Mateo County*, 901 F. 2d 762, CCA 9 (1990).

6. *Heart of Atlanta Motel, Inc. v. U.S.*, 379 U.S. 241 (1964).

7. *U.S. v. Redovan*, 656 F. Supp 121, DC Pa (1986); *U.S. v. Martin*, 710 F. Supp 271, DC Cal (1989).

8. *U.S. v. 30.64 Acres of Land*, 795 F. 2d 796, CCA 9 (1986); *U.S. v. Bertoli*, 994 F. 2d 1002, CCA 3 (1993).

9. *Steirer v. Bethlehem Area School District.* 987 F. 2d 989, CCA 3 (1993); *Herndon v. Chapel Hill-Carrboro City Board of Education*, 89 F. 3d 174, CCA 4 (1996).

10. Civil Rights Act of 1964, 42 U.S.C.A. § 2000a et seq.

11. Civil Rights Act of 1968, 18 U.S.C. § 245 and § 2101 et seq.

Amendment Fourteen

1. *Dred Scott v. Sanford*, 19 Howard 393 (1857).

2. *Rabang v. Immigration and Naturalization Service*, 35 F. 3d 1449, CCA 9 (1994).

3. *Aguayo v. Christopher*, 865 F. Supp 479, DC Ill (1994).

4. *Miller v. Christopher*, 870 F. Supp 1, DC DC (1994).

5. *U.S. v. Breyer*, 41 F. 3d 884, CCA 3 (1994); *U.S. v. Schiffer*, 831 F. Supp 1166, DC Pa (1993).

6. *New York v. O'Neill*, 359 U.S. 1 (1959).

7. *Harman v. Forssenius*, 380 U.S. 528 (1965).

8. *Colgate v. Harvey*, 296 U.S. 404 (1935).

9. *Supreme Court of New Hampshire v. Piper*, 407 U.S. 274 (1984).

10. *Crandall v. Nevada*, 6 Wall 35 (1868).

11. *Gideon v. Wainwright*, 372 U.S. 335 (1963).

12. *In re Oliver*, 333 U.S. 257 (1948).

13. *Mapp v. Ohio*, 367 U.S. 643 (1961).

14. *Pointer v. Texas*, 380 U.S. 400 (1965).

15. *Malloy v. Hogan*, 378 U.S. 1 (1964).

16. *Cooper v. Oklahoma*, 116 S. Ct. 1373 (1996).

17. *Gitlow v. New York*, 268 U.S. 1 (1925).

18. *Zinermon v. Burch*, 494 U.S. 113 (1990).

19. *Morrisey v. Brewer*, 408 U.S. 471 (1972).

20. *Goldberg v. Kelly*, 397 U.S. 254 (1970); *Wheeler v. Montgomery*, 397 U.S. 280 (1970).

21. *Matthews v. Eldridge*, 425 U.S. 319 (1976).

22. *C.B., By and Through Breeding v. Driscoll*, 82 F. 3d 383, CA 11 (1996); *Craig v. Selma City School Board*, 801 F. Supp 585, DC Ala (1992).

23. *Megenity v. Stenger*, 27 F. 3d 1120, CA 6 (1994).

24. *Bergstrom v. Buettner*, 697 F. Supp 1098, DC ND (1987).

25. *M.L.B. v. S.L.J.*, 117 S Ct. 555 (1996).

26. *Brown v. Board of Education*, 347 U.S. 483 (1954).

27. *Plessy v. Ferguson*, 163 U.S. 537 (1896).

28. *Palmer v. Thompson*, 403 U.S. 217 (1971).

29. *Loving v. Virginia*, 388 U.S. 1 (1967).

30. *McLaughlin v. Florida*, 379 U.S. 184 (1964).

31. *Bob Jones University v. U.S.*, 461 U.S. 574 (1983).

32. *Palmore v. Sidoti*, 466 U.S. 429 (1984).

33. *J.E.B. v. Alabama*, 511 U.S. 127 (1994); *Leichman v. Louisiana*, 939 F. 2d 315, CCA 5 (1991); *U.S. v. Omoruyi*, 7 F. 3d 880, CCA 9 (1993).

34. *U.S. v. Virginia*, 116 S. Ct. 2264, at page 2276.

35. 1964 Civil Rights Act, 42 U.S.C. § 703(a).

36. *International Union v. Johnson Controls, Inc.*, 499 U.S. 187 (1991).

37. *Hishon v. King and Spaulding*, 467 U.S. 69 (1964).

38. Civil Rights Act of 1991, 42 U.S.C.A. § 1981(a).

39. *Harris v. Forklift Systems, Inc.*, 510 U.S. 17 (1993).

40. *Franklin v. Gwinnett County Public Schools*, 503 U.S. 60 (1991).

41. 42 U.S.C. § 2000e et seq.

42. *North Haven Board of Education v. Bell*, 456 U.S. 512 (1982).

43. *Cohen v. Brown University*, 101 F. 3d 155, CCA 1 (1996).

44. *Mississippi University for Women v. Hogan*, 458 U.S. 718 (1982).

45. *U.S. v. Virginia*, 116 S. Ct. 2264 (1996); See also, *Faulkner v. Jones*, 51 F. 3d 440 (1995).

46. *Griffin v. Illinois*, 351 U.S. 12 (1965).

47. *Mayer v. Chicago*, 404 U.S. 189 (1971).

48. *Bullock v. Carter*, 405 U.S. 134 (1972).

49. *State v. Alabama Educational Foundation*, 231 Ala 11 (1935).

50. *Shapiro v. Thompson*, 394 U.S. 618 (1969).

51. *Plyer v. Doe*, 457 U.S. 202 (1982).

52. *San Antonio Independent School District v. Rodriquez*, 411 U.S. 1 (1973).

53.   *Vlandis v. Kline*, 412 U.S. 441 (1973).

54.   Rehabilitation Act of 1973, 29 U.S.C.A. § 701 et seq.

55.   Education for All Handicapped Children Act of 1975, 20 U.S.C. § 1401–61.

56.   *Irving Township School District v. Tatro*, 468 U.S. 883 (1984).

57.   *School Committee of the Town of Burlington v. Department of Education of Massachusetts*, 471 U.S. 359, 1985.

58.   Americans With Disabilities Act of 1990, 42 U.S.C.A. § 12111 et seq.

59.   *Anderson v. Gus Mayer Boston Store*, 924 F. Supp 763, DC Tex 1996.

60.   *Abbot v. Bragdon*, 107 F 3d 934, CA 1, 1997.

61.   *Baker v. Carr*, 369 U.S. 186 (1992).

62.   *Colegrove v. Green*, 328 U.S. 549 (1946).

63.   *Georgia v. U.S.*, 411 U.S. 526 (1973).

64.   *Upham v. Seamon*, 456 U.S. 37 (1982).

65.   *Mahan v. Howell*, 410 U.S. 37 (1973).

66.   *Abate v. Mundt*, 403 U.S. 182 (1971).

67.   *Kirkpatrick v. Preisler*, 394 U.S. 526 (1969).

68.   *Kramer v. Union Free School District*, 395 U.S. 621 (1969).

69.   *Associated Enterprises v. Toltec Watershed Improvement District*, 410 U.S. 43 (1973); *Salyer Land Co. v. Tulare Lake Basin Water Storage District*, 410 U.S. 719 (1973).

70.   Voting Rights Act of 1982, 42 U.S.C.A. § 1973aa-6.

71.   North Carolina: *Shaw v. Reno*, 509 U.S. 630 (1993), *Shaw v. Hunt*, 16 S. Ct. 1894 (1996); Georgia: *Miller v. Johnson*, 115 S. Ct. 2475 (1995); Texas: *Bush v. Vera*, 116 S. Ct. 1941 (1996); Louisiana: *U.S. v. Hays*, 115 S. Ct. 2431 (1995).

72.   42 U.S.C.A. § 1981-2000h.

73.   42 U.S.C.A. Chapter 45.

Amendment Fifteen

1.   *Harman v. Forsennius*, 380 U.S. 528 (1965).

2.   *Reddix v. Lucky*, 252 F. 2d 930, CA 5 (1958).

3.   *Smith v. Allwright*, 321 U.S. 649 (1944).

4.   *U.S. v. Manning*, 215 F. Supp 272 (1963).

5.   *Igartua De La Rosa v. U.S.*, 32 F. 3d 80, CA 1 (1994).

6.   *Voting Rights Act* of 1965, 42 U.S.C. § 1971–74.

7.   *South Carolina v. Katzenbach*, 383 U.S. 301 (1966).

8.   *Gaston County, North Carolina v. U.S.*, 395 U.S. 285 (1969).

9.   Voting Rights Act of 1965, 42 U.S.C. § 1973.

10.   1970 Amendments, Voting Rights Act of 1965, 42 U.S.C. § 1973 (aa).

11.   *Oregon v. Mitchell*, 400 U.S. 112 (1970).

12.   *Georgia v. U.S.*, 411 U.S. 526 (1973).

13.   *Houston Lawyers' Association v. Attorney General of Texas*, 501 U.S. 419 (1991); *Clark v. Roemer*, 500 U.S. 646 (1991); *Chisom v. Roemer*, 501 U.S. 380 (1991).

14.   *Hunter v. Underwood*, 471 U.S. 359 (1985).

Amendment Sixteen

1.   *Pollock v. Farmers' Trust Co.*, 158 U.S. 601 (1895).

2.   *Cheek v. U.S.*, 498 U.S. 192 (1991).

3.   *Cook v. Spillman*, 806 F. 2d 948, CCA 9 (1986).

4.   *U.S. v. Stolle*, 9 F. 3d 1555, CCA 9 (1993).

Amendment Nineteen

1.   *Prewitt v. Wilson*, 46 SW 2d 90, Ky (1932).

2.   *Duren v. Missouri*, 439 U.S. 357 (1979); *U.S. v. Ballard*, 357 Supp. 105, DC Cal (1940).

3.   *Boineau v. Thornton*, 235 F. Supp, DC SC (1964).

Amendment Twenty-One

1.   *Ziffrin, Inc. v. Reeves*, 308 U.S. 132 (1939).

2.   *California v. LaRue*, 409 U.S. 109 (1972); *Geaneas v. Willets*, 911 F. 3d 579, CCA 11 (1990); *Sammy's of Mobile, Ltd. v. City of Mobile*, 928 F. Supp 1116, DC Ala (1996).

3.   *44 Liquor Mart v. Rhode Island*, 116 S Ct. 1495 (1996).

Amendment Twenty-Four

1.   *Harper v. Virginia State Board of Elections*, 383 U.S. 663 (1966).

2.   *Morse v. Republican Party of Virginia*, 116 S Ct. 1186 (1996).

Amendment Twenty-Six

1.   *Levy v. Scranton*, 780 F. Supp 897, DC NY (1991).

Amendment Twenty-Seven

1.   *Boehner v. Anderson*, 30 F. 3d 156, CCA DC (1994).

Bibliography

General Works

Dunn, Charles W. *Constitutional Democracy in America: A Reappraisal* (Scott, Foresman and Company, 1987).

Fisher, Louis. *Constitutional Conflicts between Congress and the President* (rev. ed., Princeton University Press, 1991).

Friendly, Fred W., and Martha J. H. Elliott. *The Constitution: That Delicate Balance* (Random House, 1984).

Howard, A. E. Dick. *The United States Constitution: Roots, Rights and Responsibilities* (Smithsonian Institution Press, 1992).

Levy, Leonard W. *Original Intent and the Framers' Constitution* (Collier Macmillan, 1988).

Peltason, J. W. *Corwin and Peltason's Understanding the Constitution* (12th ed., Holt, Rinehart and Winston, 1991).

Peters, Charles. *How Washington Really Works* (Addison-Wesley, 1983).

Pyle, Christopher H., and Richard Pious. *The President, Congress and the Constitution* (Free Press, 1984).

Rohr, John A. *To Run a Constitution* (University Press of Kansas, 1986).

Sundquist, James L. *Constitutional Reform and Effective Government* (rev. ed., Brookings Institution, 1992).

Tribe, Laurence H. *Constitutional Choices* (Harvard University Press, 1986).

Introduction and History

Becker, Carl L. *The Declaration of Independence: A Study in the History of Political Ideas* (Knopf, 1958).

Beeman, Richard, Stephen Botein, and Edward C. Carter II, eds. *Beyond Confederation* (University of North Carolina Press, 1987).

Duker, William F. *A Constitutional History of Habeas Corpus* (Greenwood Press, 1980).

Farrand, Max. *The Framing of the Constitution* (Yale University Press, 1962).

Jensen, Merrill. *The Making of the Constitution* (reprint, Van Nostrand, 1979).

Ketcham, Ralph. *Presidents Above Party: The First American Presidency 1789–1829* (University of North Carolina Press, 1987).

Kurland, Philip B., and Ralph Lerner. *The Founders' Constitution* (5 vols., University of Chicago Press, 1987).

Kutler, Stanley. *The Supreme Court and the Constitution* (4th ed., Houghton Mifflin, 1990).

Lasslett, Peter, ed. *Locke's Two Treatises of Government* (Cambridge University Press, 1988).

Lewis, Anthony. *The Warren Court: A Critical Evaluation* (Random House, 1969).

McCloskey, Robert G. *The American Supreme Court* (University of Chicago Press, 1960).

Morison, S. E., H. S. Commager, and W. E. Leuchtenberg, *A Concise History of the American Republic* (Oxford University Press, 1983).

Smith, Page. *The Constitution: A Documentary and Narrative History* (William Morrow, paperback ed., 1980).

Storing, Herbert, ed. *The Anti-Federalist: Writings by the Opponents of the Constitution* (University of Chicago Press, 1985).

————. *What the Anti-Federalists Were For* (University of Chicago Press, 1981).

Warren, Charles. *The Making of the Constitution* (reprint, Rothman, 1993).

Wood, Gordon S. *The Creation of the American Republic* (Norton, 1993).

Casebooks

Barker, Lucius, and Twiley W. Barker, Jr. *Civil Liberties and the Constitution: Cases and Commentaries* (7th ed., Prentice-Hall, 1994).

Corwin, Edward S. *The Constitution and What It Means Today*, rev. by Harold W. Chase and Craig R. Ducat (14th ed., Princeton University Press, 1978).

Rossum, Ralph A., and G. Alan Tarr. *American Constitutional Law* (4th ed., St. Martin's Press, 1995).

Article One—The Congress

Davidson, Roger H., and Walter J. Oleszek. *Congress and Its Members* (Congressional Quarterly Press, 1993).

Dodd, Lawrence C., and B. I. Oppenheimer. *Congress Reconsidered* (5th ed., Congressional Quarterly Press, 1993).

Fenno, Richard. *Home Style: House Members in Their Districts* (Little, Brown, 1987).

Fiorina, Morris P. *Congress: Keystone of the Washington Establishment* (Yale University Press, 1989).

Fisher, Louis. *Constitutional Conflicts Between Congress and the Presidency* (rev. ed., Princeton University Press, 1991).

Jewell, Malcolm E., and Samuel C. Patterson. *The Legislative Process in the United States* (4th ed., Random House, 1986).

Johannes, John R. *To Serve the People: Congress and Constituency Service* (University of Nebraska Press, 1984).

Keefe, William J., and Morris S. Ogul. *The American Legislative Process: Congress and the States* (8th ed., Prentice-Hall, 1992).

Kozak, David C., and J. D. Macartney, eds. *Congress and Public Policy* (reprint, Dorsey Press, 1990).

Labovitz, John R. *Presidential Impeachment* (Yale University Press, 1978).

Morgan, Donald G. *Congress and the Constitution* (Harvard, 1966).

Ogul, Morris S. *Congress Oversees the Bureaucracy: Studies in Legislative Supervision* (University of Pittsburgh Press, 1976).

Oleszek, Walter J. *Congressional Procedures and the Public Process* (3rd ed., Congressional Quarterly Press, 1988).

Redman, Eric. *The Dance of Legislation* (Touchstone, 1974).

Rieselbach, Leroy N. *Congressional Reform* (Congressional Quarterly Press, 1993).

Sundquist, James L. *The Decline and Resurgence of Congress* (Brookings Institution, 1981).

Wilson, Woodrow. *Congressional Government* (Peter Smith, 1958).

Wormuth, Francis Dunham, and Edwin B. Firmage. *To Chain the Dog of War: The War Power of Congress in History and Law* (2nd ed., University of Illinois Press, 1989).

Article Two—The President

Barber, James David. *The Presidential Character* (4th ed., Prentice-Hall, 1992).

Califano, Joseph, Jr. *A Presidential Nation* (W. W. Norton, 1975).

Cronin, Thomas E. *Inventing the American Presidency* (University Press of Kansas, 1989).

Fisher, Louis. *The Politics of Shared Power* (3rd ed., Congressional Quarterly Press, 1992).

Germond, Jack W., and Jules Witcover. *Mad as Hell* (Warner Books, 1994).

———. *Whose Broad Stripes and Bright Stars?* (Warner Books, 1990).

Hummel, Ralph P. *The Bureaucratic Experience* (4th ed., St. Martin's Press, 1994).

Laski, Harold J. *The American Presidency* (reprint, Transaction, 1980).

Leuchtenberg, William E. *In the Shadow of FDR: From Harry Truman to Bill Clinton* (Cornell University Press, rev. ed., 1993).

Light, Paul C. *The President's Agenda: Domestic Policy Choice from Kennedy to Carter (with Notes on Ronald Reagan)* (Johns Hopkins University Press, 1983).

Lowi, Theodore J. *The Personal President* (Cornell University Press, 1985).

Margolis, Lawrence. *Executive Agreements and Presidential Power in Foreign Policy* (Praeger, 1986).

Nathan, Richard P. *The Administrative Presidency* (Macmillian, 1983).

Neustadt, Richard E. *Presidential Power* (Free Press, 1989).

Schlesinger, Arthur M., Jr. *A Thousand Days: John F. Kennedy in the White House* (Fawcett, 1984).

———. *The Imperial Presidency* (Houghton Mifflin, 1989).

White, Theodore H. *America In Search of Itself* (Warner Books, 1988).

———. *The Making of the President 1960* (reprint, Buccaneer, 1993).

Article Three—The Courts

Abraham, Henry J. *The Judicial Process* (6th ed., Oxford University Press, 1993).

———. *The Judiciary: The Supreme Court in the Government Process* (9th ed., Brown & Benchmark, 1994).

Baum, Lawrence. *The Supreme Court* (4th ed., Congressional Quarterly Press, 1991).

Blasi, Vincent, ed. *The Burger Court: The Counter Revolution that Wasn't* (Yale University Press, 1986).

Cardozo, Benjamin N. *The Nature of the Judicial Process* (Yale University Press, 1960).

Carp, Robert A., and C. K. Rowland. *Policymaking and Politics in the Federal District Courts* (University of Tennessee Press, 1983).

Carp, Robert A., and Ronald Stidham. *The Federal Courts* (2nd ed., Congressional Quarterly Press, 1990).

Carter, Lief H. *Contemporary Constitutional Lawmaking* (Pergamon Press, 1985).

Commission on the Bicentennial of the United States Constitution. *The Supreme Court of the United States: Its Beginnings & Its Justices, 1790–1991* (1992).

Cooper, Philip J. *Battles on the Bench: Conflict Inside the Supreme Court* (University Press of Kansas, 1995).

Cox, Archibald. *The Role of the Supreme Court in American Government* (Oxford University Press, 1976).

Currie, David P. *The Constitution in the Supreme Court: The First Hundred Years* (University of Chicago Press, 1986).

———. *The Constitution in the Supreme Court: The Second Century* (University of Chicago Press, 1990).

Kahn, Ronald. *The Supreme Court and Constitutional Theory, 1953–1993* (University Press of Kansas, 1994).

Magee, James J. *Mr. Justice Black: Absolutist on the Court* (Virginia Legal Studies, 1980).

McCloskey, Robert G. *The American Supreme Court* (University of Chicago Press, 1994).

Miller, Arthur S. *Politics, Democracy and the Supreme Court* (Greenwood, 1985).

Murphy, Walter F., and C. Herman Pritchett. *Courts, Judges, and Politics* (4th ed., Random House, 1986).

Neely, Richard. *How Courts Govern America* (Yale University Press, 1983).

North, Arthur A. *The Supreme Court: Judicial Process and Judicial Politics* (Appleton-Century-Crofts, 1966).

O'Brien, David M. *Storm Center: The Supreme Court in American Politics* (4th ed., Norton and Company, 1996).

Posner, Richard A. *The Federal Courts: Crisis and Reform* (Harvard University Press, 1985).

Savage, David G. *Turning Right: The Making of the Rehnquist Supreme Court* (Wiley, 1993).

Schwartz, Bernard. *Decision: How the Supreme Court Decides Cases* (Oxford University Press, 1996).

Siegan, Bernard H. *The Supreme Court's Constitution* (Transaction Books, 1987).

Westin, Alan F. *The Anatomy of a Constitutional Law Case* (Colorado University Press, 1990).

———. *The Supreme Court: Views From Inside* (reprint, Greenwood, 1983).

Wiecek, William M. *Liberty Under Law: The Supreme Court in American Life* (Johns Hopkins University Press, 1988).

Wolfe, Christopher. *The Rise of Modern Judicial Review* (Littlefield, 1994).

Woodward, Bob, and Scott Armstrong. *The Brethren* (Avon, 1991).

Article Four—Interstate Relations

Jackson, Robert H. "Full Faith and Credit: The Lawyers' Clause of the Constitution" (45 *Columbia Law Review* 1, 1945).

O'Toole, Laurence J., Jr., ed. *American Intergovernmental Relations* (2nd ed., Congressional Quarterly Press, 1992).

Article Five—Amending the Constitution

Bernstein, Richard B. *Amending America* (Times Books, 1993).

Grimes. Alan P. *Democracy and Amendments to the Constitution* (reprint, University Press of America, 1987).

Article Six—The Supremacy Article and Federalism

Berger, Raoul. *Federalism: The Founders' Design* (University of Oklahoma Press, 1987).

Elazar, Daniel Judah. *Exploring Federalism* (University of Alabama Press, 1987).

Peterson, Paul E. *The Price of Federalism* (Brookings Institution, 1995).

Riker, William H. *The Development of American Federalism* (Kluwer, 1987).

Swisher, Carl B. *American Constitutional Development* (reprint, Greenwood, 1978).

Wright, Deil S. *Understanding Intergovernmental Relations* (International Thomson, 1988).

Article Seven—Ratification

Rossiter, Clinton L., ed. *The Federalist Papers* (reprint, Buccaneer, 1990).

The Bill of Rights—General Works

Abernathy, M. Glenn. *Civil Liberties under the Constitution* (6th ed., University of South Carolina, 1993).

Alderman, Ellen, and Caroline Kennedy. *In Our Defense: The Bill of Rights in Action* (Morrow, 1994).

Barker, Lucius, and Twiley W. Barker, Jr. *Civil Liberties and the Constitution: Cases and Commentaries* (7th ed., Prentice-Hall, 1994).

Bodenhamer, David J., and James W. Ely, Jr., eds. *The Bill of Rights in Modern America: After 200 Years* (Indiana University Press, 1993).

Bryner, Gary C., and A. D. Sorensen. *The Bill of Rights: A Bicentennial Assessment* (Brigham Young University Press, 1993).

Cushman, Robert F. *Leading Constitutional Decisions* (8th ed., Prentice-Hall, 1991).

Douglas, William O. *A Living Bill of Rights* (ADL, 1961).

———. *The Right of the People.* (reprint, Greenwood, 1980).

Irons, Peter. *The Courage of Their Convictions* (Collier Macmillan, 1988).

Lipset, S. M., and Earl Raab. *The Politics of Unreason* (University of Chicago Press, 1978; ADL reprint).

Morgan, Robert J. *James Madison on the Constitution and the Bill of Rights* (Greenwood Press, 1988).

Murray, Charles. *Losing Ground: American Social Policy 1950–1980* (Basic Books, 1994).

Van Alstyne, William W. *Interpretations of the First Amendment* (reprint, Duke University Press, 1990).

Veit, Helen H., Kenneth R. Bowling, and Charlene Bangs Bickford, eds. *Creating the Bill of Rights: The Documentary Record from the First Federal Congress* (Johns Hopkins University Press, 1991).

The 1st Amendment—Preferred Rights

Religious Freedom

Beggs, David W. *America's Schools and Churches* (Indiana, 1965).

Cord, Robert L. *Separation of Church and State* (reprint, Lambeth Press, 1995).

Hook, Sidney. *Religion in a Free Society* (University of Nebraska, 1967).

Horwitz, Robert, ed. *The Moral Foundations of the American Republic* (3rd ed., University of Virginia, 1986).

Levy, Leonard W. *The Establishment Clause: Religion and the First Amendment* (2nd ed., Macmillan, 1994).

Lopatto, Paul. *Religion and the Presidential Election* (Praeger, 1985).

Miller, William L. *The First Liberty: Religion and the American Public* (Knopf, 1986).

Pfeffer, Leo. *Religion, State and the Burger Court* (Prometheus Books, 1984).

Rice, Charles E. *The Supreme Court and Public Prayer* (Fordham, 1964).

Weber, Paul J., and D. A. Gilbert. *Private Churches and Public Money* (Greenwood Press, 1981).

Wilson, John F., and Donald L. Drakeman, eds. *Church and State in American History* (D. C. Heath, 1965).

Freedom of Speech, Press, and Assembly

Canavan, Francis. *Freedom of Expression* (reprint, North Carolina Academic Press, 1986).

Friendly, Fred W. *Minnesota Rag* (Random House, 1982).

Isaacs, Norman E. *The Untended Gate: The Mismanagement of the Press* (Columbia University Press, 1986).

Leonard, Thomas C. *Power of the Press* (Oxford University Press, 1987).

O'Brien, David M. *The Public's Right to Know* (Praeger, 1981).

Rubin, Bernard, ed. *When Information Counts: Grading the Media* (D. C. Heath, 1985).

Smolla, Rodney A. *Free Speech in an Open Society* (Knopf, 1992).

Stevens, John D. *Shaping the First Amendment: The Development of Free Expression* (Sage, 1982).

Sunstein, Cass R. *Democracy and the Problem of Free Speech* (Free Press, 1995).

Van Alstyne, William. *Interpretations of the First Amendment* (reprint, Duke University Press, 1990).

The 2nd Amendment—Firearms

Halbrook, Stephen P. *That Every Man Be Armed: The Evolution of a Constitutional Right* (Independent Institute, 1994).

Kruschke, Earl R. *Gun Control* (ABC-CLIO, 1995).

Spitzer, Robert J. *The Politics of Gun Control* (Chatham House, 1995).

The 4th, 5th, and 6th Amendments—Criminal Justice

Ackerman, Bruce. *Private Property and the Constitution* (Yale University Press, 1977).

Creamer, J. Shane. *The Law of Arrest, Search and Seizure* (3rd ed., Sanders, 1980).

Dash, Samuel, R. E. Knowleton, and Richard F. Schwartz. *The Eavesdroppers* (reprint, Rutgers University Press, 1971).

Freeley, Malcolm M. *The Process is the Punishment* (Russell Sage, 1979).

Horowitz, Donald. *The Courts and Social Policy* (Brookings Institution, 1977).

La Fave, Wayne R. *Search and Seizure: A Treatise on the Fourth Amendment* (2nd ed., West Publishing, 1986).

Lewis, Anthony. *Gideon's Trumpet* (Random House, 1989).

Michalowski, Raymond. *Order, Law and Crime* (Random House, 1984).

Newman, Donald J., and Patrick Anderson. *Introduction to Criminal Justice* (4th ed., Random House, 1989).

Pound, Roscoe. *Criminal Justice in America* (reprint, DaCapo, 1972).

Silberman, Charles E. *Criminal Violence, Criminal Justice* (Random House, 1980).

Sundquist, James L. *Constitutional Reform and Effective Government* (rev. ed., Brookings Institution, 1992).

Swanson, Charles R., Neil C. Chamelin, and Leonard Territo. *Criminal Investigation* (5th ed., Random House, 1992).

Wilson, James Q. and Richard Hernstein. *Crime and Human Nature* (Simon and Schuster, 1986).

Wright, Kevin N. *The Great American Crime Myth* (Greenwood Press, 1985).

Younger, Richard D. *The People's Panel: The Grand Jury in the United States* (Brown University Press, 1963).

The 8th Amendment—Bail and Punishment

Bedau, Hugo A. *The Death Penalty in America* (3rd ed., Oxford University Press, 1982).

Berger, Raoul. *Death Penalties: The Supreme Court's Obstacle Course* (Harvard University Press, 1982).

Bowers, William J. *Legal Homicide: Death as Punishment in America 1864–1982* (Northeastern University Press, 1984).

Schwed, Roger E. *Abolition and Capital Punishment* (AMS Press, 1983).

Van den Haag, Ernest, and John P. Conrad. *The Death Penalty: A Debate* (Plenum, 1983).

The 9th Amendment—Natural Rights

Barnett, Randy E., ed. *The Rights Retained by the People: The History and Meaning of the Ninth Amendment* (George Mason University Press, 1993).

Butler, J. Douglas, and David F. Walbert, eds. *Abortion, Medicine and the Law* (Facts on File, 1992).

Kennedy, Caroline, and Ellen Alderman. *The Right to Privacy* (Knopf, 1995).

O'Brien, David M. *Privacy, Law and Public Policy* (Praeger, 1979).

The 10th Amendment—State Power

See Article Six, books on federalism.

The 12th Amendment—The Electoral System

Ceaser, James. *Presidential Selection: Theory and Development* (Princeton University Press, 1979).

Fiorina, Morris P. *Retrospective Voting in American Elections* (Yale University Press, 1981).

Flanigan, William H., and Nancy H. Zingale. *Political Behavior of the American Electorate* (8th ed., Allyn & Bacon, 1994).

Ginsberg, Benjamin, and A. Stone. *Do Elections Matter?* (3rd ed., M. E. Sharpe, 1995).

Mill, John Stuart. *Considerations on Representative Government* (Many editions, 1861).

Nie, Norman, Sidney Verba, and John Petrocik. *The Changing American Voter* (Harvard University Press, 1980).

Peirce, Neal R., and Lawrence D. Longley. *The People's President: The Electoral College in American History and the Direct-Vote Alternative* (2nd ed., Yale University Press, 1981).

Wolfinger, Raymond E., and S. J. Rosenstone. *Who Votes?* (Yale University Press, 1980).

The 14th Amendment—Citizenship and Equal Protection of the Laws

Berger, Raoul. *Government by Judiciary: The Transformation of the Fourteenth Amendment* (Harvard University Press, 1977).

Cortner, Richard C. *The Supreme Court and The Second Bill of Rights: The Fourteenth Amendment and the Nationalization of Civil Liberties* (University of Wisconsin Press, 1981).

Crain, Robert. *The Politics of School Desegregation* (Doubleday Anchor, 1968).

Curtis, Michael Kent. *No State Shall Abridge: The Fourteenth Amendment and the Bill of Rights* (Duke University Press, 1986).

Edelman, Martin. *Democratic Theories and the Constitution* (State University of New York Press, 1985).

Hochschild, Jennifer L. *The New American Dilemma: Liberal Democracy and School Desegregation* (Yale University Press, 1984).

———. *What's Fair? American Beliefs About Distributive Justice* (Harvard University Press, 1981).

Kirp, David L. *Just Schools: The Idea of Racial Equality in American Education* (University of California Press, 1982).

Kluger, Richard. *Simple Justice* (Knopf, 1976).

Loescher, Gil D., and John A. Scanlan. *Calculated Kindness: Refugees and America's Half-Open Door, 1945–Present* (Free Press, 1986).

McDowell, Gary L. *Equality and the Constitution* (University of Chicago Press, 1982).

Nelson, William E. *The Fourteenth Amendment* (Harvard University Press, 1995).

O'Neill, Timothy J. *Bakke and Politics of Equality* (University Press of New England, 1987).

Peltason, J. W. *Fifty-eight Lonely Men: Southern Federal Judges and School Desegregation* (reprint, Harcourt, Brace and World, 1971).

Schwartz, Bernard. *Swann's Way: The School Busing Case and the Supreme Court* (Oxford University Press, 1986).

Sindler, Allen P. *Bakke, DeFunis and Minority Admissions* (Longman, 1978).

Verba, Sidney, and G. R. Orren. *Equality in America: The View From The Top* (Harvard University Press, 1985).

Wilkinson, J. Harvie, III. *From Brown to Bakke: The Supreme Court and School Integration: 1954–1978* (Oxford University Press, 1981).

For books on due process of law, see 4th–6th Amendments references.

The 15th Amendment—Right to Vote

Foster, Lorn B., ed. *The Voting Rights Act: Consequences and Implications* (Praeger, 1985).

Gillette, William. *The Right to Vote: Politics and the Passage of the Fifteenth Amendment* (Johns Hopkins University Press, 1965).

Guinier, Lani. *The Tyranny of the Majority: Fundamental Fairness in Representative Democracy* (Free Press, 1994).

Keith, Bruce E. et al. *The Myth of the Independent Voter* (University of California Press, 1992).

Kessel, John H. *Presidential Campaign Politics* (4th ed., Dorsey, 1993).

Maisel, L. Sandy. *Parties and Elections in America: The Electoral Process* (Random House, 1987).

Matthews, John M. *The Legislative and Judicial History of the Fifteenth Amendment* (reprint, DaCapo, 1971).

Miller, Warren E. et al. *American National Election Studies Data Sourcebook, 1954–1978* (Harvard University Press, 1980).

Nie, Norman, Sidney Verba, and John Petrocik. *The Changing American Voter* (Harvard University Press, 1980).

Pomper, Gerald M., ed. *The Election of 1984* (Chatham House, 1985).

———. *Voters, Elections, and Parties: The Practice of Democratic Theory* (Transaction Books, 1988).

Popkin, Samuel L. *The Reasoning Voter* (University of Chicago Press, 1994).

Smith, Eric R. A. N. *The Unchanging American Voter* (University of California Press, 1989).

Smith, Jeffrey A. *American Presidential Elections: Trust and the Rational Voter* (Praeger, 1980).

Wolfinger, Raymond, and S. J. Rosenstone. *Who Votes?* (Yale University Press, 1980).

The 18th and 21st Amendments—Prohibition and its Repeal

Bordin, Ruth. *Women and Temperance: The Quest for Power and Liberty 1873–1900* (reprint, Temple University Press, 1990).

Clark, Norman H. *The Dry Years* (rev. ed., University of Washington Press, 1987).

The 19th Amendment—Woman Suffrage

Gelb, Joyce, and Marian Lief Palley. *Women and Public Policies* (Rev. ed., Princeton University Press, 1987).

Goldstein, Leslie Friedman. *The Constitutional Rights of Women: Cases in Law and Social Change* (2nd ed., University of Wisconsin Press, 1988).

Grimes, Alan P. *The Puritan Ethic and Woman Suffrage* (reprint, Greenwood, 1980).

Klein, Ethel. *Gender Politics: From Consciousness to Mass Politics* (Harvard University Press, 1984).

Kraditor, Aileen. *The Ideas of the Woman Suffrage Movement* (Norton, 1981).

Randall, Vicky. *Women and Politics* (St. Martin's Press, 1984).

The 25th Amendment—Presidential Succession

Bayh, Birch. *One Heartbeat Away: Presidential Disability and Succession* (Bobbs-Merrill, 1968).

Feerick, John D. *The Twenty-Fifth Amendment* (rev. ed., Fordham University Press, 1992).

Index